Law and Justice as Seen on TV

Law and Justice as Seen on TV

Elayne Rapping

NEW YORK UNIVERSITY PRESS

New York and London

NEW YORK UNIVERSITY PRESS
New York and London
www.nyupress.org

Library of Congress Cataloging-in-Publication Data
Rapping, Elayne
Law and Justice as seen on TV / Elayne Rapping.
p. cm.
ISBN 0–8147–7560–8 (cloth : alk. paper) —
ISBN 0–8147–7561–6 (pbk. : alk. paper)
1. Justice, Adminstration of, on television.
2. Lawyers on television.   I. Title.
PN1992.8.J87R37   2003
791.45'655—dc21   2003008856

New York University Press books are printed on acid-free paper,
and their binding materials are chosen for strength and durability.

Manufactured in the United States of America
10 9 8 7 6 5 4 3 2 1

This one is for Jon

And for all the public defenders whose names and faces never appear on television, but who toil in the trenches every day, against the greatest odds, and with little financial or social reward, in the Sisyphean effort to make our government live up to the democratic rhetoric of its own Constitution

Contents

Acknowledgments

Conversations with many colleagues, students, and friends have helped me to clarify my ideas and also to reassure me, on many occasions, that what I was attempting was indeed interesting and important, not only to those in media studies and law, but to a broader audience of academic and general readers. I want especially to thank Lee Quinby, Margaret Walker, Pat Mann, Richard Sherwin, Neil Feigenson, David Schmid, Ann Kibbey, Austin Sarat, Christopher Sharrett, Miki Iida, Christine Zinni, Ruth Barnes Shaw, Liz Hogan, the students in my graduate seminar on "Media and the Public Sphere" at the University at Buffalo, my research assistants Liz Richards and Anne Siejakowski, Eric Zinner and Emily Park of NYU Press, the anonymous reader whose rigorous review and commentary were unusually helpful, and Jonathan Rapping and his colleagues at the Public Defender Service of the District of Columbia. I am particularly grateful to the Baldy Center for Law and Society at the SUNY/University of Buffalo School of Law and the university's College of Arts and Sciences for their generous funding of much of the research for the book and the preparation of the manuscript.

Introduction

In the courtroom of honor the judge pounded his gavel
To show that all's equal and that the law is on the level . . .
And that even the nobles get properly handled
Once that the cops have chased after and caught 'em
And that the ladder of law has no top and no bottom.

—Bob Dylan

I have been writing and teaching about television for a long time. "It's a dirty job, but someone's got to do it," I usually reply when friends or colleagues ask, "How can you stand to watch all that junk?" This happens less often these days, of course, as the study of film and television has found its way into most institutions of higher learning. But it does still happen. Mostly, I suppose, because the television genres I have most often found interesting are indeed the ones most likely to be thought of as "junk": soap operas, talk shows, made-for-TV movies.

So this book, about law and justice as seen on television, represents something of a departure for me. In fact, until a few years ago, I had never paid much attention to courtroom dramas, crime shows, or—although I am an inveterate news junkie—even stories about trials, courts, or the law in general. In fact, I was about as ignorant of these issues as most Americans.

And then something interesting happened: my son became a lawyer. "Well, what's so interesting about that?" you are probably thinking. The world is full of professional, middle-class parents whose sons and daughters become lawyers. But my son Jon didn't just become a lawyer; he became a criminal defense attorney, one of the most reviled specialties of one of the most reviled professions in the nation. And he was not just your garden-variety defense attorney who—if one listens to all the jokes about them—make bundles of money being sleazy, corrupt, and soulless. No, my son chose to become the worst kind of defense attorney: a public defender—the kind who makes very little money defending the most unsympathetic and, to most Americans, the scariest segments of society. So, no proud "my-son-the-lawyer" stories for me. In Jon's office, the staff attorneys have buttons that read, "Don't tell my mother I'm a public defender; she thinks I play piano in a whorehouse." In fact, I've had friends—self-proclaimed intellectual, progressive friends—who have actually asked if my son ever feels guilty about defending "those people." Many others look at me in an odd way that I have come to recognize as shorthand for "poor kid; couldn't get a better job; what a loser." Because everyone knows that even first-year graduates from second-tier law schools are making six-figure salaries at major firms these days.

You can see where this is going. I like my son. I like and respect his idealistic, amazingly committed colleagues. I'm proud of him and the work he does. And I, at least, know that he had options, that he turned down other offers because this was what he *wanted* to do. Where, I suddenly began to wonder, did this image of defense attorneys come from? And when did it start? Since I have an obvious professional bias toward first looking at the media, I thought back to the days when, as a child, I did actually watch law shows. In those days, there was usually just one TV set in a household, and since it was the father who usually decided what the family watched, we ended up seeing a lot of shows about lawyers. The ones I remembered best were *The Defenders*, a drama about a very liberal father and son law team that took on a lot of controversial social issues; and of course *Perry Mason*, who never had a client who wasn't falsely accused and never lost a case to the sleazy district attorney who always opposed him.

By the 1980s, lawyers had gradually begun to reappear on TV. There was *LA Law*, for example. But it featured a very high-rent Los Angeles firm whose primary focus was not criminal law. But *LA Law* was the only legal series in a decade that was most notable for introducing such highly successful "quality" cop shows as *NYPD Blue* and *Homicide: Life on the Street*. In fact, as I looked back at the history of top series from the eighties, I realized that *Cagney and Lacey* and *Hill Street Blues*—the first of these lawyerly hit shows—had begun a rather intriguing new trend that I think of as "Cops with a Heart" series. All these series had a more or less liberal, even "politically correct" slant. But it was not the lawyers but the police officers whose hearts bled for the underprivileged; who anguished about sexism, racism, and poverty; and who—and this was really innovative—had complex personal lives filled with the *Sturm und Drang* of late twentieth century American life: adultery, gender violence, divorce, alcoholism, drug abuse, troubled and troubling children, and more.

These series were instructive as signs of the times, for they signaled a subtle and in many ways contradictory turn in social consciousness. They represented, as I later understood, a transitional ideological moment. Liberalism was not yet dead; far from it. In fact, the producers of these series were sixties-bred liberals themselves. But already you could sense in these series—in their very choice of law enforcers as heroes—the kind of subtly conservative "law and order" mentality that my friend expressed when he worried about my son's guilt about defending "those people." The folks who had boldly sung along with Bob Dylan when he insisted that "to live outside the law you must be honest" were no longer so sure. In fact, as they got older and more "established" themselves, their sympathies—while still ostensibly liberal, even leftist—were subtly shifting away from those who broke the law to those who protected an increasingly fearful middle class against "those people."

Of course, there were also, during these transitional years, a few series that did feature liberal, "bleeding heart" attorneys for the downtrodden, such as *The Trials of Rosie O'Neill* and *Sweet Justice*. But few TV followers reading this book will, I suspect, be able to recall them—as I myself did not until my research into TV history brought them back to mind. "Oh, right," I would think to myself as I leafed through my reference sources. "I remember that show now. It wasn't bad while it lasted." But in each case, it was these series that did not in fact last more than a season or two, while the ones that tend to come to mind rather more quickly—the cop shows just mentioned—obviously did.

If cops were largely on the rise and lawyers in decline during the 1980s, at least in fictional series, there was another media phenomenon that would soon emerge on the heels of this trend in fictional drama. It helped me understand the sudden interest—largely negative, if not downright vitriolic—in the law profession that I had been picking up in so many unlikely places: it was the sudden rise, at the beginning of the 1990s, of the live-televised criminal trial. In fact, it was the amazing impact of these early televised trials that clearly led network producers to reprise the long-dormant legal, courtroom-centered series that are now ubiquitous on virtually every network's prime-time schedule. But in its new incarnation, the genre displayed a decidedly different ideological slant than its predecessors of the fifties and sixties; for now it was almost invariably the prosecutors, not the defense attorneys, who wore the white hats. And even when this was not the case—as in series such as *The Practice* and *Philly*—the defense attorneys were a far more jaded, morally ambiguous, or at best ambivalent lot, as uncomfortable about defending "those people" as my friends assumed my son must be.

Why did the coming of the televised criminal trial, and especially Court TV, the twenty-four-hour-a-day law channel that aired the most memorable and socially significant of these trials, bring with it such a jaded view of defense attorneys? Well, to be fair, it was not Court TV, or television at all, on its own that produced such a negative attitude toward defendants and their defenders. Rather, as the cop shows mentioned above indicate, there already was a growing sense of fear of "criminals" and sympathy for the law enforcement officers and prosecutors who pursued, caught, and imprisoned them. And implicit in that growing "law and order" mentality was a parallel sense of growing distrust of those who worked to free what was more and more being perceived, by liberals and conservatives alike, as a large, dangerous, and increasingly incorrigible "criminal class."

Of course, not all Americans shared this view, but there is certainly evidence that such attitudes were increasingly common among Americans beginning, perhaps, in the 1980s but coming into clear and documented ideological dominance during the 1990s. I have therefore focused on the nineties and, in the final chapters, charted the trend's actual intensification in the years that followed. Indeed, there have been a number of significant studies by sociologists and criminologists of the widespread myths about the rise of crime in America and the growing—often unfounded—fear of crime and criminals among American citizens. Among the most detailed and thorough accounts are Steven Donziger's *The Real War on Crime* and Mike Males's *Framing Youth: 10 Myths about the Next Generation*. Both authors document the common myths that, according to polls, hold sway among Americans, and they proceed statistically to debunk them all. Donziger, for example, cites polls showing that Americans believe that street crime is increasing; that it is more violent than in the past; that more police officers are being killed; and—perhaps most interestingly—that criminals are different from the rest of us. None of this, as it turns out, reflects reality, although it all certainly does reflect recent administrations' "tough on crime" propaganda and the media's making commercial hay out of these "made for prime time" sensational myths. Males takes a similar approach to the widespread, much believed "facts" about the growth and increasing violence of youth crime. Again, he finds that polls show that most of us believe such myths, but that they are almost entirely the result of government and media propaganda and fear tactics, a subject with which Donziger also deals, along with other mythologies of crime today.[1] But it was only when the trials of these criminals were brought to TV, particularly in their most sordidly sensationalized versions, that lawyers themselves became the focus—the largely unpopular focus—of television viewers and producers in general.

This increasingly intense focus on crime and criminals as major issues in American society is indeed a relatively new phenomenon—in the twentieth century generally, but especially in the last decade or so. It has been documented by legal historian Lawrence Friedman in his thorough and authoritative *Crime and Punishment in American History.* According to Friedman, it was the federalization of so many crimes that had been issues for the states before the twentieth century that began to draw so much national attention to crime as a "problem." As he puts it, "One of the most profound trends in the history of government in this century is the drift or pull or rush toward the center," which tends to make all issues "national" and therefore subject to broad public awareness and concern. This has certainly been true of crime as a public issue. For as, in Friedman's term, the "federal leviathan" of the last century grew, the number of acts and behaviors deemed criminal grew exponentially. One such law that Friedman lists as fairly typical in the first stages of this trend, for example, was the 1923 law that made it a crime to carry "commercial sponges measuring less than five inches when wet" across state lines.

As time went on, according to Friedman, the number of such new "crimes" escalated as the government strove to create an issue that might serve as a national unifier. It was the coming of increasingly sophisticated communication technologies—especially television—that truly, in Friedman's words, made us into "one country, with one capital, one primary center of power,"[2] and, as much of this book will argue, gave the state the vehicle through which crime could be framed as a central concern for all Americans.

A brief overview of crime in American history is useful in helping to see how, by the 1990s, crime had become the dramatically central national "problem" it is today, according to the government and media. Neither Washington nor Lincoln, for example, even mentioned crime in their inaugural addresses. It was Hoover who first mentioned crime as a problem and established a task force to study it. And until the 1960s, succeeding administrations continued to build upon this focus on crime as a national problem. In the 1960s, however, as we shall see, the trend was temporarily but dramatically reversed, as an extremely liberal Supreme Court made a number of rulings favoring defendants' rights over the power of the government. This liberal turn—like so much else about the 1960s—had the effect of polarizing the nation and, as Friedman explains, by the 1980s there was "a wave of backlash" against the permissiveness of the 1960s as "a wave of conservatism swept the streets." But it was in the 1990s—when television began to focus the extreme attention on criminal justice I am analyzing—that this backlash created some of the most repressive and punitive trends in criminal justice the nation had yet seen. Friedman lists, among these trends, many of the issues I will be discussing, such as the rise in prison construction; the decline in prisoners' and defendants' rights; the rise of the Victims' Rights movement; and the reinstatement in more and more states of the death penalty.[3] My emphasis on the 1990s is thus in the context of this history of criminal justice policy and its links—as Friedman clearly acknowledges—to the centrification of national justice policy and the role of television in bringing that national focus to the broad public as perhaps the major issue of concern for Americans.

Since Friedman himself makes such a point of it, it is probably useful now to comment briefly about an issue that will come up explicitly, and implicitly, throughout this book: the power of television itself—of *viewing* these trials as opposed to merely reading or hearing about them. For one of the most important things about the coming of law to television in all its forms and genres was the very fact that television *is* a visual medium. As art historian and popular-culture analyst Erika Doss explains in discussing the power of television in the 1950s, "Sight is the dominant sense in modern Western culture." "How else explain," she writes, "the phenomenal popularity of television over radio?"[4] And it is indeed this privileging of sight over other senses in Western culture that goes far to explain why televised trials were able to capture the imagination of so many people, engage them in an intense interest in things legal, and, through the use of images that compel deep emotion, to make the case for harsh criminal justice laws.

Of course, television did not create the public interest in trials, especially sensational trials. Ever since the advent of mass media, even in its
most primitive forms, the public has had a great interest in sensational trials. As early as 1709, Dr. Henry Sacherell, an Anglican minister, delivered
a sermon before the House of Commons in England, warning about the
dangers of the Protestant dissenters to the Commonwealth, challenging
the Whig leadership's commitment to contractual government, and calling for the return of the traditional Anglican, Tory belief in obedience to
a Supreme Power. The sermon was considered seditious by Queen Anne
and the Whig majority, and Sacherell was impeached for "high crimes
and misdemeanors." The trial lasted twenty-five days and was, in every
sense, a public spectacle heretofore unknown in England's history. Pam-
phleteers and newspapers, in following the trial so carefully, made it a
matter of universal public interest and debate. While not a criminal trial,
like the Clinton impeachment, it was, in its day, an event of great interest
and heated debate.[5]

Moving closer to our own shores and public concerns, any number of
sensational trials have captured the public imagination and become
"public spectacles" despite the absence of television. The Scopes trial, the
trial of Leopold and Loeb, of the Rosenbergs, of John Hinckley, of the
Chicago Seven—all were major media events despite the absence of cameras in the courtroom. One could argue that it was not television that created the trial as public spectacle, but rather that the coming of the cameras, which allowed television—a visual medium—to become the central
venue for the circulation and discussion of such spectacles, has transformed television itself, perhaps more than vice versa. Television producers, in an age when cable TV was opening up huge new venues for new
kinds of television programming and new products, recognized the power
of the trial as a form of dramatic programming: it had the ability to capture the public imagination as few other nonfiction forms could.

But it took a very special trial, at a very special moment in our political and televisual history, to garner the kind of public attention
needed to make this transformation work. In the 1990s the right-wing
slant in political thinking, especially around issues of crime and justice,
had clearly become the dominant ideology of the day. With the rise of
cable as a prominent presence in most American homes, the two
events came together, making the major strands of the trend I am tracing become truly significant. Thus, as we shall see, it is in the 1990s that
the shift in television programming, running parallel to the shift in legal

policy itself, arises and grows. Therefore, the 1990s are the major focus of this study.

The first trial to be televised nationally to a huge, deeply engaged and enthralled public hit the homes and hearts of America in 1994: the trial of the Menendez brothers. The two young men had allegedly shot their wealthy mother and father in cold blood while the parents sat peacefully eating ice cream and watching television in their Beverly Hills mansion. They then went on a wild spending spree, buying everything from condos to gold Rolex watches, finally "swaggering" into court for their arraignments in brand-new Armani suits. Virtually everyone in America knew these details. And how did we know them? Because the proceedings were seen, in full color, gavel-to-gavel or in nightly newscast clips, on virtually every TV screen in the nation.

It was the Menendez trial that first hooked me on the topic of television and law. And it was the Menendez trial that opened the window that provided me with the route toward the answers to the question I had been asking myself since my son became a public defender: Why are defense attorneys so reviled and demeaned in public discourse and consciousness these days? Having already begun searching the media for answers to this question and educating myself about the law, the Constitution, and the workings of the criminal justice system, I watched this trial with very different eyes than most of my friends and colleagues. To them—and to the many nonlegally trained media commentators who couldn't get enough of the trial—it was a simple moral issue: these monstrous kids did it; they should pay for their horrific act, preferably with their own lives.[6]

But by then I was looking at the trial and its major players and commentators through a somewhat different, more political (if equally moral) prism. What I was seeing was less a battle between good and evil, between "innocent" victims and "evil" killers, than one of dueling ideologies about the family, gender, and generational relations. More intriguingly, I saw a battle between differing views of what a criminal trial is really about. The more I watched and listened to the arguments, objections, judicial rulings, testimony, and cross-examination of various witnesses, the more clear it became to me that what was going on in that televised courtroom—and in the minds of its living-room and press-room audiences—was far more seriously a dispute about the courtroom itself: its rules, its assumptions about relevant issues and testimony, and its actual function in American society.

To understand this phenomenon, we must recall that the legal system, like all American institutions, had not escaped the influence of the liberal ideas of the social movements of the day. Feminism, critical race theory, and other progressive ideas born of those movements had made their way into courtrooms while young attorneys who had been a part of those movements had begun to devise new defense strategies such as the "battered woman defense." They challenged the system to expand its interpretation of "guilt" and "innocence" by including newly minted ideas— for example, that defendants' previous experiences might reasonably lead them to commit acts of violence previously viewed in more black and white terms. The Menendez defense, centered largely on issues of emotional, physical, and sexual child abuse by a brutally authoritarian patriarch, was clearly indebted to those movements. As Donziger, Males, and others document, however, a new "law and order" mentality was setting in—in a sense a backlash against the admittedly brief but extremely influential interventions of the sixties. Issues of gender, race, family dysfunction and abuse, gay rights, and other issues politicized by the sixties' social movements had inevitably affected the legal system as young, radicalized law students entered the arena. The Menendez trial was, among other things, a battle of competing ideologies: one on the rise, one in decline.

But ideology itself does not make for great drama. Something else transformed these ideological issues into great drama: television. For television—as I have noted and as the Menendez trial made vividly clear—relies far more than print or radio on emotion and dramatic intensity for its appeal. The Menendez trial was nothing if not emotionally intense: tears, stories and images of outrageously vicious acts against children and parents; heated battles between opposing attorneys as well as judges and attorneys; unusually depraved and villainous witnesses as well as heartbreakingly sympathetic ones; and a set of defendants and attorneys who were themselves unusually telegenic in personality and style. All of this made for terrific television.

But at the end of the day, while the defense team was masterful in its own use of these techniques—so masterful, in fact, that the actual jurors could not agree on a verdict in what the prosecution had assumed was a slam-dunk case—the larger, public audience was not only shocked but outraged. In fact, the Menendez brothers became symbols of a system gone woefully astray, in which the courts had become so befuddled by psychobabble and "abuse excuses" that they were allowing cold-blooded killers to go free, at least temporarily.

Two major factors were responsible for this widespread indictment of the outcome of the first Menendez trial. The first was the growing right-wing sentiment against "soft on crime" judges and juries, the growing fear of crime, and the desire, on the part of more and more Americans, to see criminals, no matter what the reasons for their actions, given harshly punitive convictions and sentences. The second trend under attack by the public and most of the media was more subtly political. Television drama depends foremost on "closure," what Bertolt Brecht once cynically described as "Happy endings/Nice and tidy." While it is true that "closure" can be achieved by any number of definitive conclusions, including, for example, an acquittal of an innocent defendant—the mainstay of early legal series such as *Perry Mason* and *Matlock*—the rising anti-crime/criminal mentality of post-sixties America created an audience of viewer-citizens who were increasingly demanding a particular kind of closure: the conviction and punishment of the evil offender. One need not watch trial coverage of murder cases and hear the hue and cry for blood by friends and loved ones of crime victims to recognize this syndrome. One need only watch the news or read the print-media columnists to know what I am talking about. Whether it is the "war on terror," the "war on crime," or the "war on Saddam Hussein," what the president promises, the media encourages, and the polls indicate is that most Americans today want "revenge" against those deemed "evil." But the complexities and subtleties of the issues raised by the Menendez defense team—by the social movements of the sixties themselves—did not lend themselves to this or any other kind of closure.

The Menendez trial, then, was emblematic of a variety of interlocking themes that I want to explore in some depth in the bulk of this book. It marked a moment of high dramatic conflict between opposing views of justice—and other, much larger social issues—one liberal, one increasingly conservative. But it also marked a moment when—largely due to the demise of sixties' activism—the courtroom was increasingly replacing other, more traditionally political arenas as the major sphere within which vexed social and political issues of all kinds were being debated and ruled upon, both institutionally and publicly. This is one of the major themes I want to explore in this book. For, if television has made of these trials the kind of nationally unifying public event traditionally reserved for political and natural "disasters," then television has also played a major role in politicizing the legal system in ways that have made it the primary arbiter of important social and political policy issues.

The Menendez trial, and the others we will examine, illustrated an important and problematic trend that television did not "cause" but which its inherent dramatic appeal helped to promote: the "legalization" and "criminalization" of a host of issues traditionally seen as being social, cultural, or political and assumed to be best handled by the institutions established to deal with them. Indeed, the turn to the legal system for "solutions" to social issues had serious consequences: it implicitly precluded any idea that social forces and institutions might be responsible for these problems; and that, in turn, these forces and institutions should perhaps be attacked or amended in order to "solve" them.

In other words, root causes of social decay and corruption were passed over, ignored, and eventually even eliminated from public debate by the far more simplistic turn to criminal justice as the sole arbiter of these matters. Was there a problem with teen-age rebellion? Take it to the courts and let the judge and jurors decide what to do about it. Was family violence on the rise? Then criminalize and legalize the issue and let the courts determine what to do about it. Indeed, almost all issues that had, in earlier, more liberal periods, been seen as products of larger social forces and institutions were suddenly being seen as matters that could most cleanly and finally be disposed of by defining them in legal, often criminal terms. Those involved could be treated as perpetrators and victims of something far more cut and dried—indeed black and white—than the panoply of social, economic, and political forces that had previously been impugned. Now it was simply the evil of crime, of the criminal act or character, that was to be blamed for our major troubles.

The solutions offered by this construction of social problems were also those used by the criminal justice system: the array of penalties—fines, probation, community service, incarceration, and, ultimately, death— that the criminal justice system is set up to order and enforce in all cases brought before it. It is not surprising, then, that in such a context of thought and drama, not only the criminal defendants but also their advocates came to be seen as the bad guys, the un-Perry Masons who worked so hard to let these rabid criminals run loose upon our streets to mug and burgle and maim and kill again. Ergo, the birth of the defense attorney as villain.

One can see the appeal of this kind of simplistic thinking. Family, gender, and generational disputes are clearly among the most vexed of current social issues, as families unravel in threads of increasingly visible and televised "dysfunction." Issues of racial violence and unrest and apparent rises in crime, especially youth crime, are at play, too.

It may seem odd to be discussing fictional series and hard-news broadcasts as though they were more or less interchangeable. But, in fact, one of the main themes of this book is that, although there *are* major differences that largely have to do with issues of race and class, the two types of programming share an ideological similarity in their approach to the causes and cures for social problems of all kinds. This approach is the one offered by criminal justice, with its white-hatted prosecutors and police officers and its black-hatted defense attorneys, and with its ultimate focus on the narrative closure that punishment, retribution, and banishment from society of the "criminal" conveniently brings with it.

Thus, as I will argue and demonstrate, there is an increasingly blurry line between what is "in the headlines" and what shows up on dramatic fictional series. While the fictional or entertainment versions of legal justice are in many ways less realistic than the more serious documentary forms, it is the fictional portrayals that are more likely to have been seen, and intellectually and emotionally digested, by viewers. Most people, after all, have some familiarity with *Law and Order*. But fewer people are likely to be as familiar with the many newer series, on Court TV and elsewhere, that give far more detailed, if ideologically biased pictures of the criminal justice system as it actually works.

As someone who teaches university students, I am all too aware of the influence of fictional television on public thinking. Class discussions more and more frequently reference shows such as *Law and Order*, *The Practice*, and even *Ally McBeal* in discussions of legal and criminal justice issues, as if these fictional representations were not only "torn from the headlines," as advertised, but are virtual representations of legal reality. Indeed, a friend of mine told me about an incident in her own classroom. When she asked what, if any, newspapers her students read, one young man raised his hand and said, "I don't read the paper but I watch *Law and Order* and that's how I keep up with what's going on in the world."[7]

Which brings me back to where I began: the fictional series I first began studying in my early attempts to understand the widespread animosity toward defense attorneys. The impact of Court TV, and of trials like the Menendez trial, was broad and far reaching. Although the success of the fledgling cable network ironically led to its ultimate fall in ratings as more and more networks began doing what Court TV had proven to be so lucrative—covering, commenting on, and investigating the workings of the criminal justice system—its impact on television programming generally has been profound.

In fact, my friend's student's reference to *Law and Order* is not as surprising as it may at first seem. By the time the Court TV bug had infected most of America, the networks had already figured out that the time was ripe for the return of the dramatic legal series. The first and most successful of these was *Law and Order*, the longest-running series still on the air, with two successful spin-offs and an endless run of reruns on both TNT and A&E. All of these reflect the new turn to the "law and order" mentality I have been describing. Since the debut and astounding success of this series, almost twenty new law series have surfaced, some still around, most more short lived. Nonetheless, the dramatic success of any new television genre is a marker of some significant social turn. These new law series are, as I will show, among the most telling markers of our current political times.

I will begin my discussion with these fictional legal entertainment forms, which are so widely seen and discussed by many of us, and will then go on to investigate the less familiar nonfiction legal genres, primarily those invented or suggested by the success of Court TV. Because the power of live trials and the many venues that now comment and elaborate on them have proven to have a hold on the American imagination, we must also deal with the fact that this imaginative hold has generated a large number of fictional and fictionalized legal series—and a huge number of devoted viewers.

I have divided this book into two major sections. In Part One I analyze the popular and familiar series that most clearly mark the shifts in television's dominant ideology about law and justice, crime and punishment, and the way these shifts have coincided with broader trends in legal and political policy and history. Chapter 1 analyzes, in more generic terms, two of the most popular, long-running dramatic series: *Law and Order*, which employs the conventions of film noir, and *The Practice*, which is pure melodrama. My intent here is to demonstrate the second major thematic thrust of the book as a whole: how such stylistic and generic choices tend to lend themselves particularly well to liberal or conservative readings. For while *Law and Order*, the earlier series, features prosecutors, its noiresque features in fact make it noticeably less conservative than the more recent, and far more melodramatic, *The Practice*, even though this series features defense attorneys as heroes. Thus, the interplay of aesthetics, politics, and legal history come together in complex and often contradictory ways that need to be understood in order to fully understand how television "makes meaning." Chapter 2 deals with *Cops*, which, because it is a "reality" series using live footage of police officers on duty, provides a realistic view of those the police most often tend to apprehend, and why. However, the show does this in a form so distorted by visual and dramatic technique that it is hard to see it as less fictional than the fictional series we are more used to.

Finally, I look at a new series which, I believe, while perhaps ahead of its time, marks a new and important trend in series television: the prison drama, as exemplified by HBO's bold and innovative series *Oz*. This is the first series to go beyond the police station and courtroom and look at what happens after sentencing, when the convicted defendant is actually incarcerated. Although "highbrow" in the world of television series, this show is in fact much closer in tone and conservative implication to the tabloid "reality" series discussed in chapter 2 than the earlier "transitional" series such as *Law and Order*. Thus, the turn to more conservative ideological slants in entertainment programming, as I will also argue, tends to produce a shift in all these genres toward more melodramatic, and often brutally violent and expressionistic styles and conventions. While the tabloids reflect a more socially realistic view of the typical "criminal," if not the crime fighter, there is enough blurriness between the two forms to produce an admittedly contradictory and complex picture, but one which, nonetheless, reflects an inherently conservative turn in programs addressing issues of law and justice in general.

To see the blurriness, with all the contradictions inherent in the turn from fiction to nonfiction, we turn in Part Two to a primary focus on nonfiction television programming, which presents itself as less entertainment oriented and addresses the viewer far more definitively than the series discussed in Part One: as a *citizen* meant to take seriously what is being shown and to think about its implications. I begin with a long chapter charting the history of the coming of cameras to the courtroom, the rise of Court TV, and the parallel rise of the live televised trial as major media event. For it is on Court TV that law most dramatically and explicitly becomes entertainment; and it is on Court TV that the blurry line between the two categories becomes most evident and problematic. The inherent conflict, in a commercial medium, between producing serious educational fare and making money through ratings has always been a vexed issue. As one critic put it, "While Court TV's avowed goal is to educate . . . production decisions to cut between trials as well as decisions about what trials to be aired, are reflective of the network's sensitivity to luring audiences more used to afternoon soap operas than dense trial coverage."[8]

Nonetheless, as I have already suggested, there is something to be said for the seriousness of trials that deal with what critics blithely dismiss as "soap opera fare." The issues on which Court TV focuses, while aimed at a broad audience drawn to sensationalism, are also often among the most vexed social issues of the day. The very fact that they are now being framed as criminal issues not only demonstrates the blurry line between "entertainment" and "serious programming," but also, as I show in this section, the very real dangers of criminalizing issues that are more appropriately handled by other discourses and agencies.

The chapters that follow deal with major social issues: gender violence, juvenile delinquency, family dysfunction, and the coming of a major new social movement, the Victims' Rights movement. This is arguably the most influential new movement of our time, one which fits perfectly with the rightward drift of legal and political thought and practice of recent years. I have not chosen these particular issues at random. Throughout the book I demonstrate the ways in which the criminal justice system and, in turn, Court TV and the other discussion and documentary series it has spawned, has increasingly moved toward a broadening of what is considered "criminal behavior." More and more, it includes issues that have traditionally been understood as family or social issues handled through extralegal agencies. For this reason, while we watch these trials or the spin-off series that discuss them we are increasingly being led by the media to understand these matters in terms of criminal justice concepts and processes of resolution. My choice of topics thus reflects the realities of what is actually going on in real courtrooms today and then reframed and revisited on television: what I call the criminalization of American life. Gender issues of all kinds, for example, are now being negotiated primarily within the arena of the criminal justice system. And to a lesser but increasing extent, so are issues of family dysfunction and deviant or rebellious youth behavior.

Similarly, in courtrooms across America, the presence of so-called victim impact statements, from friends and family members of victims of crime, play an increasingly large role in determining the punishment for convicted offenders. This is a dramatic switch from the more liberal tendency dominant—if increasingly under siege—from the 1960s through the 1980s, when the courts were still at least nominally committed to protecting the rights of the accused. This switch has helped to shift the pendulum toward the public's major concern with the punishment of "wrongdoers" who are often already judged and condemned by the media before a trial even starts. Thus, the particular issues I discuss in this section have been "chosen," so to speak, by the legal system and media themselves, and are therefore of particular importance in understanding the drift of criminal justice policy and the ways in which television has tended to support and advance it.

In all of these chapters, I have followed a particular strategy. I start by tracing, historically, the trends in both criminal justice and media treatments, using different genres for each issue. I first compare the earlier, generally more liberal treatments in traditional genres with the far more politically problematic representations of these issues in current versions of traditional genres. But finally, and most importantly, I turn in each chapter to the much imitated Court TV, focusing primarily on its *Crime Stories* series which, in the style of "reality TV," edits down to one hour mini-docudramas the actual footage of trials.

All chapters include historical analyses of how the traditional and classic forms have also shifted—sometimes radically, sometimes more subtly—toward more conservative ideological biases along with the changing political times. But it is in the rise of the increasingly popular and influential Court TV and its imitators that we see most starkly the radical shift in political perspective produced by the framing of these issues in narrowly limited legal contexts. For the chapter on gender violence, for example, I compare early, and then later, docudramas with typical Court TV trials that focus on these issues. I try to demonstrate how, historically, the ideological shift crosses genres while it still appears more starkly and explicitly in documentary programming of the Court TV variety. To show the criminalization of the family, I trace the shifts in early and then later daytime talk shows to demonstrate how this ideological slant crosses genres as times change. To show the demonization of youth, I use earlier and more current cinematic treatments of "juvenile delinquency" as a way of identifying shifts that cross genres, while also focusing on the more explicitly ideological nature of that shift in the Court TV–inspired newer genres.

Why is this shift most explicit on Court TV's programming? The reasons are several. First, single-issue networks such as Court TV have an unavoidable need, in the interest of filling all their airtime, to show much more clearly the class, race, and gender biases of what seems a far more egalitarian system on the fictional shows than actually exists. But perhaps more significant is the fact that programs like Court TV's *Crime Stories*—which, unlike fictional series or even a series like *Cops*, demand to be taken seriously and engage us as thoughtful viewers—come complete with editorial narrative commentary from legal "experts" who lead us to the "correct" political conclusions.

Even here, however, there is a good deal of complexity and contradiction. The Pandora's box of social issues—racism, gender violence, the death penalty—has now been opened wide. Even a series such as *Crime Stories* must at least express its awareness of and concern about these issues, even when its commentators manage to sabotage and distort their alleged concern through the use of the narrowing ideological lens allowed by the arena of the courtroom, and by the use of specific visual and dramatic conventions made possible by post-trial editing and commentary.

Thus, contradictions, complexities and generic norms notwithstanding, the general ideological slant of recent programming is more or less visible across genres, even as it waxes and wanes in emphases and explicitness from series to series and from genre and genre. For television, like all popular culture, is never as simply and simplemindedly monolithic as its most fervent critics, of both the left and right, often suggest. If it were, it would be far less intriguing—and certainly less powerful—than it is. Nor would we need books like this one to help us tease out its more confusing, if often beguilingly seductive, ways of playing with our hearts and minds.

Finally, in Part Three, I conclude with a summary and elaboration upon the major theme of the book: the criminalization of American life. For as everything that comes before will demonstrate, there is indeed a widespread national tendency to define and approach all social issues and problems within the narrow terrain of criminal law. And television—conveniently if not necessarily intentionally—has been, and continues to be, a useful handmaiden to those who have an interest in maintaining this broad consensus. Indeed, even as I write, such programming is proliferating more quickly than I can incorporate it, and there is no sign of its abatement in the near future. And so, in conclusion, I will look at the rise and flowering of this trend and raise some questions about its problematic consequences. For in shifting to programming that favors punitive, often vengeful "solutions" to social problems in general, it turns us away from the larger, more complex, and difficult approaches to these problems in ways that are often self-defeating and certainly questionable in their social and moral implications.

PART I

Fiction and Entertainment Genres

1

The Return of the Attorney-Hero
Politics and Justice
in the Prime-Time Courtroom

What ever happened to the defense-attorney hero on television? Where are the Perry Masons? The TV versions of Atticus Finch, or the fictionalized Clarence Darrows of *Inherit the Wind* and *Compulsion*? A one-time staple of TV series about crime and justice, this staunch advocate for the poor, the powerless, the unjustly accused has slowly receded from TV screens to be replaced by heroic policemen and D.A.s. Even in pulp fiction and popular movies, it's the chasers and prosecutors of the "bad guy" criminals who, with certain exceptions that prove the rule, have long reigned supreme. Defense attorneys, more often than not, appear as sleazy, corrupt, and unscrupulous, tainted by some suspiciously radical political agenda, or, at best, as hopelessly inept—the strawman foils of those who represent "true justice."

It was not always thus. In the 1950s and 1960s, the number of series featuring defense attorneys was surprisingly large. By the late 1970s, however, as I noted in the Introduction, law series—and the arena in which issues of law and justice were negotiated in general—gave way in popularity to the new wave of sophisticated, dramatically complex cop series. *Hill Street Blues*, *Cagney and Lacey*, *NYPD Blue*, and *Homicide* were popular.[1] Here lawyers were secondary characters and the search for justice took place out on the streets, where cops hunted down criminals, and the arrest, not the trial, marked the moment of narrative closure. But for the most part—and this was a sign of the times—law enforcers representing the power of the state to track down criminals became the major defenders of justice; and the legal arena, in which more subtle and nuanced definitions and portrayals of "justice" might appear, took a back seat.

There were law series on television even as early as the 1940s. But far from having any particular ideological slant, these series—produced when television was taking its first baby steps and neither the cold war nor Vietnam had forced the new medium to confront tricky issues of ideology—were innocently free of any clear bias. *Famous Jury Trials* and *They Stand Accused*, both of which ran from 1948 to 1951, presented trials in which each side was presented and then a verdict given. In the former, actors played all the roles, and in the latter, while actors played defendant and witnesses, the audience itself played the role of judge and jury. The latter series did not even have a script. And while the cases often concerned murderers, the audience/jury was left with the task of deciding if insanity, self-defense, or premeditation would determine the actual verdict. And then, in 1957, *Perry Mason*, the first legal drama to become a hit, was born—and continued to run until 1974. Mason was a defense attorney who never lost a case. But he was really more a detective than a lawyer, since his role was, invariably, to find the evidence of who *really* did it, and thereby free his invariably innocent client. Nonetheless, although social issues did not intrude upon these "who dunnits," Mason was the first role model for the defense-attorney hero on TV.

By the 1960s, however, issues of inequality and injustice in American society were becoming more and more prominent, in public policy and in mass culture. A significant number of legal series featured defense attorneys, many of whom specifically sought to serve the indigent in the interest of social justice and the righting of broader social injustices. The best known of these, *The Defenders*, which ran from 1961 to 1965, was written by Reginald Rose, a black-listed Hollywood screenwriter, and the issues taken on by the father-son partnership were often controversial indeed. Abortion rights, labor issues, and even the black list itself were among the themes the series explored from a decidedly liberal stance.

Indeed, from 1961 until 1976 a surprising number of series featured similarly socially conscious defense attorneys. The least political was the 1965–66 series, *The Trials of O'Brien*, which dealt more with the personal chaos in the life of a successful, attractive defense attorney. But others were more meaty. *The Law and Mr. Jones*, which ran from 1960 to 1962, featured a compassionate fighter for the underdog who was fond of quoting Oliver Wendell Holmes and tireless in his fight for his clients' freedom.

By the late 1960s, law series were at least as liberal, if not more so. *The Lawyers*, which ran from 1969 to 1972, featured three partners, each with different talents but all committed to working for unpopular causes. *Judd for the Defense*, which ran from 1967 to 1969 (and is still rerun on the TV Land Network), tackled issues such as labor, civil rights, and even draft evasion, as Judd defended clients from a variety of "radical" groups, including antiwar activists. In 1970 two series, *Storefront Lawyers* and *The Young Lawyers*, featured lawyers, in the latter case students, who set up offices in impoverished neighborhoods to serve the indigent. Among the most popular of these series, running from 1971 to 1974, was *Owen Marshall*, another defense attorney modeled after the heroes of *The Defenders*. And finally there was *Petrocelli*, which ran from 1974 to 1976 and featured another valiant fighter for justice who, although Harvard educated, chose to set up office in a trailer, often causing his family to suffer financial difficulties because of his commitment to serving the poor.

And then, abruptly, lawyers seemed almost to disappear from prime time to be replaced by the increasingly popular "cops with a heart" series—*Cagney and Lacey* and *Hill Street Blues*—both of which ran from the early to the late 1980s. There were, it is important to note, two law series that did appear during this period and did very well. *Matlock*, which ran from 1986 to 1995, was a kind of clone of the old Perry Mason series. It featured a feisty lawyer whose clients were always innocent. He never lost a case and did more detective work than trial work in his quest to find the real criminal and free his often unbelievably naive and victimized clients. One important new law series was much more realistic and certainly popular and successful. *LA Law*, which ran from 1986 to 1994, featured a firm made up of upscale corporate lawyers who, while sometimes trying criminal cases, devoted most of their billing hours to the problems encountered by their wealthy Beverly Hills clients.

The 1990s, however, as we have seen, made things far more interesting. During this decade, in the wake of the conservative Reagan-Bush years, Clinton Democrats—fearful of losing votes in an era in which conservatism seemed to rule the day—also moved distinctly to the right. They helped to form a national consensus on many issues, criminal justice being one of the major ones. And it is in the 1990s—indeed, we can mark the exact date as 1991—that the shift in television programming, and particularly television's approach to criminal justice issues, becomes markedly apparent. Not that this shift was without its contradictions, false starts, and misleading tendencies at the start. In fact, if one were to look at a list of series introduced during the decade, one might seriously question whether the shift existed at all. Although the dramatic legal series did return, not all the early courtroom dramas were particularly conservative. Indeed, several were markedly liberal. The renewed interest in things legal was unambiguously clear, since several new legal series quickly emerged in the wake of the coming of Court TV in 1991 and the growing interest in criminal trials it produced. But as with Court TV itself, as we shall see, the early years of renewed interest in the law on television did not immediately reveal a strongly conservative bias. Rather, as in the case of crime series such as *Cagney and Lacey* and *Hill Street Blues*, there were more contradictory moments during the 1990s when it seemed as though the producers and networks were feeling their way into new political territory, uncertain which way the wind might blow.

However, a close look at the variety of new series, with an eye toward the staying power of certain series and genres, as compared to the short lives of others, does indeed reveal a long-term, and by now deeply embedded, orientation to the right. In fact, as we shall soon see, even a law series like *Law and Order*, which has proven to have very long legs indeed, expressed more liberal positions in its earliest seasons than it did later. While other factors, too numerous to list here, contributed to the success or failure of series addressing criminal justice issues introduced in the 1990s, the willingness of producers to move, ideologically, with the times—as Dick Wolf, producer of *Law and Order*, did—has been a clear factor in determining which series lived and which did not.

The Darwinian Nineties and the Survival of Television's "Fittest"

In 1991, as Court TV started up, so too did two new courtroom series—the first since 1976. The first, produced by *Cagney and Lacey*'s Barney Rosensweig, was *The Trials of Rosie O'Neill*, a drama about a public defender from a wealthy family, which mixed the heroine's personal traumas and her commitment to the work her family strongly scorned. The second was Dick Wolf's *Law and Order*. We know which one had the staying power: *O'Neill* lasted less than two seasons; *Law and Order* has become an institution—and, again, it became more conservative as it has evolved.

There were a few other liberally slanted legal dramas in those years as well. John Grisham's *The Client*, based on his novel of the same name, ran from 1995 to 1996 and featured a female liberal defense attorney, who, like O'Neill, had as many personal problems as her clients had legal ones. In 1994 another series lasting less than two seasons, *Sweet Justice*, also featured women defense attorneys, one black and one white, who were concerned primarily with issues of civil rights in the southern city in which they practiced. There was also David Kelley's *Picket Fences*, which, while not narrowly a legal drama since it dealt with many issues confronting the small town in which it was set, tended to end each segment in the courtroom, where the serious and complex moral and ethical issues addressed brought the series and its creator (himself an attorney) quite a bit of critical acclaim. What is most interesting about this liberal-leaning series is that its relatively long run—from 1992 to 1996—was followed immediately in 1997 with Kelley's even more successful and still-running *The Practice*, which, as we shall soon see, tended increasingly, if subtly, to take a more clear-cut "law and order" stance than its predecessor. Another short-lived law series, *Murder One*, which was produced by *Hill Street Blues*' Steven Bochco, ran from 1995 to 1996. This one, more in the style of Bochco's *LA Law* than the others, presented a highly jaded view of the defense bar. Here the main character—another Beverly Hills player—was as cynical and manipulative as people had by then, in the wake of the Menendez and Simpson trials, come to see the high-powered defense attorneys of the LA rich and famous. This series, which attempted to follow a single story for an entire season, had more than ideology going against it. It was difficult to expect audiences, in the age of cable TV, to set their Palm Pilots to the same time slot each week in order to follow the story as it developed. What was left standing by the end of the decade, therefore, was *Law and Order* and *The Practice*, the two series we will be looking at in some depth because of their success in setting a standard for the many legal series that have followed.

During these years of touch-and-go efforts to produce legal series with a liberal bias, other developments in TV programming were doing much better at surviving. More significantly, they were setting the political tone for what audiences, now enthralled with criminal cases, would be watching in great numbers for years to come. The most obvious, already mentioned, was Court TV itself, which made "reality" programming centering in the legal system a major focus of TV programming throughout network and cable channels. Still another new genre, the tabloid crime series, also emerged—and proved to have strong legs—during those years. *Unsolved Mysteries*, a series hosted by Robert Stack, who played FBI agent Elliot Ness in the 1959–62 series *The Untouchables*, presented scarily grotesque reenactments of actual crimes yet unsolved, and often asked viewers to help solve them. The series actually began in 1988 but reached its height of popularity in the 1990s. It is still running nightly, mostly in reruns, on the Lifetime cable channel, five nights a week. Two other tabloids, *Cops*, which we will look at in detail in the next chapter, and *America's Most Wanted*, also presented reenactments of unsolved crimes, this time with the cooperation of the FBI. It managed to tote up a good number of arrests helped by viewers who looked for and sometimes found the wanted offenders. *Cops* began in 1989 and is still going strong. And *AMW*, whose host, John Walsh, the father of a kidnaped boy who was found dead and a leading founder of the Victims' Rights movement, began in 1988 and is also still a hit. In fact, in recent seasons, it has beefed up its title, which now reads *America's Most Wanted: America Fights Back*.

As we look back over this intriguing decade, it is clear that the winners were the law series that kept up with the conservative beat of the time, and the tabloid reality series that, in terms of television programming, can be said to have led the charge to the right. *Law and Order*, now rerun almost endlessly on TNT and its home network, NBC—certainly began the trend toward courtroom drama series. It is responsible, so far, for two popular spin-off series, *Law and Order: Criminal Intent* and *Law and Order: Special Victims Unit*, and it is in serious contention to become the longest-running series in TV history. The closest relative to *Law and Order*, and certainly its major competition in terms of popularity, awards, and ratings, is *The Practice*, whose heroes are defense attorneys, not prosecutors. Even though some of these series might, at first glance, seem to be "liberal" in thrust, upon closer examination, more often than not, they have embedded in their very foundations an implicitly conservative bias.

To demonstrate this point I have chosen to use *Law and Order* and *The Practice* because they are so popular and influential, and because they are such classic examples of law series today; indeed, they are the models for the many new series that have followed. While both *Law and Order* and *The Practice* usually present a conservative (if often contradictory) bias in criminal justice, in keeping with the times, *The Practice*, despite its ostensibly liberal *bona fides*, is actually far more conservative than its predecessor largely *because* it is less straightforward in its expression of its underlying political values.

It is important to note, however, that while these series are probably the most popular and influential courtroom series to date, there are many other new series that differ in significant ways from the two I am discussing. Because television producers always search for ways to plug into current successful programming trends, with a somewhat different spin on each new contender, many law and crime series have sprung up in recent years. Some, like *CSI: Crime Scene Investigation*, were immediate hits, with almost immediate spin-offs. Others, such as *Family Law*, have lasted barely two seasons. Many, such as *CSI, Crossing Jordan, The Shield, 100 Centre Street*, and *Judging Amy*, tend to incorporate generic and thematic aspects of series that are very different in style and ideology, making them often fascinatingly contradictory ideological hybrids. They pick and choose from a variety of conventions common to both tabloid and the more "quality" series such as *Law and Order*, mixing serious attention to legal procedure with often gory scenes of sordid violence on seedy landscapes.

Moreover, no trend, no matter how influential, is ever monolithically dominant. Old forms tend to survive as new ones develop and evolve, so there is always a good deal of overlap at any given time among and between series formats. Demographics plays an important role as well. How else can one explain the long run of "old-fashioned" series such as Angela Lansbury's *Murder She Wrote* and Dick Van Dyke's *Diagnosis Murder*? There is always an older audience tied to older cultural traditions, just as there is a young audience hooked into newer, soon-to-be major genres before the vast majority of mainstream viewers are even aware of them. Class, race, and gender differences also account for the wide variety of subtle, and not so subtle, differences in existing crime and law series. I will say more about some of these older series as well as up-and-coming new series in the Conclusion to this book. But for now I will focus on the most generically "classic" and highly rated series of the day.

Down These Mean Streets: Crime and Justice in Law and Order

Since *Law and Order* is the Daddy of them all, so to speak, I will begin by looking at the way it presents crime and justice, and the changes it has gone through in the many years since its inception. In comparison it will be easier to see how very different, and subtly conservative, *The Practice* is. *Law and Order* belongs in a tradition of crime and legal fiction that goes back to the early days of classic Hollywood movies based on the dark, cynical writings of authors such as Raymond Chandler and Dashiell

Hammett in an era, at the end of World War II, when American life was undergoing intense social and economic upheaval. Vivian Sobchak, in writing about some of these films, cites the "the increase in crime . . . the destabilization of the . . . domestic economy and consequent 'deregulation' of the institutionalized and patriarchally informed relationship between men and women" as major sources of anxiety which films like *Double Indemnity, The Maltese Falcon, The Big Sleep,* and others reflected.[2] Like these films, *Law and Order* is set in the dark, sinister streets, in the seedy bars and clubs of urban nightlife. We see the images of middle- and upper-class homes in which intimacy and security are mere façades covering the raw truth of family breakdown, violence, and perversion. They also have in common the emphasis on deviant psychological motives; the hostility and suspicion in gender relations, especially sexual ones; the portrayal of women as either dangerous but seductive villainesses or virtuous mothers, secretaries, and girlfriends; and the hero as a cynical, damaged loner, who tends to straddle the fence between the worlds of law and justice and those of the criminal elements he stalks as he works to ward off, if not defeat, the forces of decadence and corruption symbolized by the criminal.[3]

Law and Order has gone, over the years, through a number of shifts, castings, and major characters, though it roughly follows the same format. However, in the earliest years liberal concerns were given more serious attention, while more recent segments have reflected the more punitive New York criminal justice system, which has restored the death penalty and instituted other changes that make criminal prosecution easier and criminal defense more difficult. In the early segments, the chief assistant district attorney, Ben Stone, was a level-headed but tough prosecutor who lacked the strain of angry, often vengeful determination to convict incorrigible criminals that has come to typify the current chief, Jack McCoy. Assistants were first a race-conscious black male named Robinette and then a fairly liberal feminist, Claire Kincaid. Since then, each assistant, always an attractive white woman, has been increasingly less concerned with "politically correct" morally troubling issues and more extreme in the pure pursuit of conviction at all costs. Jamie Ross was a former defense attorney, fed up with her high-powered firm's legal tactics. Abbie Carmichael's tough-on-crime stance was given no explanation. And from there on, each successive woman has simply followed the tough-on-crime pattern now established by the series, with none of the ideological anguish typical of Robinette and Kincaid—not to mention

McCoy and Stone—in the early days of the series. The central administrative role, that of the head of the detectives' department, was first played by a white male named Kragen, who now plays the same role on the spin-off *Law and Order: Special Victims' Unit*, which itself features a tough female detective. The administrator's role is now played by an African American woman named Anita Van Buren, who is both race and class conscious but tough on crime because, as is often noted, it affects her own community and her children's lives.[4]

These attorneys play out their roles in the second half-hour of the series, after the suspect has been captured. They are seen in various negotiations with suspects, defense attorneys, and judges about how the trial will be handled and then, finally, we see the trial itself. Often this section involves new developments in which the original suspect is eliminated and the real criminal is finally found. Often, the prosecutors will lose a case and leave the court house philosophizing about society, the legal system, and the morality of what they do.

The first half of the show centers on the conduct of the criminal investigation, and also, quite often, on a series of dead ends the detectives run up against before they actually catch the person they believe is guilty. The earlier segments featured a shifting number of central detective teams in segments tending to involve the two central cops in moral arguments about their cases. Early segments, for example, often featured the devout Catholic detective in arguments about abortion with his younger, more cynical partner. For the last several years the team has been headed by Lenny Briscoe, an older, former alcoholic, a much-divorced guy whose sexual relationships and failed parenting flaws have left him cynical and hard boiled to a fault. His longest-running partnership was with a Latino named Rey Curtis, a family man whose own personal code of honor was sometimes in conflict with his partner's cynicism, but who was also prone to more passionate outbursts of violence against suspects—especially those who use racial slurs—than the more sanguine Briscoe. Curtis has been succeeded by an African American man named Green who is perhaps the most violence prone and least philosophical of them all.

In these segments, the police run down leads and typically spend a lot of time insulting the suspects they pursue. They even get involved in street fights with the criminal element they pursue. They express an equal or even larger amount of contempt for the morality, hypocrisy, and corruption of those they decide to place on the "wrong" side of the law when the suspects are upper class.

In most respects, *Law and Order* resembles the world of the classic crime dramas of the Golden Age of Hollywood: the seedy neighborhoods and bars; the alienated, hostile, suspicious people of the streets; the emotionally barren homes, offices, hotels, and restaurants of the wealthy, in which secrets, lies, devious schemes, and perverse relationships prevail; the recurring theme of evil temptresses or out of control, psychologically damaged street criminals; and the general sense of breakdown in the social and moral fabric. While the specific historic features of postwar urban life may have changed, its sense of anxiety, concern over the breakdown of traditional gender and family relations, and the ever-changing economic and social order has only intensified over the decades. Thus the popular style that dramatizes the loneliness, cynicism, paranoia, gender antagonisms, incipient violence, dramatic economic inequality, and breakdown of traditional values which define the urban landscape has endured. *L&O*, like its classic movie models, adheres religiously to this dark, pessimistic vision.

The heroes—both cops and lawyers—engage in cynical, hard-boiled dialogue. "I've seen it all" cynicism sets the tone of the urban environment in which crime occurs. The protagonists are not above bending the rules a bit in the name of an ever-illusive justice, in a city and system in which laws, institutions, and characters—the criminals as well as the heroes—are less than perfect. What is different is that the heroes in this series—and in all the crime series of the 1990s—are not independent private investigators like Sam Spade and Philip Marlowe, but representatives of the state itself as police officers or prosecutors. Assistant District Attorney McCoy and Detective Briscoe may seem very much like Spade and Marlowe in personality and lifestyle: they are cynical loners; current or recovering drinkers who drink (or drank) alone in seedy bars; men with dark pasts marked by conflicted and failed family and romantic relationships. Their determination to catch "the bad guys" and put them away drives the weekly narrative. But their victories are always temporary and they are often foiled in their efforts to achieve moral closure by the flaws in the system and the deviousness of criminals and defense attorneys.

Commentators on this series, which has gained critical acclaim for its intelligent and complex representation of how the criminal justice system really functions in urban centers, have often noted that it is the system itself that is the series' main character. "Roles are dictated by process rather than personality," according to one critic, for "the real star of *Law and Order* is the criminal justice system itself. . . . Here process is king and woe to those naive enough to think they have some control over its mysterious ways."[5] There is much truth in this statement. *Law and Order* gives detailed attention to the ways in which not only criminal justice specifically but urban cities generally—from the smallest neighborhood dynamics to the largest institutional structures—work together as a coherent system in which all players, including the lawyers and cops, are cogs in the complex machinery of modern urban society. Like the psychologists, medical examiners, forensic experts, judges, white-collar criminals, gold-digging temptresses, street criminals, gang lords, parents and teachers and juvenile offenders—but unlike the outsider heroes of Hammett and Chandler—McCoy and Briscoe belong, first and foremost, to a body politic whose workings they can neither wholly control nor elude.

There is a moral ambiguity in the series. For this model of criminal justice is offset, for generic reasons, by the need for real heroes who concern themselves with matters of right and wrong, judging criminals not simply in terms of their psychological flaws, but also in terms of the "badness" of their acts. Thus, as Diane Keetley has insightfully noted, there is a "persistent unsettling of the notion of 'crime'" in the series, "as it puts into play the two primary elements of a crime—*actus reus* (guilty act) and *mens rea* (guilty mind). The show repeatedly asks the audience to consider not only 'Who did it?' but 'were the defendant's actions actually criminal?' Even if it is clear that the defendant did commit the crime, his or her state of mind and thus his or her criminal responsibility are often put in doubt."[6]

But, I would add, rarely by the prosecutors themselves. In fact, over the years McCoy and his series of associates have become increasingly impatient with psychological assumptions and solutions to the problem of crime. McCoy, especially, expounds regularly on his belief in "pure evil" and his impatience with defenses based on "psychobabble" and "sob stories about sad childhoods." Each successive associate has become increasingly strident and harsh in her or his law-and-order position. The first two, Robinette and Kincaid, tended to be far more liberal in their concerns than their successors. They worried over issues of race and gender equity and had serious qualms about issues such as the death penalty. In a particularly moving episode, aired the year that the death penalty was reinstated in New York, the tensions around this issue and its effects on the principals who were made to watch their first execution were palpable. Kincaid in particular was visibly shaken while McCoy was hard boiled and "business as usual" throughout. She complained of "feeling ill" and took the day off; he kept to his schedule, becoming perhaps more unyielding than ever in his meetings with defense attorneys over possible plea bargains.

But it was on this very segment that Kincaid was literally killed off, to be replaced by the third associate, Jamie Ross, a disillusioned former defense attorney who was far tougher and more hard boiled than either Kincaid or Robinette. The fourth and fifth associates, Carmichael and Southerlyn, have never met defendants who they felt didn't deserve the stiffest possible punishment, including death. These shifts in character and script writing have had a clear, if often subtle, impact on the underlying political slant, if not the generic basics, of the series. For no matter what the apparent political biases are of the revolving cast of principals, they remain heroic figures fighting for justice against opponents who invariably represent the socially or politically "wrong" side.

To demonstrate, I will offer two more or less thematically similar segments—one dating from the Ben Stone–Claire Kincaid era, in which Kincaid had just joined the team; and the other a more recent segment in which the McCoy-Carmichael characters were in charge of the legal proceedings. Both deal with race and racism. In the first, a white supremacist, angered when his mother is mugged by black youths, goes on a serial killing spree in which four people of color are murdered. Stone, Carmichael, and the actual D.A., Adam Schiff, are determined to convict this guy because they hate what he stands for and has done. The defendant's sister wants her brother to plead insanity and thus qualify for psychiatric treatment. But the clever defendant, paranoid indeed and unwilling to take such a route, hires an excellent black attorney who manages to win the case. The attorney's motives? He is tired of the low-rent, low-media-exposure ghetto he is stuck in, defending black defendants, and he wants to get national attention and join the high-profile, big-bucks league of the likes of Alan Dershowitz and Gerry Spence. (This segment predated Johnnie Cochran's rise to national fame.) In the end, the acquitted man kills again, then is killed himself by the daughter of his last victim. Both deaths are viewed, sorrowfully, by Schiff, Stone, and Kincaid as tragically unnecessary. If only the insanity plea had been accepted, perhaps a less bloody conclusion might have been possible. The liberalism of this segment, and the passion with which the prosecutors express their frustration at their loss, is palpable. So is the scorn heaped upon the black defense attorney, who is seen to have no principles and to be as sleazy as the other defense attorneys on this series.

On the more recent segment, however, the liberal tone is decidedly absent. It is replaced by a growing sense of anger and vengefulness—in tune with the increasingly conservative times—at the leaders of the black community who allegedly use their position to keep law enforcement officials, whenever possible, from convicting blacks, no matter how corrupt or heinous their crimes, by "playing the race card"—as, in these post-O. J. days, we now say. This time the story involves the internecine warfare of two equally corrupt black power organizations in which one black leader is murdered by followers of the second. The lawyer for the accused is another hot-shot black attorney, fashioned, in appearance and style, after the controversially radical New York activist Al Sharpton. He tries the case on purely racial grounds, riling up passionate community support for the corrupt and self-serving defendant, and so befuddles the jury. Again, the guilty man goes free. Again, the D.A.'s office is frustrated, although clearly more passionately enraged by the evils of human nature than sadly frustrated by its weaknesses. And again, the defense attorney is shown to be an opportunistic sleaze. But the racial politics of the two segments are alarmingly different even as the heroic roles of the prosecutors, trying to squeeze an ounce of blood-red justice from the socially and politically complex "turnips" they are forced to work with each week, remain central and clear. They may now be more vengeful and enraged than saddened by the flaws in human nature, but they remain on the job, doing God's work in trying the best they can to rid society of its dangerous "bad guys."

Thus, despite its sophisticated social and institutional intricacies and its often intriguing ways of presenting complex and contradictory approaches to serious social issues, *L&O* is, on another level, a series in which individual heroism and ideas of morality and justice still play the decisive role. Jack McCoy and Lenny Briscoe are socially damaged men who have somehow survived with an intact core of human decency and morality to bring the moral closure that contemporary viewers expect. But again, unlike the Sam Spades and Philip Marlowes of classic Hollywood, who maintained their cores of decency by eschewing *all* connection to established institutional power, McCoy is smack in the middle of it: he is its powerful representative. Thus we get the overtly conservative slant of the series—whether the specific cases play to the sympathies of a liberal audience or to a more conservative one. Its virtuous hero is no outsider but an establishment power broker, and the role he plays is that of the avenging, punishing prosecutor, impatient with social, political, or psychological defenses, and increasingly more avid in his desire to judge and punish than treat or rehabilitate.

Back to the Future

The issue of the "guilty act" versus the "guilty mind" has long been a major concern of those who theorize about crime and its role in modern life. In modern times, with the rise of therapeutic discourse, we have seen attention focus away from traditional moral concepts like "good and evil" and "right and wrong" toward more sociological and psychological explanations—*away* from the guilty *act* as the primary factor in determining punishment and toward the guilty *mind* of the defendant. We might call this view of criminal justice "defendant centered" since its primary focus is the psychology of the actor and the social environment that formed him or her. Thus the modern fascination with serial killers and other examples of extreme deviance. Ted Bundy, Jeffrey Dahmer, the Son of Sam—all are cultural icons of recent history whose family and social experiences are scrutinized with intense interest in scholarly journals, Op-Ed pieces, and TV talk shows, while their victims' names are quickly forgotten. "*Why* did the actor act as he or she did?" is the prime question in series like *L&O*; the moral significance and consequences of the act—the suffering of victims, for example—are largely thrust into the background. As often as not, they are the McGuffins upon which the narrative depends for its logic, but hardly the key players in the drama since they are generally dead early into the story.

Such a view of crime, and of the importance of the criminal's motives and mindset, is particularly suited to liberal democracies in which therapeutic rather than physical punishment were more in vogue. But recently, as liberalism has increasingly given way to a more conservative strain of political sentiment, the legal concern with "guilty acts" is increasingly in the foreground and punishment of the most extreme and brutal kind is once more called for. In fact, we might call the current ideas about criminal justice "victim centered" rather than "defendant centered." As Alison Young has argued, we are living at a time when notions of a body politic, in which individual units can be studied and repaired, have given way to a sense of "shared victimization" and "a shared awareness of risk and danger" as the markers of community unity and belonging.[7]

In such a world, the criminal is no longer the sick individual but the alien "other," threatening to disrupt the fragile sense of community stability with deviant acts of violence and plunder.[8] The *act* of the criminal— now seen as a dangerous outsider—becomes the focus of concern as public debate shifts dramatically from the "why" of the crime to its moral nature and consequences. With it come such signs of the time as the dramatic rise of the Victims' Rights movement, with its emphases on the "badness" of the criminal act and the suffering of its victims; the return of the often vengeance-driven cry for the death penalty; the growing popularity of public "shaming" punishments and calls for public executions; and the increasing derision, and ineffectiveness, of psychological- and social-based defenses such as insanity pleas and so-called abuse excuses.

The Politics of The Practice

In the series *The Practice*, however, it is clear upon immediate viewing that we are dealing with a different perspective of criminal justice and the social context in which it operates.

Far from the cynicism of *Law and Order* and its theatrical models, *The Practice* wears its sentimental bleeding heart on its sleeve, featuring an attractive team of idealistic young defense attorneys. Unlike *Law and Order*, its central premise is not that the law exists to keep at bay the ever-threatening decay and downfall of Western civilization as we know it. Rather, its lawyer-heroes are struggling partners in a less-than-posh law firm who live for the chance to try cases in which real issues of morality and justice are at stake. The series' ensemble cast has been fairly constant. Bobby Donnell, the founder of the firm, is a practicing-Catholic hunk who attempts at times to rule with a more authoritarian hand than his partners are willing to put up with. His partners include Lindsay Dole— now his wife—a crackerjack lawyer who often has serious qualms about her cases. Her best moments have been when she has successfully taken on corporate opponents—tobacco firms, corporate polluters—and, in a David versus Goliath style, brought them to their knees. In one episode her opponent was her law school mentor who expressed disdain at her choice of defending low-life criminals when she could be climbing the corporate ladder. She herself has agonized about the conflict—faced by most defense attorneys, even the most idealistic—between staying financially solvent and representing often despicable people, especially drug dealers.

The other characters are Ellinor Shutt, a truly exceptional TV star because she is successful and even sexually active at times despite her often-discussed obesity. She agonizes over her clients' sins too often, especially anti-Semitic hate crimes, which particularly distress her because she is Jewish. Eugene Young, however, is perhaps the most interesting character, an African American who must often deal with the problems of trying to raise a son to be moral and law abiding while he himself is defending criminals. This conflict was in fact the cause of his divorce. The Italian character, Jimmy Berlucci, is the least effective member of the group—a sweet if not terribly impressive counsel who often finds himself in tricky situations. Finally there is Rebecca, an African American woman who began as a feisty secretary, went to law school at night, and ultimately became a partner in the firm.

This is an extremely attractive group of multicultural friends and partners. Their practice of law is more often victim centered than defendant centered. To survive as a firm, they must take on the kinds of cases that most defense attorneys must take—drug deals, assaults and murders, sex and child-abuse. In most segments the drama revolves around the conflict between the lawyers' own moral values and the often "disgusting" people and cases they are forced to deal with "in the name of the law."

But the moral ambiguity is not always cut and dried, and there is indeed an effort, in many episodes, to balance the moral equation by giving serious attention to the actual democratic, constitutional principles on which they based their choice to join the defense bar. In one episode, for example, the firm was being sued by a defense witness—the brother of a murder victim—for having suggested, in the interest of freeing their own accused client, that he might even have killed his own sister. Most of the defense case actually centered on the fact that the accused lawyer felt guilty, "sick," and "disgusted with himself" about his behavior in this and other cases and had even considered leaving the profession because of this guilt. But in closing arguments, the lead attorney in the firm's case made an impassioned statement about the "honor" of their work since it was their responsibility to make sure that the state did not unfairly confer harsh punishment on a client they "knew" to be innocent. It is noteworthy that in a subsequent segment, however, the very client in question was revealed to have been a serial killer, guilty not only of the previous crime but many others. And thus the ironies and contradictions in the series go on.

These contradictions are often intriguing. But at the end of day—or of the case, to speak in terms of narrative closure—it is more often true that the contradictions are overridden by the more conservative orientation of the series as a whole. For unlike *Perry Mason* or the heroes of the popular and more liberal John Grisham novels, these lawyers more often than not find themselves defending clients whose acquittals are not cause for celebration, but a sense of moral anguish. This does not happen in a John Grisham novel or *Perry Mason* episode because the heroes of these narratives are always, and more easily, on the "right" side, defending those who are truly innocent and whom the system has wrongly accused.

Nonetheless, if the series were truly advancing the view—so central to our Constitution—that every defendant, no matter how odious or guilty, deserves the very best defense possible so that our democratic system can function properly, they would not experience moral anguish and disgust when they win their cases. The cynical crime fighters of *Law and Order* are at least clear about their role in the system, and, though they are often frustrated and uneasy about failing to gain a conviction—they can sleep well at night. The system itself may thwart them, but, in their own eyes, they fight the good fight.

Not so the lawyers in *The Practice*. This is true because in most instances they are not positioned within the justice system as advocates for the innocent and/or abused (although they do at times make reference to these ideals). But they do not often enough, or consistently enough, stand for the more progressive (if increasingly reviled) view of lawyer-heroes like Clarence Darrow, whose principled defense of the despised and powerless—whether Eugene V. Debs or Leopold and Loeb—was rooted in a commitment to the constitutional principle that every defendant deserves the very best possible defense so that the powerful engines of state will be forced to meet their burden of absolute *proof* of guilt before any citizen can be deprived of liberty or life. The idea that one is innocent until *proven* guilty, after all, is at the heart of our democracy, which differs—I would say admirably—from systems of justice even in other Western democracies.

In fact, when the series is at its progressive best, it is not necessarily through its discursive assertion of any particular legal or democratic principle, but rather in the more purely dramatic, emotional depictions. Probably the most moving and ideologically vexed segment concerned the death penalty. Shot in documentary style, the segment involved a death-row inmate in the last hours before his execution. A documentary filmmaker was shooting these last hours in real time and Jimmy, against his will, was appointed to represent the firm and stay with the prisoner, while the filming took place. The condemned man awaited his final moment and, at hour's end, was executed. Jimmy, a strong believer in the death penalty, was, as the hour began, vehemently opposed to his assignment.

The segment never revealed whether the man, an African American, was guilty or not. But as he and Jimmy sat together in his cell, making small talk, sharing sports lore, playing cards and, in the most moving moments, sharing the condemned man's last tearful meeting with his wife and children, the mood of the segment, and of Jimmy himself, shifted dramatically. The audience was allowed to experience Jimmy's growing affection for and identification with the prisoner and his growing doubts about the death penalty itself. Both Jimmy and the viewing audience were allowed to see the convicted man as a total human being, whose entire life was not, as the criminal justice system often implies, defined by what may have been his worst act. Finally, as the increasingly sympathetic man was dragged off to the gas chamber, Jimmy was seen to be visibly shaken in a life-altering way.

It is this kind of thing that makes the series, and its characters, more contradictory and complex than most television series. But if such ambiguity and idealism are not entirely absent from the series, they are hardly the usual driving forces of the lawyers on *The Practice*. Unlike Atticus Finch, Clarence Darrow, or the Grisham-style lawyer-heroes who resolve the "gap between law and justice" by exonerating the unjustly accused or socially abused, the lawyer-heroes of *The Practice* more often experience deep grief and guilt because they have served "the law" but not the ideals of justice. Indeed, far from feeling empathy for their unfortunate clients, in many of the most dramatic episodes the lawyers clearly despise them—and themselves—for having to defend them. And while they may occasionally make high-minded speeches about the honorable work of defense law, it is in the sufferings and self-doubts enacted in most of the episodes that the deepest dramatic truths about their dominant attitudes toward their work and their clients shine through.

This slant was made more explicit with the addition of a hard-line female prosecutor named Helen Gamble. She is Lindsay's former roommate and best friend and Bobby's former lover. In real life, as I have seen it, it is actually quite rare for defense attorneys and prosecutors to be more than cordial acquaintances. The ideological differences between them too often cause friction that does not abate when the court goes dark. Rather, each group, especially defense attorneys, tend to hang with their own, so to speak, because they feel increasingly under siege by their unpopular public image. Helen is often in anguish about her job. When she finds herself forced to prosecute a defendant in ways that challenge her own morality, she is seen to agonize over her own role as an "officer of the court" and lose more than a night's sleep. One segment even ended with Helen going tearfully to the home of an innocent defendant's family to apologize for having convicted their loved one. At times, she and her defense attorney friends even collaborate, in moral unison, in highly unorthodox if not wholly unethical ways that real lawyers would rarely risk, to achieve true "justice" in spite of the "legal technicalities" imposed by an amoral, technocratic "system." Thus there is a balance between the moral anguish they often experience and the positive references to the constitutional principles upon which our adversarial justice system has been based since the eighteenth century.

Still, it is far more often the case that the subtextual contradictions that make this series more than a cartoon are defeated dramatically by the ultimate narrative closure. There is more often anguish about getting the "bad guys" off than a sense of honor and pride. In my experience, most principled defense attorneys do feel good about winning against the heavyweight state apparatus and supporting true constitutional democracy. Not so here. For example, in one episode Eugene defended a child molester whose behavior and attitude, during the entire lawyer-client relationship, often provoked Eugene to verbal abuse. When the man was acquitted, so outraged and guilt-ridden was Eugene that he proceeded to personally beat up his client, right in the courtroom.

On another episode, another member of the firm, Lindsay Dole, won acquittal for a rapist-murderer and then was attacked and nearly killed in her office, presumably (it was at first assumed) by the very man she set free. Her partner and lover, Bobby Donnell, overwrought by grief and anger, went into the courtroom the next day and, during the presentation of his own case, actually excoriated his own client, a petty thief. Writhing in agony at the moral conflict which forced him to defend such "degenerates"—"because our Constitution requires that every defendant have an adequate defense and fair trial," he yelled sarcastically at one point— he turned to his client and screamed, "You're just going to go out and rob somebody again, aren't you?? Aren't you?? Because you have the IQ of a moron and the morals of an animal," as he grabbed the poor man by the shoulder. "But we have to uphold your constitutional rights, don't we?" he nearly sobbed.

In another episode, Rebecca, the newest member of the bar, defended a man against a robbery charge of which he was clearly innocent. But in the course of preparing for the trial, she realized that he was almost certainly a serial killer who could not have committed the robbery because he was a few blocks away molesting and killing a young girl. Seeking to be removed from the case, she was told by the judge that the law requires her do the best job she can, and that she, the judge, would be watching her to make sure she did. The man was acquitted and sent off, we presume, to rape and kill again. And Rebecca, in a state of abject pain, yelled at the judge who had required her to fulfill her legal responsibility to her client: "Legal, what about moral??" Thus the gap between law and justice is hardly bridged, as it is in classic legal melodrama, but rather exacerbated.

Another way in which *The Practice* confuses its viewers' understanding of the criminal justice system is in its highly unrealistic portrayal of the roles of the attorneys. We have an adversarial system in which opposing attorneys are in fact *opposing* because they have different jobs to do: one to convict, the other to acquit. Too often morality stands in for justice—as the Constitution clearly defines it—in ways that may be dramatically compelling but are highly subversive of the real role of our legal system, which is to insure that the rights of the accused are upheld. Indeed, the prosecution has a legal obligation to dismiss a case, or not pursue it all, once they know that their case does not qualify as a valid one or that the defendant is actually innocent. For political reasons, of course, in the real world, prosecutors do indeed on occasion pursue cases that may win them points under such circumstances. The issue of "morality," then, in the actual legal system, is not the ultimate marker of justice that *The Practice* would have viewers believe. For it is as likely for the prosecutors to be on the side of "right" or "wrong" as the defense attorneys.

Thus, there is no moral or political distinction between defense attorneys and prosecutors. "Heroes," on either side of the courtroom, are those who strive to uphold the moral order which the collective conscience of the day demands.

Thus, from beginning to end, the dramatic contrast between cynical series like *Law and Order* and the more emotional *The Practice* is clear. The opening credits for *The Practice*, for example, feature no dark scenes of police cars roaming the seedy, dangerous streets of the urban night or grim attorneys and ominous courthouses set firmly in the midst of city decay and dirt. Instead, there are shots of the stately courthouse in broad daylight, a single symbolic image of justice set outside the context of its urban setting. Where *L&O*'s credits feature shots of suspects being roughly frisked and cuffed by cops, *The Practice*'s only image of (assumed) violent crime is a single close-up of a handgun, suggesting the intense drama, rather than the setting and circumstances, of the criminal act and its consequences. In fact, there are no scenes of urban landscapes at all, and the shots of the protagonists are also in close-up, their highly emotive faces looking anguished, even grief stricken, in their pursuit of justice. If McCoy and his associates are hard-boiled, the lawyers on the *The Practice* are pure marshmallows, ready to weep at the drop of a moral conundrum. While both series end on notes of moral ambiguity, *L&O*'s final scenes—in which the attorneys comment upon the justice or injustice in which they have just participated—tend to show the attorneys cynically remarking on the situation.

The Practice, however, typically ends with one or more of the heroes suffering agonies of guilt or collapsing in exhausted relief at the turn that the particular week's events has taken. Indeed, tear-filled eyes and outbursts, often violent outbursts, of frustrated emotion are the hallmark of the series' most dramatic moments, especially when, as in the examples above, they are forced to set dangerous criminals free. Bobby and Lindsay are the Heathcliff and Cathy of legal melodrama, whose unbridled passions, for each other and for ideals of justice, lead them to moan, wail, gnash teeth, and more. Indeed, their emotions are so often out of bounds that it is the legal system itself, with its strict laws of conduct and process, that serves as the agent of "recuperation, helping the protagonists to take their proper role in the social and domestic order; disciplining their unruly passions and desires."⁹ But if the producers clearly share the lawyers' contempt for most of their clients, they do not share their *self*-contempt. For these lawyers, as written by the creative staff, achieve a kind of sainthood, no matter what their actions, because they always "feel" the proper anguish, grief, and guilt about what they've done. In fact, the lawyers themselves, in their suffering for the *victims* of injustice, and in many cases their powerlessness to heal the wounds, become themselves suffering victims of the unjust system they serve. Thus—win or lose—they appear virtuous and innocent.

But perhaps the most distinctive feature of the series, and the one that works most effectively to mask its conservative orientation, is its lack of social, political, or psychological context. Like the lawyer-heroes of *Law and Order*, *The Practice*'s heroes must operate within a world in which moral ambiguity and failed justice rules. But these lawyers do not function in an institutional environment in which the processes of criminal justice are seen as part of an integrated social body where police officers, psychologists, forensic experts, and the dynamics of the families, schools, neighborhoods and other institutions in which the guilty exist figure prominently. On the contrary, police officers never appear in the series, and family and schoolmates or teachers generally appear as character witnesses, if at all. Similarly, the use of psychiatric and forensic experts generally occurs within the dramatic context of the trial itself, where it functions more to lay out the moral dilemmas of the case—typically something like euthanasia—than the workings of the legal system. The emphasis is on "sensibility and sentimentality . . . inflation of personal conflicts . . . and internalization of external social conflict."[10] For this is a world in which social issues figure prominently, but they are viewed outside the social, economic, or political contexts in which they occur, and redefined wholly in terms of personal morality.

The way in which law and lawyers function in this series is very close to the way in which they function in daytime soap operas, among the most unrealistic of all popular forms.[11] As in soap operas, emotion and inherent morality are everything while the portrayal of actual institutions and social processes is absent or wildly unrealistic. There too, emotional outbursts and violence in courtroom scenes are common. But on soap operas justice always does prevail because the link between social reality and fantasy has been wholly dissolved. On *The Practice*, however, which must follow the conventions of realism that serious prime-time drama demands, justice is often left lying dead on the courtroom floor, and the heroes are left to suffer agonies of guilt and failure.

All of these issues do indeed make the series complex and contradictory enough to make for often intelligent, even riveting, drama. Like the protagonists on *Law and Order*, moral issues plague them in ways that are often emotionally moving. In fact, in most segments, there is enough subtextual conflict in the minds and hearts of these attorneys to lend their apparent liberalism more than a pinch of authenticity. On occasion they are even shown making impressive speeches about the virtue and value of what defense attorneys do in the name of democracy. For, as they will at times declare in purely Darrowesque rhetoric, it is a constitutional necessity that every American, no matter how odious his or her character or deeds, is entitled to the best possible defense.

Outsiders but Not Outlaws:
The Practice as a Dramatic Version of Friends

One might argue, I suppose, that the very premise of the series, that the system does not in fact work because "real" criminals go free to rape and plunder citizens again and again, renders it more critical of the system than *Law and Order*. But that argument holds only if one believes— as the founding fathers certainly did not—that the role of the courts is to free the innocent and imprison the guilty. However, as unpopular and even hard to understand for many of us today as it may be—in large part because of series like *The Practice*—that is in fact not the ultimate purpose of the American system. Rather, as I have said, the real job of the system is to force the state to prove its case beyond a reasonable doubt or to let the defendant—powerless against a state that does not honor this code—go free. We may wish that the issues involved were as morally clear-cut as they seem on *The Practice*—or for that matter on soap operas—but they are not. In fact, what makes the series most problematic is the fiction it presents that a "morally good" person can actually know "the truth" in a criminal case. But this is a misunderstood idea, and criminal trials are not, at heart, about "the truth" at all. They are about insuring that the rights of the less powerful among us are protected from those with the enormous power to use the law to serve its own political purposes, though every defendant does have the right to counsel. Therefore, the early series, in which defense attorneys did indeed fight for the underdog, were so much more progressive than the series we see today.

The contradiction in *The Practice*—its desire to have it both ways, creating characters on the side of law and order who must nonetheless represent rather than prosecute criminals—is what makes this series so politically problematic. For unlike *Law and Order*, which puts its conservative political bias on the table, *The Practice* obscures and muddies its politics by making its crime- and criminal-hating heroes appear as the outsiders, reviled by establishment firms and always fighting an uphill battle to survive. But this contradiction can only appear even vaguely credible because the series so thoroughly removes the institutions and processes of law and justice from their actual social, political, and economic contexts. For if it clearly makes no sense, psychologically or politically, for these attorneys to be on the side of the criminal element, the heroes of *The Practice*, no matter where they stand in the larger social and political system, are, by virtue of their moral "feelings" and values, as innocent as babes.

The Practice in fact functions more like the kind of "workplace-family" sitcom Ella Taylor analyzes in her study of *Prime Time Families* than *Law and Order*.[12] Unlike the dingy, dark office in which McCoy sits grimly at the end of a hard day, contemplating the dark urban landscape, the offices on *The Practice*, like those on *Murphy Brown* or *Mary Tyler Moore*, are a home away from home for a group of single, professional friends. For them the workplace has become the major site of intimacy and support. Its lawyer-heroes are members of a close-knit "family" in which values such as loyalty, compassion, and traditional morality are central. Donnell himself is a practicing Catholic who often seeks out clerical counsel for his moral dilemmas. And the others fight vigorously—often even physically violently—among themselves whenever one or the other seems, by the group, to be acting in ways that push the envelope of moral decency farther than their consciences might allow.

Moral conflicts among firm members are in fact among the most dramatic elements in the series. Has Lindsay gone too far in her efforts to gain financial security for the firm by taking so many drug lords as clients? Has Ellinor's sexual relationship with a client blurred her moral judgment about his guilt or innocence? Is Jimmy's defense of a family member accused of employment discrimination morally defensible? In the latter case, the answer is so obvious that Jimmy ends up feeling so guilty about representing the "wrong" person, rather than the woman whose rights have clearly been violated, that he ends up asking her out on a date—which she understandably declines. But "You're a good guy, Jimmy," she assures him, recognizing that his heart is in the right place because of his obvious suffering over the position he has taken. Indeed, this is a law firm characterized by its "good guy" membership, in which the identifying badge of entry is deep and sincere suffering. It is a community of the just and virtuous trying valiantly to survive in the nasty world of criminal justice without losing its soul. It's a heartwarming picture, but one that leaves much to be desired in the way of actual social commentary because it is founded on a view of justice so narrow and sentimental that it leaves no room to ask where the heroes actually stand ideologically.

Indeed, *The Practice* is, on one level, pure escapism in a way that *Law and Order* is not. As in soap operas, the lawyers behave in ways that are so unbelievable to anyone who has ever entered a criminal court room as to be ludicrous. In fact, virtually every one of the principals would by now have been disbarred, or at least held in near permanent contempt of court, for their unconscionable courtroom behavior. But on another level, it can hardly be called escapist because it is presented as a serious drama in which real and pressing social issues are dealt with in every episode. It works not to *escape* reality, but to reconstruct it in such a way that viewers are purposely confused about the actual message about law and justice it presents.

Is this how ethical, principled, *democratic*-minded defense attorneys actually feel and behave? Clarence Darrow, or even contemporary defense attorney Gerry Spence, might not think so. They might, in fact, be appalled at these lawyers' attitudes and actions—but not for the reasons the series suggests. It is not their tactics—always a cause of moral anguish for the group—which make them "ethically challenged" as members of the bar. It is their contempt for most of their clients and their failure—except on the rare occasions noted—to represent defense law as a morally and politically honorable, even heroic, profession. Series like *The Defenders* and novels and movies based on the Grisham model have been much more successful in this portrayal. For while the lawyers on *The Practice* fulfill their obligation to provide a vigorous defense for every client they do so, too often in a state of guilt and anguish which must surely, if only implicitly, bolster the arguments of those pushing for harsher criminal justice policies. Like the most sensational tabloid TV show or the fire-and-brimstone rant of a right-wing politician or talk-show host, the series consistently presents images of criminal defendants as totally odious and hateful. No one, not even a defense attorney—and certainly not an audience of potential jurors and voters—could possibly love, much less feel compassion for such beings.

Thus we have two series, *Law and Order* and *The Practice*, which are, in very different ways, representative of the current trend in criminal justice policy toward a more and more reactionary and punitive system. But there is a major difference in the implications of the two approaches. In *Law and Order*, as we have seen, it is the system itself that is the hero, while the individual players are symbolically interchangeable. Cast members change regularly, but their roles do not. And it is primarily the casting of the heroes as prosecutors of the presumably guilty, rather than defenders of the innocent, or socially powerless, that determine the series' implicitly conservative politics. For the system these prosecutors serve is not so much dysfunctional as dispassionate, based as it is on science, psychology, and other techniques of detection and evidentiary proof to reach a case's ultimate conclusions. Thus, when a guilty person is not convicted or an innocent is sent to prison, the fault lies not with the players themselves, but with inherent ambiguities or loopholes in the criminal justice code itself. "Win some, lose some" is the attitude of the protagonists at the end of each segment, as they walk off screen until the next episode, when they will be back on the court, ready to play the game one more time, do the best they can, briefly celebrate or mourn, and chalk it up to legal experience.

There are of course various levels of ideological and even moral contradiction in this series. Nonetheless, even in the early years, when the feminist Kincaid or race-conscious Robinette often expressed strong liberal views, the loss of a case to a system unwilling to respect such views was presented in a more cynically resigned than tragic way. And even in recent years, as McCoy and his increasingly hard-nosed assistants have become more outspokenly vengeful and punitive in their personal views of crime and criminals, there are still moments of ideological contradiction as they disagree among themselves, and with the judges and juries who determine the narrative closure of each segment. Still, they would never dream of subverting the system they serve—especially through violent or illegal actions—in order to force their own moral positions on the system they proudly serve.

But this is exactly what the heroes of *The Practice* do quite often, if sometimes unbelievably so. For on this series the players are clearly the heroes or villains, and the system is a largely dysfunctional institution in which justice, presented here as synonymous with morality, is to be found primarily in the interstices of the legal code when the actors are able to work around the system to force morality out of it by brute force—metaphorically and sometimes literally. The series itself would have us believe that the problem with the system is that it does not really care about morality or justice but only about its own heartless, impersonal rules—a very popular view among many journalists and lay people. More and more we want retribution and vengeance and are impatient with a system that doesn't provide that kind of reassuring closure.

A tremendous confusion is implicit in such an assumption, which series like *The Practice*, and more recent television programs we will look at in following chapters do much to reinforce. The legal system, as the founding fathers who wrote our Constitution structured it, was not based on the idea of vengeance or retribution, or even, to its credit, on the importance of punishing the "bad guys," as TV series are fond of referring to suspects and defendants. It was based on a far more radically democratic idea: that one is innocent until proven guilty; that the burden is on the state to prove "beyond a reasonable doubt" the guilt of a defendant; and that—most radically—it is far better to let a hundred guilty persons go free than to wrongly imprison, or worse, execute, one innocent one. When we watch television or read the pundits these days, however, it is increasingly difficult to remember, or even comprehend, these ideas. When Eugene or Rebecca or Bobby weep or attack their own monstrous clients, the audience is of course meant to *feel* for them—"feel" being the operative term. They are on the side of the angels, after all. But, as Clarence Darrow and those who follow in his footsteps understand, the courtroom is not a place where angels, or devils for that matter, have a role to play.

2

Aliens, Nomads, Mad Dogs, and Road Warriors

Tabloid TV and the
New Face of Criminal Violence

As we have seen, issues of law and order, crime and punishment, have been a generic staple since the earliest days of television. As times change—politically, culturally, socially—so too do these genres shift in style and ideology, to fit the tenor of the day. And, as we have also seen, stories of crime and punishment, sometimes more and sometimes less directly, tend to reflect shifting views of the role of the criminal justice system. In times of dramatic paradigmatic change, the media, especially television, have for the most part tended to reflect these ideological shifts in the broader public world.[1]

The 1990s, as we have also seen, were such a time. With the Clinton presidency, we saw what can only be viewed by future historians as a radical shift in the very meaning of the terms "liberal" and "conservative." A new consensus emerged in which Democrats joined Republicans in a middle ground far to the right of the traditional political "center"; and the basics of liberal, progressive policy—welfare, affirmative action, health care, education—increasingly fell prey to policies driven by the discourses of privatization, self-sufficiency, and race- and gender-blind notions of equality. The Bush presidency has escalated this trend.

Even as social spending on education and social welfare declined, government spending rose dramatically in crime control. By 1997, prison construction and management had become the single greatest growth industry in the nation. The imposition of more harsh and punitive measures—three-strike laws for simple, often nonviolent offenses; harsh mandatory sentences; the rise in legalization and enforcement of the death penalty; the trying of youths, often in single-digit age groups, in adult courts; highway chain gangs; punishments involving public identi-fication and shaming of offenders and ex-offenders; and so on—defined an increasingly repressive society in which those in power grew more and more fearful and hostile toward those they worked to control.[2] With the dramatic increase in the war-driven "anti-terrorism" legislation, already begun by Clinton, in which the civil rights and liberties of all Americans have been ever more seriously threatened, the Bush administration has managed to escalate this trend with even more public support than shown in the Clinton years.

Nonetheless, for all the hype that the rising crime rates justify these policies, the actual rate of violent crime fell rather dramatically in those years. Still, new inmates arrived in droves to fill the newly constructed prisons—some now even privately run for profit—for longer and longer terms. Who were these dangerous criminals? For the most part, they were people convicted of nonviolent offenses involving drugs, prostitution, and other activities associated less with human aggression or greed than sheer survival—both psychological and material—in an increasingly harsh and hopeless world. Not surprisingly, most of those incarcerated in this period were members of minority and underclass populations. In-deed, studies showed that by 1994 "one out of every three African-Amer-ican men between the ages of 20 and 29 in the entire country—including suburban and rural areas—was under some form of criminal justice su-pervision."[3] Members of immigrant populations were also increasingly visible among the prison population. And the fastest growing segment of all among the chronically incarcerated in the 1990s was women, previ-ously a negligible problem for law enforcement officials, but whose num-bers, across all racial and ethnic lines, rose dramatically.[4]

The newly imprisoned are not for the most part armed robbers or murderers or even—media hype to the contrary notwithstanding—serial killers or child molesters. They are nonviolent drug users and other cul-tural and social outsiders and misfits, people who have increasingly fallen through the system's cracks or never been allowed to enter its gates. They pose a serious problem for the state not so much because they are vi-ciously aggressive by nature or motive, but because they do not easily fit lawfully into the newly restrictive and intolerant version of American democracy. And so it was, as Stanley Aronowitz has suggested, that by the late 1990s—as the slashing of "big government" and the globalization of the economy rendered many of its previous functions obsolete[5]— the major role of the state had become internal security and domestic repression, what he rightly describes as "criminal detention and prosecution (misnamed criminal 'justice')"[6] of an ever more broadly defined "criminal element" of the population.

In the last chapter we saw the rise, in the 1990s, of three important new justice-focused genres: Court TV, the prosecutor-centered legal series, and the tabloid crime genre. In this chapter I want to look more closely at this last genre, for it is in these increasingly popular series, rather than in the more upscale, ideologically complex and sophisticated "quality" series such as *Law and Order*, that we can see most dramatically how television has played to the new, more punitive sentiments and policies of the last decade or so. Nor is this situation surprising. For it is very often in the "lower," less-established genres that cultural innovations and shifts tend first to emerge. When one turns to these newly minted forms of crime drama, what one sees is an image of "crime" and "criminality" that is markedly different from what we are used to seeing on prime time. It is an image, however, which is eerily suited to the political climate at century's end, one in which paranoia, intolerance of difference, and a laissez-faire attitude toward repressive police tactics seem to be the order of the day.[7] It is one which, as we shall see in chapter 3, and later, in Part Two, has increasingly marked the presentation of criminal-justice programming in general.

"Down These Mean Streets": The City as Traditional Crime Site

Crime drama—whether it features lawyers, police officers, or a combination of both, as in *Law and Order*—has, like all long-standing cultural staples, incorporated certain standard features that mark them and give them social relevance. The crime drama, first and foremost, gives us an image of the landscape within which social order must be maintained, within which the endless rituals of social disruption and the return to harmony and peace are performed. Second, the crime drama sketches out the human (or subhuman) contours by which we distinguish "deviance" from "normality," the "outlaw" from the good citizen who lives "within the boundaries of the law."

In traditional crime drama, the landscape of crime has been the city—the urban centers of industrial Western society down whose "mean streets" Raymond Chandler's characters stealthily tread. For "the city is a concrete embodiment of the achievements of industrial society" which "embodies our civilization and the degree to which we are successful in maintaining that achievement."[8] And so its fall into disorder or violence represents a grave threat to our common survival and well-being. Crime drama thus has an important social function: it is the nightly ritual through which we collectively experience the dread of the chaos that violence symbolizes, and the reassurance that comes when the violent are captured and restrained.

On television, the crime genre begins in the 1950s with *Dragnet*, a series about a straight-arrow cop who was as baffled as his audiences by the iniquity he saw evolving in the city streets. More recently, the genre has been updated to fit a time when even TV audiences (perhaps especially TV audiences) are cynically savvy enough to know that good and evil are not so easily distinguishable. But more recently, in series of the 1990s such as *Law and Order*, *NYPD Blue*, and *Homicide*, crime and criminality are no longer portrayed as wholly different from the more "normal" characteristics and actions of the law abiding among us. On the contrary, in these highly sophisticated series—closer to Chandler and Hammett than *Dragnet*—criminals and their actions are portrayed as more or less exaggerated versions of what are normal, even unavoidable, moral and emotional flaws and failings common to most people living in contemporary industrialized societies. The city—still the sign of our ultimate social achievement—is a far more inherently flawed and ambiguous symbol. While it is still worth the risk of life and limb to protect, it is nonetheless a rather shady, tainted arena in which cops themselves are not above cutting corners. Worse, it has become hard to bring about the increasingly difficult moment of reassurance and closure.

Because the dominant images of crime and violence portrayed in these series are so familiar, so "naturalized," in our common imaginations, it will be useful to briefly review and analyze some of them. I will do so from a perspective somewhat different from the generic one we examined in the last chapter so we can see, as vividly as possible, how different the assumptions and conventions of the newly emerging tabloids really are. I have again chosen *Law and Order* in my comparison, because it provides the most thorough, systematic picture of the workings of the criminal justice system—from criminal act to investigation to trial—as they are typically presented on network television's classic "quality" crime series. It is worth mentioning once again that this series shows no sign of losing viewers and in fact has become something of a cottage industry for its creator, Dick Wolf. However, as series like *The Practice* suggest, even as *Law and Order* maintains its front-running position, newer, more expressionistic forms are also arising, creating interesting questions about the direction of crime and law series as a whole. Many are melodramatic; others, like the tabloid series we will be examining here, are simply more cynically violent and brutal. Moreover, it was already clear by the 2001–2002 season, with the FX network's surprise hit *The Shield*, that the conventions of tabloid crime—which are nothing if not cynical and brutal—have already infiltrated more traditional genres. Although they are radically different from the melodramatic hysteria of *The Practice*, they similarly embody a hostile, vengeful view of criminality and the proper way for the justice system to deal with it.

So, let us now revisit *Law and Order*, this time focusing on its representation of the workings of law enforcement in classic crime drama rather than on stylistic conventions. Since setting and character are key to understanding how these series produce meaning, we will begin with the matter of setting and then turn to issues of character. Set in the mean streets of Manhattan, *L&O* devotes half its hourly time slot to the investigation and arrest of a suspect, and the rest to his or her criminal prosecution. Typically, the cops employ a variety of psychological and forensic methods to ferret out the offender; and then the prosecutors use similar techniques to decide upon and negotiate a proper punishment.

On one segment, for example, a young woman was found dead in an alley of a drug overdose. In their search for answers to why a well-dressed young woman would end up in so downscale a setting, the cops were led from the Lower East Side crime scene to a Central Park West apartment to a Wall Street office to a graduate student hangout. The answer—involving drugs and money—involved the greedy, unprincipled executor of her parents' estate, who had been giving the young woman and her Ivy League brother money to feed their mutual drug habits in order to keep them quiet while he skimmed from their considerable trust funds. On another segment, a drug bust in an inner-city neighborhood seemed to implicate an outstanding black Princeton scholarship student. As it turned out, this young man, an Ivy League outsider, had been coerced into buying drugs for his wealthy white classmates as a way of buying social acceptance. And on still another segment, a thirteen-year-old boy fatally shot a schoolmate with his father's sports pistol. Was it an accident, as he claimed, or something more sinister? The answer emerged through careful interviews and investigations of the divorced parents, who had complex psychological and financial reasons for keeping the truth about their son's history and psychology hidden.

Each of these segments—no matter the age, class, race or socioeconomic background or status of the apprehended and punished offender—was informed by a common set of assumptions about crime, criminality, and human nature. Criminals were seen to act out of a common if complex set of psychological, social, and economic motivations easily recognizable as "human" to members of the viewing audiences. Greed, social acceptance, anger, revenge, the desire of a parent to control a child, the desire of a child to please or rebel against a parent—these were some of the universally understandable factors driving the players in these stories to their various immoral or illegal acts. Crimes were planned in advance or carefully covered up after the fact. The city—from its highest social reaches to its lowest—was portrayed as an organically unified community in which all members—regardless of race, class, or gender, regardless of ghetto project or Park Avenue address—shared a common human nature. All, even the ghetto dwellers (for "Quality TV" is nothing if not politically correct, at least rhetorically), were reasonably intelligent, articulate, and rational. All were conscious that their deeds were "wrong" but were driven to them through failure to control certain common, understandable desires and needs.

Nor were the cops or lawyers on these segments in any way different—socially, morally, intellectually—from those they investigated and tried. They too revealed commonly recognizable social and moral foibles and flaws. They too had skeletons in closets, corners hastily cut, peccadilloes they wished to conceal. Over the course of the series run, viewers came to know all of these things, and to see how the heroes—like those they charged and tried—were also part of a common, flawed but functional, social entity, a city of diverse but still socially integrated individuals and institutions. Their methods of interrogation were often harsh, even at times physically brutal; and their legal maneuvers and deals—from arrest to interrogation and confession to trial—often less than morally or even legally satisfying. But what was always clear was their concern for the social welfare and smooth functioning of the city, of the victims, and, even, in a sense, of the criminals themselves. For while the fate of the offender, after capture or conviction, was rarely portrayed, the universe in which crime was negotiated was one in which such terms as "correction" and "rehabilitation"—staples of liberal criminological discourse—were implicitly assumed to apply.[9] These were not, after all, scenes from a police state. They were scenes from an institutional environment informed by humane, relatively liberal assumptions about human nature and its appropriate treatment. Such has been the world of television crime drama, in which—so the conventions of the genre imply—cops, prosecutors, and the myriad professional workers in tangential institutions with whom they collaborate serve a system in which values and assumptions are clear and universal; and the means to correcting injustice and reforming those who deviate are theoretically known, available, and relatively effective.

In the "Quality TV" series sketched above, then, murderers, muggers, even inner city drug dealers and gang members are portrayed as very much like us, except that in a moment of weakness they have given in to their most dangerous and antisocial impulses. They have acted upon the selfish desire for wealth, power, social acceptance, or even revenge—emotions we all share but manage to keep in check. "Who dunnit?" is answered with sociological, psychological, and moral analyses that make sense to us all, as "motives" in a criminal trial must make sense.

That these two forms coexist is worth commenting upon, for it is important to recognize that dominant ideologies—and the cultural forms that arise along with them—do not simply knock each other out of the box, so to speak, in one fell swoop. On the contrary, new ideologies and forms tend to overlap in periods of major ideological shifts such as we are now experiencing. Even when one ideology does become clearly dominant, in public discourse and in cultural forms there will still be residual elements of earlier ideas and tastes. Thus the process by which the ideas and forms that emerge as dominant is rather subtle. Even the 1950s, which many recall as being highly monolithic and conservative, had the Beat generation and the emergence of teen rebellion films like *Blackboard Jungle* and *Rebel without a Cause*. At the time, however, these "subcultural" strains were not necessarily known or taken seriously by mainstream observers and commentators. And so it is today. *Law and Order* is gradually becoming more conservative while maintaining its traditional form even as *Cops*, often dismissed as marginal or trashy, is emerging. And to complicate things more, the strains of tabloid stylistics—the gory settings and scenes, the borderline city and neighborhood settings—begin to enter into, and complicate, even the newer traditional series such as *Crossing Jordan* and *CSI: Crime Scene Investigation*, making for a fascinatingly complex form of cultural and political transition.

At the Borders: From Deviant Misfits to Alien Invaders

To turn to the tabloids after watching a series like *L&O* is to feel more than disoriented: the conventions of setting, narrative, and characterization are radically different. Criminals are no longer "just like us," only a bit "ill" or "defective" or "morally weak" and therefore easily correctable; on the contrary, they are increasingly, incorrigibly, "other," and "alien." For the creatures policed and apprehended by these cops are not capable of internalizing or abiding by the norms and values of a liberal democracy. They are far too irrational, too uncontrollable, too inscrutable for such measures to be effective. They are part of a newly constructed image of "crime" and "criminal violence" in which more harsh and repressive measures than those suggested on series like *Law and Order* are suddenly necessary to maintain social order, because those who threaten that order are—or have suddenly become—inhuman brutes and freaks.

There have been many examples and varieties of tabloid TV: the *Hard Copy* and *Inside Edition* "shocks, horrors, and sensations of the day" version; the *America's Most Wanted/Unsolved Mysteries* "they're still out there" version; the *American Detective* and *Top Cops* "let's ride along with Officer Jones" version. They have come and gone, most rather quickly, since the genre first emerged in the 1990s.[10] But all share more than a prurient interest in the more irrational forms of criminal behavior—both minor and extreme—as either the major or sole subject matter. They also share a low budget, "video verité" style based on documentary interviews, tapes of actual police work, and, in some cases, dramatic reenactments of past, but not yet solved, crimes. Of all of these, *Cops* is the one which most dramatically reveals the contours of what I am arguing is a newly emerging construction of criminal violence.[11] *Cops*, for one thing, focuses exclusively on crime and crime control, with no detours to other sensational matters, as do popular shows like *Hard Copy* that include a variety of themes and formats. But more importantly, it is the series which most thoroughly jettisons the traditional paraphernalia of crime drama to present a radically new vision of the landscape and nature of crime, criminality, and law enforcement. It is a vision so expressionistically marked as to allow a striking glimpse of key assumptions and implications of current political trends.

Immediately upon tuning in to this program, we know we are *not* in Raymond Chandler country. There are no savvy New York cops, lawyers, and experts who work and live within a coherent, if darkened and flawed version of the political imaginary which television, since the 1950s, has constructed, amended, and preserved in our collective social conscience. *Cops* is set in a metaphoric border territory—literally, "out where the buses don't run." The families and neighborhoods that set the standard for "normality" against which criminal deviance is defined on shows like *L&O* are gone. The theme of the family in danger—a staple, as George Lipsitz reminds us, not only of crime drama, but of most mainstream TV forms[12]—is largely dispensed with here, because the political imaginary within which *Cops* is set is far from any community in which traditional family life might thrive. This is a landscape of highways, strip malls, trailer parks, and convenience stores, where churches, schools, office buildings—the institutions that make up "normal" society—have no place. While the landscape may resemble places we have all seen and visited, somehow it seems—despite the *echt*-verité quality of the representation—more "foreign" than any American landscape we may have entered.

Each week *Cops* follows a police officer, in some area of the United States not typically seen on TV, as he[13] makes his (usually) nightly rounds, patrolling the highways and answering calls about neighborhood and domestic disturbances. Each week the program begins by introducing the viewer to the city or town being visited, showing a collage of random shots of local denizens, each more strange, menacing, or simply pathetic than the last. Against a soundtrack playing an upbeat version of the reggae song "Bad Boys" ("Bad boys, bad boys, whatcha gonna do?/Whatcha gonna do when they come for you?"), we see a barrage of fast cuts: a drunk about to strike out or simply wobbling on the point of collapse; a black, dreadlocked rollerblader dressed only in a scant bikini; an armed "offender" of some kind being violently apprehended and cuffed as he puts up a wild but hapless struggle; a cop comforting—or even diapering—a wailing, unkempt baby as the parent is dragged away. All are intercut with road marks identifying the city and county in question.

There is no narrator or voiceover giving direction to the series. The cop who is featured each week—always clean-cut in appearance and articulate and civilized in manner and speech—speaks directly to the audience, eschewing all traditional televisual apparatus, letting viewers know they are in familiar media terrain. Here we are confronted directly with "real life," it is implied, with no Tom Brokaw or Hugh Downs to spin it to us. In this way, the series smoothly if disingenuously signals the viewer that it will eschew the artificial constructions by which traditional TV series smoothen the edges of reality and sugarcoat the horrors of what *real* cops, in the *real* world, are up against. And yet, of course, the distortions of media convention—of a less familiar variety—are as salient here as anywhere on commercial television.

The cop begins by introducing himself in simple, down-home terms. He explains a bit about his own background, his motives in becoming a cop, the gratifications and frustrations he receives from the work, and so on. "I wanted to be a priest," says one officer, typically, "but I began to think I could serve better in law enforcement." Another recounts his admiration for his own father, who was also a cop. Always there is a sense of altruism and service of a kind more reminiscent of Joe Friday than Sam Spade or Philip Marlowe. The cops—who of course always know, even if the audience is lulled into forgetting, that the camera is running—present themselves in the most cleaned-up, wholesome of terms. They are deliberately constructed, indeed self-constructed, in the image of traditional American male heroism that audiences so much want to believe in, and which police officers—in these post–Rodney King days—are eager to help them believe. Because these officers are so pure and altruistic, the contrast between them and those they police is as dramatic as possible.

The half-hour segment takes the viewer from site to site—usually six or seven "cases" are covered in the twenty-two-minute period. The cop will answer calls on his car radio, chase down and stop suspicious cars on the streets and highways he patrols, and apprehend strange-acting individuals who happen to be walking along the generally unpopulated roads or highways. Intoxicated, drugged-out drivers, domestic and street brawls, out-of-control or suspicious looking loiterers—these are the "crimes" the officers on *Cops* are most likely to attend to, week after week,[14] as they drive their police cars through the rough-and-tumble roadways and trailer park settlements they endlessly police, looking for trouble. The structure of the series thus follows a serial format rather than the narrative arc—crime, investigation, capture, and punishment—of traditional crime drama. Crime itself, as we have been taught to understand it by the media,[15] is thus radically reconstructed. No more do criminals plot and scheme toward nefarious goals or act out of jealous rage or greed or anger and then hide out, dissemble, and attempt to cover their tracks as in traditional narratives. Now we have a set of characters apparently driven not by reasonable, if reprehensible desires or goals, but by brute instinct or chemical derangement. They lurk, wander, or simply break down within a spiritual and physical wasteland somewhere outside society's orderly boundaries. Since the structure precludes any knowledge of what might have come before, who the person is, and what her or his social and psychological background might be, the impression of sheer unmotivated madness is driven home. Thus, in place of the orderly plot structure of conflict, crisis, and resolution, we have a series of endless irrational "disruptions."

In such a format, the traditional construction of violence itself, as we have come to understand it through crime drama, is also radically transformed. For in traditional series, we have a motivated act of violence at the beginning of the hour, driving the rest of the action: the concerted effort to find the criminal by figuring out his motives, tracking him down, and arresting him. The violence—itself an isolated event that stands out from the rest of the action—is thus causally connected to a story about the perpetrator in which, by hour's end, a rich mesh of sociological and psychological life circumstances has usually emerged to explain his act. The criminal, in such a narrative, no matter how amoral or vicious, is thus still a human being whose defects are theoretically understandable and therefore correctable. For this reason, even the most vicious of traditional crimes can be understood within the context of a general view of the criminal mind and nature in which all other, lesser crimes also fit.

This construction still applies even to the most extremely demonized of criminals and criminal acts—serial killers and child molesters, perhaps—as seen on traditional crime dramas and in (serious) news media. But on series like *Cops*, and in the newer entries such as *The Shield* and *Oz*—that we will analyze in the next chapter—such medicalized, psychological, and sociological views of criminal behavior are gone. Instead, we are presented with a view of the criminal mind and behavior as less than human, as brutish, irrational, and inherently incapable of understanding or abiding by any legal code, or—more to the point—of being rehabilitated through the methods of medical or social science. That both visions of the criminal mind and act should coexist at this point in history is not surprising. Indeed, in series like *Crossing Jordan* and *CSI: Crime Scene Investigation*, for example, as mentioned in the Introduction, we see a blending of the two. For in periods in which radical revisions of dominant assumptions about important issues occur, as has already been noted, the shift is always uneven, and the older, declining visions do not simply disappear to make room for the new. Such a culture shock would be hard to digest. Rather, the process is slower and more uneven. Old visions and ideas tend to persist while newer ones are absorbed over time. Some even stay in sight for some time, often in the interest of older viewers who remain loyal to them. This has become especially true with the rise of cable TV and its need to continue to rerun lapsed series in order to fill their airtime. Moreover, as already noted, the newer visions are often first seen in forms and venues viewed as "low" or "trashy" by critics and educated viewers. Nonetheless, we need to pay close attention to these newer visions because—as in the case of rock 'n' roll, for example—while they may at first appeal to a mostly younger, less educated audience, they may represent a wave of the future.

This is certainly the case with series like *Cops*. Critically damned, rarely even mentioned in the same reviews or conversations in which series like *Law and Order* are discussed, the show nonetheless has been running for almost a decade now, often many times a week or even in one evening. Thus, its staying power, and the vision of the criminal mind and act it presents, needs to be watched carefully. For among its more interestingly telling features is that, in its demonic view of the criminal—so different from what we see on *Law and Order, Homicide,* or *NYPD Blue*—we can see that it reflects the view of crime that is increasingly presented on regular news programming. In fact, with twenty-four cable news channels stuck with the problem of how to fill up all that airtime and whisk viewers away from the competition, it has become common to see endless hours of footage and talk about the most horrific of current crimes and perpetrators. The Jeffrey Dahmers and Andrea Yateses of the world get enormous amounts of airtime while more common crimes, the bulk of actual police work, get short shrift. For, as Ray Surette argues in his discussion of "Predator Criminals as Media Icons," "the crimes that dominate the public consciousness and policy debates" are not common crimes but the rarest ones, for "the modern mass media have raised the specter of the predator criminal from a minor character to a common, ever-present image."[16] Surette rightly concludes that such imagery does indeed support arguments for policies that stress punitive measures for criminals rather than attacking the root causes of crime itself. Surette himself includes among those punitive approaches "intensive individual rehabilitative or educational efforts" of the kind that still adhere to the assumption that criminals are theoretically correctable and reformable.[17]

On *Cops*, however, because of the way in which violence itself is represented, even this vestige of liberal policy assumption seems no longer to apply. For the offenders on *Cops*, while certainly inherently violent or prone to violence, are rarely predators. They do not molest children or go on killing sprees. They do not threaten our homes or prey on city streets looking to mug, rob, or rape "our" women. In fact, on the most obvious level, they are far less threatening than the criminals seen on other crime series—or on the nightly news, for that matter. Their acts are not generally directed *toward* anyone or anything; they usually do not even do much serious damage except, perhaps, to themselves. Nor are their worst violent acts generally of the sensational, explosive variety that is most anxiety provoking to the general population. Rather, they seem to embody a constant proneness to random, sporadic violence represented as a permanent condition of human—or rather subhuman—nature: they are simply inherently violent in ways that make no sense at all. We get no clues, no "story" of any kind, onto which we can hang a diagnosis or criminal profile. And because of this representational technique, treatment or rehabilitation—the implicit solutions to the threat posed by predator criminals of even the most demonized kind, as Surette himself suggests—are not options.

Indeed, even when the cops attempt to get at the bottom of things, they rarely get a coherent story from anyone involved. Sometimes this is because the witnesses and victims are incoherent, either because of drugs or because they speak another language. More often they simply tell incoherent narratives or contradict one another. And again, since we see each person only in this isolated moment when his or her actions are most irrational, out of control, and potentially dangerous, we can never know if there is more to the story than meets the always faithfully "truthful" eye of the trusted video lens. Indeed, so powerful is the appeal to "reality" held by documentary footage that the missing context—social, emotional, narrative—seems irrelevant or, worse, is never even considered.[18]

Beyond the City: The Border World of Tabloid TV

The implications of *Cops'* construction of criminal violence must surely strike fear in the hearts of viewers. The creatures portrayed—inscrutable, uncontrollable, and beyond the ken of traditional criminological "expertise"—are after all "somewhere" very near to us, for we see actual road signs identifying actual American locations. And because of this visually implied proximity to "normal" society, they are likely, so it is ominously implied, to seep through our borders and spread their chaos to our own vulnerable communities if left unchecked.

But who are these creatures, and where is the landscape they inhabit, which seems, at once, so near yet also a world away? On traditional crime dramas, the place is the city, and the criminal—as we have come to know him—is someone who lives within the city's boundaries. In recent times there have been two dominant images of the dangerous urban criminal. The most common has been the inner-city black male. Indeed, this image has been an unfortunate staple of crime drama as well as news reporting, demonizing the African American inner-city male as emblematic of the American criminal.[19] If series like *L&O* have tended to clean up these portrayals in the interest of "political correctness," there are other genres, particularly the local news, which have taken the opposite tack. They present ever more brutalized images of young black males—"superpredators" is the increasingly popular term devised by Princeton criminologist John Diulio—to fit the growing conservative discourse on crime and punishment.[20] This criminal, though he is fenced off into a separate area of the city, still inhabits the city's borders and is free to move within it.

The other dominant image, more recent and more menacing perhaps, is the one Surette describes: the predator criminal who commits the most gruesome of violent acts. He, too, is a creature of urban centers, particularly fearful because he is less easily identifiable on sight. Often dwelling quietly and unobtrusively on our own streets and working in our own office buildings, he may seem the epitome of "normality" until his urge for blood sets him off on a crime spree. Other genres, too, are filled with tales of this character who suddenly "snaps" and beneath his deceptively mild surface reveals a mania-driven bloodlust.[21] Here, too, however, we have a city dweller, a person we may pass in the streets or sit next to on the subway.

When we enter the world of *Cops*, however, we are somewhere else, somewhere far from the urban streets where the crime we are used to occurs, in another universe entirely. We may often have gone to the kinds of places pictured here—bars, strip malls, low-rent apartment complexes, convenience stores—but somehow they do not look or feel quite the same now. Due to the way things seem to happen—with no before or after, no why or wherefore—and the limited nature of the *kinds* of things that happen, combined with the absence of cues or information about who these people are and how they happened to be where we find them, we cannot imagine actually finding ourselves in such a constructed universe. For it is a world in which *nothing but* brawls and bars and hookers and mental breakdowns and outbursts ever occur, and we can never comprehend any of it in any human or social terms.[22]

Of course the footage is real. These are real people encountered in real areas of a real America. In fact, if we want to attempt a sociological profile of the most common types of people and neighborhoods encountered, we can fairly safely do so. These are people who are habitually in trouble with the police, depicted in the kinds of places in which such people tend to live and hang out. The real segment of the population from which this select group of "police regulars" is drawn—as caricatured and distorted as the representation of them may be—are those who are permanently down on their luck for a variety of reasons, momentarily or chronically dysfunctional, or inveterate "outsiders" and misfits of various kinds who can't or won't conform to social norms. At worst, they are of extremely weak character and prone to the worst kind of judgments. When encountered, most are under the influence of drugs or alcohol. Many are petty criminals: hookers, purveyors of illegal gambling games, scam artists so incompetent that they are always apprehended. Others are immigrants who do not speak English well and have not found a way to integrate themselves into "normal" American life. And still others are homeless, because of drug or alcohol problems or because they are mentally ill. Indeed, mental illness seems to be a very common problem among those the cops deal with each week. But since this very concept has no place in the universe of *Cops*, they are simply part of the mix of people who are endlessly, violently out of control and in trouble with the law.

Of course, as in traditional urban series—and certainly in the news itself—a great number of these people are black. For no matter what the genre or the actual setting of crime, in our society it is predictable that a hugely disproportionate number of those who fit the "criminal profile" will in fact be people of color. And *Cops* does not diverge from this stereotype (although it does redefine its terms, as we shall see). Opening credit segments of each episode almost invariably feature black men and women, swaggering or staggering on their way to being apprehended, knocked down, cuffed, and carried off. In a typical episode, several of the incidents the officer of the evening encounters will involve black people in the throes of one kind of violent, out-of-control act or another.

Nonetheless, the way in which race—and the black "criminal"—is presented in this series is significantly different from the way such a person is presented on series such as *Law and Order*. For these are black people who no longer inhabit the urban centers where organized gang warfare, drug dealing, robbery, muggings, and murders are acted out by people whose motives are clear and whose actions—no matter how repellent—make sense to the viewer. Rather, these are blacks who have seriously hit the skids and drifted out of the inner-city communities where traditional crime normally takes place on series TV. They, like the other sad subjects of *Cops*, have lost their way. They can no longer function even in their own traditional communities and have become border dwellers in a world in which race does not have the same highlighted significance as in the rest of society, at least to those with whom they finally come to live and associate (if not necessarily the audiences who watch the show). Rather, as with the homeless, their racial identities are in a sense absorbed into a more multicultural hodgepodge of losers and drifters whose "home" communities, no matter where they might have been, have been lost to them.

Thus *Cops* gives the impression that there is a world "out there," in "those neighborhoods" in some other part of town, where human life as we know it simply ceases to exist. This world—symbolically and expressionistically contrived out of an infinite amount of videotape from which only a relatively small amount of footage is ever actually put on the air—is filled with people of a variety of racial and ethnic backgrounds who are indeed aliens, freaks of nature, subhuman primitive beasts whose words make no sense and whose actions are bizarre. This is a particularly postmodern universe, for it is a world unmoored from the very bases of civilized life and order in which a potpourri of cultural, ethnic, racial, and sexual "types" are thrown together in generic otherness. Cut loose from community and cultural cohesion, they are set adrift along a metaphoric border territory at the very fringes of "normal" life, where all hope of a better future—and the liberal rhetoric which fuels it—disappears.

Within this quintessentially postmodern cultural mix, three types stand out in particular: the drug abuser, the sexual "deviant," and the immigrant. The rhetoric of the right is of course thick with jeremiads about the dangers of sexual promiscuity and deviance, of drug abuse and other forms of chemical indulgence, and of the economic and sociological threat posed by the hordes of immigrants who, we hear, are flooding our borders, contaminating our heritage and traditions, and sapping our social services. It is these very people—representing multiculturalism in all its demonized symbolism—whom we see in their most degraded and chaotic formations on *Cops*. Here white characters are as degraded and deranged as black; women are as aggressively violent as men; and there are any number of ethnic characters, mostly immigrants from Middle Eastern and Latin nations, who mix and match with the others indiscriminately. Their households are not stable or permanent and do not follow any socially "normal" pattern of domestic life. They may contain interracial couples and families; groups of racially and sexually mixed boarders of various ages; immigrant groups for whom English is still a foreign language and whose clothing and furnishings clearly mark them as "foreign"; drug and alcohol abusers, flagrantly identifiable gays and transvestites, and so on. Often, neighbors and even house members seem not to know each other. And it is implied that virtually every arrangement is temporary and expedient.

To examine specific images and encounters in more detail is to get a clear sense of the qualitative differences etched between those who police and those who are policed. We see how clearly the latter are represented as being inherently different and inferior—and especially violent—in ways which no means of therapy or correction could possibly affect. When called to a domestic disturbance or forced to subdue a driver on the highway, the police invariably—as far as we are allowed to see—find a person so horribly out of control that he or she reacts only to brute force. In these cases, the producers will allow the tape to roll longer, often focusing starkly and steadily on a person becoming more and more out of control, in ways which are in the end painful to watch. Often, the person will be wildly, violently rebellious and hysterical. Unkempt, often barely clothed and surrounded by filth and chaos, he or she is allowed to gyrate and gesticulate as the cops show saintlike restraint and patience. This stark visual contrast between the hysteria and violence of the offenders and the calm and patience of the cops is among the most vivid ways in which tabloid criminals are marked as subhuman and different from "normal" Americans like the police.

On one case, for example, a black man who was stopped for erratic driving refused to give up his knife and surrender. He kept shuffling down the middle of the highway, clearly in a state of derangement. But the cops—five or six of them—simply followed him at a distance, calling over and over again, "Hey Buddy, just drop the knife and we can help you." After several moments that were excruciating for viewers, they were forced to subdue him and in the process he was shot and seriously disabled. As he jerked and shook while being cuffed and taken into custody, the cops congratulated themselves on a job well done. "You really showed restraint, man," they kept saying to the shooter. And indeed, under the watchful eye of the video camera, he certainly had, in a way which could only make Rodney King wish he lived in this border territory instead of the one in which he barely escaped with his life on a similar road.[23] But while we learned a lot about the virtues of the police force in this segment, for all its excessive length we knew no more at the end about the apprehended man than at the start. He was simply one more mad-dog road warrior, unfit to drive, surely, and unfit to live in civilized society, so bizarrely incomprehensible were his actions.

This implication of irrationality and even bestiality is particularly offensive when people of color are involved. On a typical incident, for example, a Middle Eastern couple—he in turban, she in long dress and sandals—were having a physical fight, it seemed. The woman was incoherent, flailing on the ground, wailing, and pointing to her bleeding leg. The man paced outside the house, incoherently mumbling as though in a trance. Neighbors were asked to explain, but no coherent story emerged. The issue—and this would surely have been articulated on *L&O*—was domestic violence. But the shocking, humiliating visual imagery, along with the incoherent, irrational physical and verbal behavior of the couple, shifted the emphasis to something very different: the repellent, embarrassing irrationality, hysteria, and violence of "foreigners." In this way, *Cops* works to dehumanize and barbarize a range of cultural and sexual difference so emphatically that only the police are left to represent "real" human nature—a calm, superior conquering army assigned to patrol the settlements in which a primitive, subhuman, barbaric tribe dwells.

And calmly patrol they do, unflappable in the face of the most "freakish" of events and characters. On one segment, a black prostitute was apprehended as she staggered into the road, having narrowly escaped from a violent john who had slashed her face with a knife. As it turned out, she was a transvestite—high on something and in high drag—with whom the cop was familiar. Out of control and incoherent, she attempted to flirt with the cop as he worked to subdue her and get her to a hospital. From there, the cop went on to a house call in which a drug-crazed young man wildly waved a gun and staggered about as the woman who had made the call—to whom he referred as "my wife-type" although she seemed at least twenty years older than he—cringed in terror. This couple was interracial, as were another couple on the scene who looked on in an apparent stupor as a child, a girl of perhaps three, filthy and unkempt, hovered nearby, sobbing. All four adults, high and in possession of drugs and paraphernalia, were eventually arrested as backup came to assist the cop, and the child was lovingly calmed, cleaned up, taken into custody, and assured that she would be taken care of as she clung desperately to the heroic cop. What happened to the child—or indeed anything else about her or the others—was of course not shown.

As I have suggested, one of the two central roles of crime drama is to mark out and delineate the contours of "deviance" by sketching a portrait of a "normal" and legal standard against which the "outlaw" is measured in various periods of social history. It is therefore particularly important to take note of the dramatic ways in which the tabloids reconfigure that image. Since the 1970s, when British cultural studies theorists such as Stuart Hall and Dick Hebdige began the important study of subcultures and deviance as cultural constructs, the links between cultural studies and criminology have become clearer and clearer. For, as criminologist Jeff Ferrell has put it, "many social groups and events traditionally conceptualized as 'criminal' are in fact," in modern times, "defined in their everyday operations" less by criminal actions than by the "subcultural meaning and style" of their appearance and social behavior.[24]

But on the tabloids, criminals are no longer constructed in terms of simple "deviance" from accepted norms of a recognizable coherent community. The people observed on *Cops* are better described in terms of "anti-style" than any common style. For there is nothing holding any of them together culturally or behaviorally except the very absence of any particular style or ritual that would bind them to a true community—even a criminal community. They are not so much "deviant" from "normal" behavior as simply "others," "aliens," hovering at our borders, held back only by the thin blue line of police who are presented as the true saviors of American civilization.

New Paradigms for New Times:
The Criminal as Domestic Terrorist

What is the policy implication of the situation encountered on *Cops*? Clearly there is no sense that preventive or corrective measures should be taken. As we have seen, the editing techniques preclude all sense that so-cial contexts or conditions, much less racial or economic inequality, play a role here. Rather, the conditions under which these people live—filth, squalor, chaos—are seen as of their own making, a result of their own de-graded natures. Even drug treatment programs seem irrelevant here, since again and again we see junkies stopped who are well known to the cops, who have been in and out of rehab, and who simply grin sheepishly when caught and arrested yet again. The same is true of the general violence, which is also seen as a choice of lifestyle or, more accurately, a condition of nature. Women in domestic disturbance incidents, for example, are usually presented as "regulars," who—as the cops shake their heads and exchange looks—seem incapable of "learning their lesson" and leaving their violent partners. More often than not, the women themselves are ac-cused by the partner or witnesses of being the aggressors. We get no talk-ing-head "expert" testimony here to give context and meaning to the plight of battered women and the forces that keep them in place. Prosti-tutes too are seen as simply perverse by nature, determined to continue in their wayward paths and exhibiting only the most weary annoyance when stopped by the cops.

What is most striking and unnerving about the image of the various outsiders and misfits pictured on *Cops* is that they are even seen as crim-inals. For they are clearly people with a variety of economic, social, psy-chological, and cultural problems, whose violent acts are far less threat-ening to the public than to themselves. The criminalization of "quality of life" issues is not new in American society. Drug addiction and prostitu-tion have long been criminalized in lieu of addressing the broad social and economic factors that cause such behaviors, and attempting to correct them. But *Cops* extends the implications of this trend to a far broader range of people and behaviors, dragging off virtually everyone encoun-tered who cannot be readily subdued. People of other cultures and lan-guages, the homeless, the mentally imbalanced—anyone who is momen-tarily out of control for any reason—will find themselves apprehended and hauled off to jail by these cops. And more often than not, the means by which this is accomplished is both brutal and free of all reference to civil or, indeed, human rights. Rarely are Miranda rights read to anyone on *Cops*, at least on-screen. Even more rarely does anyone ask for a lawyer. And this, we are led to believe, is no more than appropriate, for these people are uncontrollably irrational beings who cannot compre-hend the rules by which we live.[25]

If concepts such as deviance, delinquency, reform, and rehabilitation no longer seem adequate to describe the world of crime and punishment that is being constructed on tabloid TV, what discourse, what rhetoric, might be more appropriate? I would suggest that the criminal—or the criminalized other—just described bears a striking resemblance to another relatively new media icon meant to strike terror in the hearts of good, law-abiding citizens: the terrorist. For like the terrorist, the tabloid criminal is an alien, an outsider who poses a threat to social order because he does not conform to the psychological and moral norms by which we, in Western society, have learned to live peacefully together. Terrorists are irrational, inscrutable, and inherently violent. They threaten to infiltrate our porous borders, bringing fear, chaos, and disorder. Furthermore, they cannot be "reformed" or "rehabilitated" according to traditional correctional methods, because they neither recognize, nor respect, the codes to which such measures apply.

There is of course a literature of terrorism—both political and cultural—in which just such qualities are described in an effort to convince us that new, harsher methods of repression are needed to combat this new breed of antisocial being. Terrorists are marked, in the media, by dramatic signs of difference, both physical and psychological. These signs are so repellent and horrifying as to easily justify the use of measures previously unthinkable in the enforcement of "normal" criminal law—because terrorists are not, of course, "normal" criminals; they are alien, inhuman, monsters.

In a fascinating study of the rhetorical image of the international terrorist, legal scholar Ileana Porras uses just such terminology to describe the terrorist as cultural image. "Terrorism," she writes, "has come to be the thing against which liberal democracies define themselves; . . . the repository of everything that cannot be allowed to fit inside the self-image of democracy; . . . the terrorist has become the 'other' that threatens . . . the annihilation of the democratic "self" and an external force against which democracies therefore must strenuously defend against."[26]

"In the expert literature on terrorism," she writes, "the terrorist is transformed from an ordinary deviant into a frightening foreign/barbaric/beast," a "border violator" who does not recognize laws or family ties, and who must be subdued and repressed by "extra-normal means." The political and legal implications of this cultural construction are clear to Porras: "The rhetorical transformation of terrorists into frightening alien outlaws," she writes, "suggests a justification for repression by the state and an excuse for . . . authoritarian regimes." In fact," she writes, "repressive measures short of military dictatorship are virtually recommended by the literature on terrorism . . . because the failure to use all possible means to combat terrorism is to put society at risk of falling into chaos."[27]

I would suggest this description is very close indeed to the image of the border criminal depicted on shows like *Cops*. Out of control, primitive and subhuman, incapable of reason, of abiding by law, or of maintaining family ties, he or she is a creature to be repressed, to be kept out of our borders by the harshest possible measures. For to allow him or her in is to invite the very chaos Porras suggests the terrorist represents. The actual acts committed by the tabloid criminals are of course not nearly dangerous enough to be compared with acts of terrorism. But the idea of inherent "otherness"—which marks the immigrant, the sexual deviant, and the drug addict—and the grotesquely expressionistic conventions by which the tabloids represent these people makes the comparison in kind, if not deed, emotionally resonant. The border dwellers on *Cops* are the dregs of society. But rather than presenting any cultural, political, or social context that might explain their deplorable state of life or even suggest ways to remedy it, these shows choose to represent these outsiders as alien, depraved, and inferior, and thus to suggest that only the most repressive policies are appropriate for them. It may seem to viewers of the series that this kind of treatment is more than justified for such subhuman, irrational creatures. But policies set in place to apply to designated, demonized scapegoats—as these aliens, addicts, and misfits of various kinds have become—can all too easily be used against everyone, especially in a postmodern world in which the designation of "otherness" has, in one way or another, come to be a floating signifier that may attach, at any time, to any of us.

The issue of terrorism and its links with criminality in general in so much of current media discussion of the issue, has of course become particularly resonant since the attack on the World Trade Center in September 2001. In fact, when I first wrote about tabloid crime series in a much earlier version of this chapter, I had no idea how ominously prescient the analogy would soon become. It is an issue we will return to later in the book, since it is impossible to avoid it in any serious discussion of television, law, and criminality. However, the next chapter, which completes

our study of the evolution of entertainment genres devoted to law enforcement, will deal with a different, equally recent and ominous development in fictional television: the coming of *Oz*, the first series ever to be
set inside a maximum security prison—or in any prison, for that matter—
in which the demonization of the criminal escalates even further, and on
the most "quality" of television venues, HBO.

3

Signs of the Times

Oz and the Sudden Visibility of Prisons on Television

As I was beginning to write this chapter on *Oz* and the representation of prisons on television, I read an inspiring story about a group of citizens who personally put up $100,000 to finance a federal civil rights suit against the state of Georgia.[1] At issue were the barbaric conditions and treatment of the nine- to seventeen-year-old male and female inmates in the juvenile detention center located in their small Georgia town. Among the atrocities cited in the suit were crowding so severe that as many as five children slept on floors, near open toilets, in rooms meant for one; routine sexual abuse of inmates; lack of such basic necessities as eyeglasses and toothbrushes; and the absence of any educational or psychological programs or staff. So unbearable were the conditions of the center that suicide attempts were common.

This story was extraordinary because it is almost unheard of for middle- to upper-class citizens to *accept* the placement of such centers in their communities much less investigate, feel sympathy for, and take action, *at their own significant expense,* on behalf of what criminologists and media reports have typically portrayed as youthful "superpredators" deserving of extreme punishment. But it is more than altruism and a community's concern for "others" that made this story worthy of comment. For in reporting it, the article also brought to light some of the Clinton administration's legacy of criminal justice legislation that is generally as unknown as the deplorable, inhumane conditions under which most inmates—juvenile and adult, male and female—are living. Certain features of President Clinton's 1996 "anti-terrorism" bill made it necessary for these citizens to finance the suit privately. Most notably, the bill curtails the ability to bring such suits by refusing to allow any attorneys who receive federal funding—including most of the Legal Aid and public defender lawyers who typically represent indigent clients—from filing suits on behalf of prisoners.[2]

I suspect that very few Americans read this story. Unlike the many stories about crime and criminal justice picked up and sensationalized by television news, magazines, and talk shows—tales of serial killers, school shooting sprees, and child abuse and murder cases—this one attracted no television crews or cameras. With certain laudable exceptions, most other stories of prison abuse and repression that are the daily reality for prisoners all over the nation, especially since the coming of commercial prisons—which are run strictly for profit and are unregulated by local authorities—are not picked up by mass media. What the media do focus on with great regularity and sensationalism are the legislative initiatives, both state and federal, that produce the laws that allow such conditions to thrive. But as a rule these stories tend to present such legislation in an upbeat tone that stresses the government's efforts to "get tough on crime" and are often peppered with quotes by government officials. Such cries have been successful in garnering public support for harsher criminal legislation. A clear example is the successful California referendum that mandated the "three strike" law, by which anyone convicted of a third felony crime, no matter how severe or minor, is now automatically imprisoned for life.[3] The success of such laws is almost certainly, at least partly, a result of the misleading and incendiary ways in which the media cause viewers to have often unreasonable fears about the rate of crime, its nature, and its likelihood to affect them. In fact, as criminologists V. Kappeler, M. Blumberg, and G. Potter have shown, the media are among the most important creators and circulators of the socially constructed "mythologies" of crime and justice that become "commonsense" public opinion. For, as these authors document, the media consistently use techniques meant to confuse and mislead the public.[4] Among these are the construction of criminal stereotypes; presentation of opinion as fact; masking of opinion by seeking out expert sources who will agree with their preformed opinions; use of value-loaded terminology; selective presentation of fact; management of information through framing and editing techniques; and vague references to unnamed officials or "those close to criminal justice theories and policies." As a result, many Americans support the "War on Crime"[5] with passion. They are determined to keep themselves safe in what they perceive as a social landscape filled with mass murderers run amok, with teenage "superpredators," and with murder and mayhem around every corner. In reality, statistics show a dramatically declining crime rate.

Before we turn to media representations generally, and to *Oz* in particular, I will put current trends in criminal justice policy and representation into historical and political perspective. We might begin by looking at the context in which prisons, and punishment generally, came to be hidden from public view in the first place, first physically and then electronically. Although crime news and crime fiction are among the most permanent and popular of television fare, such coverage and representation have, until very recently, stopped short of the prison gates. In the age of the monarchies, harsh physical punishment of criminals was often made into a public spectacle meant to instill in the public consciousness the meaning of crimes against the state and give citizens the satisfaction of seeing it ritualistically punished.[6] In the modern age of liberal democracies this process was increasingly considered inhumane. And so came the creation of the modern prison, hidden from public view, in which those convicted of crimes were subjected to disciplinary treatment devised by the new "scientists" of psychological and social "management."

Until quite recently, this shift away from public punishment as an edifying public spectacle was reflected in many television crime dramas. The search for the criminal, through the use of techniques of detection and psychological analysis, and finally the apprehension marked the moment of narrative closure, when justice was carried out and the community was made safe once more from the defective, sick, and dangerous individual. Even with the coming of TV law series such as *Law and Order* and *The Practice*, and televised trials on Court TV, the moment of narrative closure was most typically marked by the jury's verdict or, occasionally, with the sentencing hearing in which punishment was meted out by the judge. What happened next—the actual removal of the convicted man or woman to prison—was left to the imagination. The prison routines and experiences of the men and women in twenty-three-hour lockdown, solitary confinement, and death row, and the procedures by which death sentences have been carried out—all of this was as invisible to the television viewer as to the average citizen. In fact, if Court TV and its fictional counterparts have made the general public more aware of the juridical aspects of the criminal justice system, no such trend had—until the late 1990s and the coming of *Oz*—emerged to represent for public consumption a factual or fictionalized version of the inner workings of American prisons.

The coming of *Oz*, one of the most critically acclaimed of recent TV series, is therefore a significant sign of the times. Most significantly, it marks a shift in both criminal justice policy and mainstream media approaches to the issue of punishment. It turns away from the model of a publicly invisible, relatively benign and "corrective" form of punishment, suited to liberal democracies, to something much more resonant of earlier eras in which punishment for crime was not only physical and brutal, but also publicly visible: a ritualistic spectacle that served both as a warning and as a moral education for a public socialized to see crime in terms of evil, of unforgivable and unacceptable social transgression.

The idea that punishment should be seen as a public warning against social transgression is, in many ways, a throwback to earlier times, before the rise of liberal democracies introduced the notion of therapeutic "correction" performed by "doctors" of the new sciences of criminology and psychology. In this older version of the role of punishment, public displays were seen as a way of publicly separating and shaming those who broke the rules that hold us together as a society, and as a warning to the rest of us of the wages of such antisocial behavior.[7] In this more traditional view, to quote the social thinker Emile Durkheim, "punishment does not serve, or else only serves secondarily, in correcting the culpable." Its true function is "to maintain social cohesion intact, while maintaining all its vitality in the common conscience."[8] Such a view of punishment as having a primarily public, symbolic purpose—of maintaining and reinforcing what the Standards and Practices departments of network TV call "existing social standards"—is very much in keeping with the rise in televisual spectacles of trials. Now, with the coming of *Oz* and other cable programs, such as Court TV's *Inside Cell Block F* and *Lock and Key*, we see the aftermath of the guilty verdict so familiar to TV viewers by now: the incarceration and punishment of those found guilty. What better way to do this than to display, for all to see, representations of the consequences of social transgression in their most visual and dramatic aspects.

Thus the coming of prison drama to television marks a powerful moment in the history of crime drama on TV. *Oz* is regarded by critics (not to mention its creators, who compare their work to the tragedies of Sophocles and Shakespeare[9]) as among the most "highbrow" of television programming. The show is on the outskirts of mainstream television, of the "trash TV" of the tabloids; but also, more recently, it is on the premium channels that do not depend on commercial sponsors, where new trends tend to surface first. "Trash" series like *Cops* have changed the way in which criminality is represented on TV in ways that serve to justify the most extremely brutal and inhumane treatment of those suspected, much less convicted, of crimes. But so, I would argue, has *Oz*. Indeed, I would argue further that what *Cops* and *America's Most Wanted* started, with their demonization of unapprehended and unincarcerated criminals, *Oz* has continued. The show gives horrifying images of these inhuman brutes and monsters once they have been tried, convicted, and locked away in the dungeons that earlier television series considered off-limits to the public eye. If *Cops* and *AMW* gratify a public eager to see monstrous and alien "criminals" apprehended and taken away in police cars, *Oz* takes the next step by assuring us that—as the new "law and order" sentiments rise in popularity—these incorrigible demons are being properly disposed of.

Indeed, it is intriguing to look at the figures cited in a *New York Times* report that cites the results of a Gallup Poll, listed in five-year increments from 1950 to 1999, on what issues most troubled Americans. From 1950 to 1990—with a brief blip between 1965 and 1970 in which campus unrest and juvenile delinquency appeared, and quickly disappeared—the issues of concern were primarily war and foreign affairs, racial problems, unemployment, and other economic issues. But in 1990, drug abuse appears as the second most troubling issue; in 1995 crime and violence rise to number one; and in 1999, "ethics, morality and family decline," followed by crime and violence, top the list.[10] Television has been quick to pick up the trend, if at first—as is typical—in the upper and lower margins of its programming arena.

The Clinton Era, "Crime Control," and the Coming of Prison TV

To understand fully the significance of the coming of *Oz*, and its critical and popular reception, we might look at the ideological and political context in which it emerged, and chart briefly the rise of the ideas and policies it so vividly reflects and reinforces. As criminologists Franklin Zimring, Gordon Hawkins, Geoffrey Alpert, and Kenneth Haas have documented, theories of punishment dictating prison policy underwent several ideological shifts in the second half of the twentieth century. "For most of the past 200 years, the dominant purposes of corrections have gradually moved from a strictly punitive philosophy toward the ideal of rehabilitation . . . the belief that criminal offenders can be reformed and taught to live socially productive, crime free lives became a major goal of correctional policy in the 1950s and 1960s," according to Haas.[11]

But by the 1970s, a debate among criminologists about the effectiveness of rehabilitation arose, spurred largely by the fears engendered by civil rights and antiwar protests and rebellions. Indeed, according to Haas and Alpert, it was Richard Nixon—whose paranoid fear of these protestors led him to criminal actions that ultimately led to his resignation, in the face of near-certain impeachment—who actually planted the first seeds of the now dominant conservative trend in criminal justice policy, back in the days when liberal ideas were dramatically dominant. Nixon's "law and order" policies, according to Haas and Alpert, led to "some of the most repressive legislation concerning civil rights and civil liberties seen in many years" (a record surpassed, as *New York Times* columnist Anthony Lewis has documented, only by William Jefferson Clinton).[12]

As Nixon's repressive policies became more fashionable in the 1980s and 1990s than they were in his own day, rehabilitation as a theory and policy grew increasingly unpopular. Other theories—deterrence, retribution, and incapacitation—grew in popularity. But deterrence, according to Zimring, lost credibility with liberals and conservatives alike, if for different reasons: liberals dismissed it as ineffective, while conservatives preferred more morally informed policies featuring retribution and punishment. The liberals were correct in their assessment of the ineffectiveness of imprisonment as a deterrent to crime. But since they had no coherent alternative to suggest, the conservative desire to see crime as a form of "sin" to be punished as harshly as possible, and criminals as unregenerate sinners who needed to be removed from society, increasingly carried the day. They saw the death penalty, ultimately, as the best possible answer to both demands, and "incapacitation" became the dominant theory dictating both prison administration and sentencing-law policy.[13]

These shifts in penal theory and the underlying assumptions about human nature and the "criminal mind" they reflect follow the general shifts in the broader political climate of the nation, as the twentieth century moved toward its final years. As Haas suggests, Richard Nixon, the first in a long line of Republican presidents to hold power after the Kennedy-Johnson years, sowed the seeds of political reaction before their time had come. But if Nixon's "law and order" mentality was out of sync with his own times, it was well suited to the later Reagan/Bush years. The rise of the right and the backlash against the progressive agendas of the 1960s and 1970s—feminism, civil rights, the war on poverty, gay rights, and the Warren Court's commitment to the rights of criminal defendants and inmates—rose to ideological ascendance with a vengeance. The Supreme Courts that succeeded the liberal Warren Court were increasingly dominated by conservative Republican appointees like Anthony Scalia and Clarence Thomas, whose animosity toward civil liberties and criminal defendants and convicts was intense. By 1976, attacks on the Eighth Amendment, which forbids "cruel and unusual punishment," began to increase.

The first important case to begin this slide toward "law and order" and the erosion of the liberal bent toward defendants' rights was *Estelle v. Gamble*, in which an inmate claimed that he was deprived of adequate medical care. This case resulted in a decision which, while acknowledging that such deliberate deprivation, if it resulted in "torture or a lingering death," was indeed "cruel and unusual," denied that "the conscience of mankind" would be offended if such suffering was the result of an accident or mere negligence. In other words, we had reached a point where the actual suffering of an inmate was no longer seen by the court as a matter of moral concern, or, indeed, of human rights discourse. Rather, the emphasis was now placed on the prison personnels' *intent*. Negligence, which in criminal *trials* still stands as a basis for prosecution, was no longer seen in the same way when the *negligent* person or persons were employees of the criminal justice system itself.[14]

In time, decisions such as these multiplied in ways that increasingly ate away at the human rights of prisoners and left them open to the kind of physical abuse which for so long had seemed obsolete. Indeed, by 1990, the Court, with such additions as Anthony Scalia and Clarence Thomas, had shifted so far to the right that Sandra Day O'Connor and William Souter found themselves on the "left" in many decisions. In the case of *Wilson v. Seiter*, for example, the Scalia Court ruled that for a punishment to be "cruel and unusual," someone must have deliberately inflicted it. In *Hudson v McMillian* (Justice Thomas's first significant written opinion), the Court ruled that "mere" prison conditions or practices could not be construed as "punishment" at all. Thus, prison officials and staff were given a virtual license to ignore the human needs of prisoners and to inflict outrageously inhumane suffering on them.[15]

During this same period, the civil rights of prisoners were being similarly eroded. In 1988 and 1989 two cases, *Thornburgh v. Abbott* and

Kentucky v. Thompson, approved censorship of prison publications and the limiting of prison visits. With the media-aided popularity of such "anti-crime," pro-punishment rulings, "New Democrats" like Bill Clinton and Al Gore were quick to follow suit, initiating crime bills in 1994 and 1996 that stripped criminal defendants of the right to file suit using attorneys receiving federal money; to meet with press; to appeal decisions—including death sentences—after a time period too brief for most legal aid attorneys to meet; and more. The Clinton administration's affirmative measures included the erosion of Fourth Amendment protections against illegal search and seizure by widening the berth given police to make such searches and to use seized property in court cases. Most importantly, the bill authorized the building of huge numbers of new prisons, making it economically unfeasible for the government, and the local communities receiving these institutions, to keep them unfilled. Thus, arresting, incarcerating, and retaining even more of the population in prisons for longer and longer periods, and for lesser and lesser "crimes," became a de facto necessity. The bills also cut funding for such standard privileges as the right to attend college classes and have access to exercise equipment and other leisure activities. At the same time, the use of physical shock devices to control prisoners, the authorization of the death penalty for an increasing number of crimes never before considered capital offenses, and similarly vengeful and cruel punishments were becoming commonplace.[16]

The Blurring of Left, Right, and Center
in Penal Theory and Practice

It is indisputable that the George H. W. Bush and Bill Clinton years engendered a rash of harsh and inhumane attacks on the rights of prisoners. However, even in more liberal eras, a close look at penal policy and theory reveals a rather muddled and contradictory set of practices that make it clear that those in charge of the system have never really had a clear idea of what it was they were trying to do. In fact, one of the most troubling aspects of the prison system has been that the most "liberal" of administrations and legislations, those most bent on providing "rehabiliation" in the belief that, theoretically, all human beings, even those guilty of the most blood-curdling acts, were capable of change and even redemption, have never really clarified the distinction between "physical" punishment and other forms of discipline.

Indeed, throughout the twentieth century, no matter what the dominant ideological bent of any given era—whether rehabilitation, retribution, deterrence, or incapacitation—in practice, within the confines of prison walls invisible to the public, there was always a mix of practices. Thus, there has been a blurry line between what was physical punishment and what was discipline, what was theoretically "rehabilitative" and what was physically and psychologically brutal. The original justification for solitary confinement, for example, was that it gave a prisoner the solitude to meditate on his actions. As early as 1777 the Quaker reformer John Bradford, for example, declared that isolation from "the society of his fellow prisoners, in which society the worse are sure to corrupt the better, is calculated to raise up in [the prisoner] reflections on the folly of his choice and expose his mind to such better and continued sentences as may produce a lasting alteration in the principles of his conduct."[17] Yet, as practiced in prisons like Alcatraz and the newer supermax prisons dubbed "high-tech dungeons and torture chambers,"[18] this practice is anything but reformative. And herein lies the great irony of today's prison system, with its mishmash of theories and potpourri of arbitrary practices that do not necessarily jibe with the theories of the time, written and legislated by those who may not ever be in charge of implementing or monitoring them. For the truth is that in practice, the very distinction between "discipline" and "torture" is often as lost on those who administer prisons as is the distinction between rehabilitation and retribution.

Prisons are at best ineffective and at worst still the most horrifying of places. In keeping them hidden from public view, the (all too often) physical abuses and indignities suffered by inmates, even in the most liberal times, have largely gone undiscussed and unacknowledged by the wider public. It is no surprise, then, that even under the most liberal regimes, policies meant to rehabilitate were often far different and less "helpful" to prisoners looking for a better life than distant lawmakers could know. It was therefore easy to convince "liberals" like Clinton and Gore that "rehabilitation" simply didn't work. Because it was already obvious to anyone familiar with the statistics on recidivism and on the lack of correlation between murder rates and the death penalty that "deterrence" was a totally ineffective policy, liberals were left with no coherent response to the right-wing call for incapacitation as the only real policy with any teeth in it. According to the rhetoric, it was the only way to insure that criminals would permanently and decisively be kept from committing further crimes. From there, the death penalty was an easy sell. What better form of "incapacitation," after all, than death itself.

Of course, common sense—or better yet, firsthand knowledge or experience of the prison system as it really is—tells us that prisons, unless they involve life sentences with no chance of parole or death itself, do the very opposite of what they promise. Far from keeping inmates from committing further crimes, they tend to give even those who are capable of rehabilititon what amounts to a university-level course in crime as a lifetime profession. The infliction of harsher and harsher treatment on those already hardened in the ways of crime, and the rescinding of the few privileges and opportunities for change they may have had in the past, in many cases—as statistics about recidivism attest[19]—simply reinforce and harden them further in what they have come to know as a lifestyle. Indeed, hard time and harsh treatment have made a prison system in which crime itself flourishes, as there are no other options offered for survival—inside or out.[20] Yet these prisons, according to the sensationalized rhetoric spouted by politicians and dramatically reinforced by the media, have become a social necessity and therefore need to be constructed and filled.

From Cool Hand Luke to Hannibal Lecter: The Transformation of the Classic Prison Drama

Herein is the importance of the media. As long as the actual punishment of convicted criminals was well hidden behind closed prison doors, prison conditions remained virtually invisible to the public: no one asked, and no one told. Because of current right-wing calls for physical punishment and public shamings, and because executions have become popular with so many Americans, it was inevitable that television would need to go where it had never gone before—inside prison doors. For prison series are the logical extension of shows like *Cops*. Indeed, the tabloid crime shows almost cry out for this kind of "sequel," in which the brutes we have come to know and fear so well are taken away for good to places where their likes will never need to frighten or threaten us again. And this is exactly what shows like *Oz* and the clones that are bound to follow will provide. For what we see here is a version of that life which, hardly surprisingly, fits perfectly with the political rationale for incarceration, brutality, incapacitation, and death. We do not see the truth about the reality of prisons and what happens to the women and men who are placed there for long periods of time.

Which brings us at last to the link between criminal justice policy and media representation. It was not until HBO began running *Oz* in 1998 that prison life was even glimpsed by television audiences. When it did air, it was in the context of the rise and popularity of the new criminal justice policies that gave the stamp of approval to atrocious prison practices and conditions—only a public convinced by government and media rhetoric and imagery that those convicted of crimes were indeed subhuman creatures, no matter what may have driven them to their "crimes." *Oz* presents a vision of hell on earth in which inmates are so depraved and vicious that no sane person could possibly think they should ever again be let loose upon society.

We have no earlier TV series to compare to *Oz*, of course, but we do have many examples of Hollywood films about prison life. This genre has been a staple of movie-making for decades. Just like early TV series about lawyers tended in general to show a far more liberal orientation than the more recent series, so did earlier Hollywood films. In fact, even today Hollywood produces prison films with a surprisingly liberal slant, with a far different perspective on prisons than *Oz*. Especially in the late post–cold war 1950s and 1960s, when liberal sentiments were becoming more common, the prison film genre produced a few classic films that gave audiences a view of prison life from a point of view that was extremely sympathetic to convicts. In dramatic contrast to current television depictions of and assumptions about "criminals," in and out of prisons, these movies portrayed inmates—even those guilty of the crimes of which they were accused—as essentially decent and humane, capable of deep interpersonal bonding, loyalty, community solidarity. Their strong sense of justice and willingness to fight back against institutionalized *in*justice was truly noble and inspiring.

Occasional prison movies will still show sympathy for inmates and contempt for their brutal and malicious treatment by guards and wardens. But it is significant that these more recent films draw far smaller audiences than the earlier films. Most people, for example, have probably never heard of *Murder in the First*, arguably the best of these films, which was produced in 1994 and went almost directly from studio to video rental after failing colossally at theaters. *The Shawshank Redemption*, produced in the same year, while more widely seen, was also less dramatic in its portrayal of institutional abuse and far more concerned with the personal redemption of individual inmates. It is also worth noting that both films were set in the 1930s and 1940s, not the present. *Murder in the First*, which dramatically and passionately exposes the brutality of prison life and its personnel, was billed as the story of "the trial that brought down Alcatraz." That infamous institution did not actually close its doors until 1963, over two decades after the 1941 case on which the film was based. Nonetheless, these two films, and their 1962 classic counterparts, *Cool Hand Luke* and *The Birdman of Alcatraz*, are all dramatically, if not shockingly, different from TV's *Oz*. The differences are important to note before we can truly understand the harshness of the TV series that has garnered so much acclaim even from liberal audiences.[21]

As noted earlier, in practice there is a very blurry line between what passes for "correction" and what is sheer brutal punishment, what is deemed rehabilitative and what is simply retributive and incapacitating. But in the four films just mentioned, this confusion is viscerally clarified. All, in one way or another, feature protagonists who are in some sense resistant to the prison system that holds, humbles, and harasses them. All four also feature clear presentations of these prisoners, whether "guilty" of the crimes of which they are convicted of or not, as men of dignity and worth. Some are broken by the system and some undergo remarkable transformations, but all are heroic figures whose fates—before entering prison and during their incarceration—are seen to have been molded by the conditions in which they are forced to live. More importantly—the most striking difference between the prison film genre and its new television version—all four movies portray prisoners whose salvation, or symbolic significance, is rooted in their deep bonding with other human beings, whether prisoners, supporters, or attorneys.

Cool Hand Luke is a movie which fairly reeks of its 1960s birth date in its glorification of rebellion against authority, and nonconformity in general. Luke (like McMurphy in *One Flew over the Cuckoo's Nest*) is a born rebel, a nonconformist whose very posture is meant to question and defy authority. He is serving two years for knocking off the heads of parking meters, symbols of the mechanization and regulation of modern life. Unable or unwilling to hold a "steady" job or "settle down," he is the generic outlaw Americans have always loved (and envied), as the gray flannel–blue collar discipline of industrial society clamped down on the individualism that Jeffersonian democracy was meant to foster. In prison, of course, he finds an even more constraining form of discipline, as the rules and regulations of daily life make it virtually impossible to make a free move or decision. The prison to which Luke is sent is a work farm where prisoners are sent out in chain gangs to clear weeds from highways. But as humiliating and dehumanizing as this routine is, Luke's "cool" insubordinate attitude makes him a symbol of resistance to the other men. He is fearless and contemptuous, apparently able to withstand any discipline—including nights "in the box"—and emerge as spunky and defiant as ever. But finally he can take no more, and his continuous escape efforts, and subsequent prison reprisals, finally break and ultimately kill him.

What is interesting about this film is its black-and-white portrayal of the system: the inmates are good old boys; the guards and warden are vicious, brutal, and inhuman. Unquestionably, prison is meant to break rather than reform these men; what passes for discipline is in fact a form of brutal physical and psychological punishment. The issue of discipline and its ultimate goal of turning men into mindless automatons rather than better souls is made explicit in *Birdman of Alcatraz*, the based-on-fact story of Robert Stroud, a hardened killer who spends fifty-four years in a maximum-security prison, most of it in solitary confinement. Again, the warden is an inhuman, mean-spirited man whose goal, as he rises in the ranks of federal prison bureaucracy, is to break the spirit of every prisoner so that he will "behave the way you want us to," as Stroud, in a climactic "debate" with his keeper, brazenly tells him. "When these men leave here they can't think for themselves, can't function as human beings," he lectures. "They have had all their creativity and individuality taken from them" and have lost "the dignity they once had."

Stroud is seen, at first, as an antisocial loner, incapable of relating to anyone in a respectful or civil manner. But in this case, he is indeed "rehabilitated" in prison, but not through the disciplinary regimes of the warden. On the contrary, this occurs through the friendship of a decent guard who teaches him to treat others with civility, a fellow inmate with whom he communicates through the bars, and the love of a woman who shares his love of birds and their commitment to finding cures for their diseases. Furthermore, he finds a vocation by accident, when he nurses a baby bird found in his exercise space, eventually becoming an expert on birds and the keeper of a small menagerie. He publishes articles and becomes a national celebrity, which allows him to expand his solitary cell and even start a business with the woman he marries.

None of this takes place in Alcatraz, however. The Birdman is in Leavenworth Prison, where things are run far more loosely than contemporary audiences would find comfortable. But the warden, who left Leavenworth for Washington while this change transpires, returns to take vengeance on Stroud. He has him transferred to the new, "modern" prison at Alcatraz, and deprives him of all access to birds, publishing, and his bird rehabilitation business. "Look at this," the warden tells him in a climactic interchange, as he points to the pristine splendor of the new, high-tech disciplinary compound. To this, Stroud replies with a lecture about human dignity and creativity. And so, again, we have a critique of prison life in which discipline is seen as debilitating to the human soul, while friendship, work, and love—even in the confines of an amazingly free prison environment—has the power to rehabilitate a hardened criminal into a loving, productive man. Here again we had a prisoner whose basic dignity and refusal to conform to humiliating, spirit-breaking regimens—his resistance to authority—made him heroic and spiritually victorious, even though he dies in prison. We never know what made Stroud the violent killer he was, but we do see what freed him. All this is in dramatic contrast to the assumptions and practices of two generations of penal theory that destroy, spiritually and physically, the men who succumb to them.

The Shawshank Redemption is a period piece which seems, in the context of the other three films, to be almost unrealistically dreamlike (which is not surprising since it is based on a Stephen King story). This fictional prison, supposedly set in the same time period as *Birdman of Alcatraz,* is similarly free of overt physical punishment except for early scenes in which the hero, Andy Dufresne, is—as is the case in the previous two films—put to the test of surviving physical abuse in order to "prove" his manhood. For Luke it is a boxing match with the prison bully who befriends him when he refuses to quit even when beaten, and several nights in the horrifying "box." For Stroud it is an early stay in a dungeonlike "hole" where rats crawl over his face; and for Dufresne it is the continuous rape by other prisoners, which he survives without breaking or ratting. But even here it is the basic dignity of the hero, and his bonding with the other inmates, that saves him. He uses his accounting skills (he was a banker, unjustly convicted of murdering his faithless wife) to make himself indispensable to the (again) inhumanly cruel warden. And he is clever enough to bargain for perks for the other men. Finally, through his implacable serenity and patience, he manages to dig his way out of the prison he will never be allowed to leave legally, given his financial indispensability to the warden, and makes his way to an island retreat where he lives peacefully as a hotel keeper, awaiting the arrival of his friend Red, who eventually is released and joins him.

Human dignity, bonding and brotherhood, and the hope of fulfilling a dream in which one's creativity and individuality can be expressed, are the characteristics that save Dufresne and Stroud. Cool Hand Luke, on the other hand, has no such salvation but lives on as a symbol to other prisoners of the power and importance of resisting institutionalized tyranny, even at the risk of death. This is also the fate of the doomed prisoner, Henri Young, in *Murder in the First*. Set in Alcatraz in the 1930s and early 1940s, this is a truly horrifying depiction of the total physical and psychological destruction of a human being within the deep recesses of a prison dungeon hidden from the view of even the warden, who oversees three prisons and rarely visits any of them. Henri, imprisoned for stealing five dollars to feed his starving young sister when he is unable to find work during the Depression, is caught in an escape attempt and lives for three years without light, air, exercise, or human company before being returned to the general population. His first act then is to kill, out of sheer animal instinct, the inmate who ratted on him.

The film tells the story of Henri's relationship with his wealthy Harvard-educated public defender and of the heroic resistance of both men to a system—legal and penal—in which injustice, brutality, corruption, and hypocrisy rule. Again, there is the defiance of authority on the part of one man—the defense attorney, Stamfield—and the rehabilitation of the other, Henri, to a state of human dignity through the friendship of another person. Catatonic and nearly subhuman at first, Henri ultimately is brought to heroic, if martyred, action when he testifies to the conditions that drove him, someone who had never hurt anyone before he was incarcerated while still almost a child, to subhuman, bestial violence and rage. Refusing to testify at first, because he prefers death to returning to Alcatraz, he finally overcomes his fear and acts in a way which, according to the highly fictionalized film, helps to bring down the unbelievably brutal and inhuman prison system. Returning to his cell, he carves the word "Victory" on his wall before his dead body is found on the floor of his cell a few days later.

Is this the Alcatraz of Robert Stroud's old age, with its pristine, disciplinary technology? Hardly. But the power of neither movie is diminished by the type of facility, or by the discipline methods or the social goals any of these fictional or fictionalized prisons are meant to depict. What is true of all these prisons, all these heroes, and all these films is their very similar message: that prison itself is a dehumanizing, ineffective, and ultimately counterproductive institution. Once viewed from the prisoners' perspective—or indeed from the perspective of any decent, intelligent person—such a place cannot be justified. This is perhaps made most explicit in *Murder in the First* during the trial scenes in which Stamfield essentially yells "j'accuse" at the entire system. "I was the weapon," says Henri, when he finally finds the courage to speak, "but I am not a murderer." And in pointing a finger at the prison system itself for its role in fostering and breeding the violent behavior it is meant to reform, or at least incapacitate, the film points at the very crux of what is wrong with the current theories of incarcerations as a means of ending crime.

The American prison system is itself a crime, and moreover it breeds multitudes of other crimes. For "if," as one commentator suggests, "one views the U.S. prison system as a reasonable response to lawbreaking, then crime, violence, and drugs seem like problems that can never be solved." Thus, as one prisoner has eloquently explained, "Prison teaches that violence not only works, it works quickly. People are manufactured into explosive machines and released without decompression. The explosion will come but not necessarily here. [Prisoners] will explode—but individually when they're out in the community."[22]

Thus, as those favoring incapacitation rightly believe, there is no answer except to keep prisoners locked away forever. If it seems hard to justify this irrational system, by rational criteria it clearly is irrational. But the beauty of drama—on TV, film, or the stage—is that it relies heavily on emotional manipulation to convey and convince audiences of its message. And *Oz*, with its brutally dramatic portrayal of inmates as the ultimate bullies, and its presentation of the prison staff as more good-hearted, well-meaning victims than bullies, makes a brilliant emotional case for a system that is, in rational terms, quite hard to justify.

Oz and Its Emerald City:
We're Definitely Not in Kansas Anymore

One of the few television analysts to take note of the absence of prisons on television is sociologist Connie McNeeley. She has noted that "programs focusing on prisons are almost nonexistent in the overall scheme of television programming production and content." In the interest of supporting the existing social order, she explains: "Television emphasizes repression of criminal conduct as the most important function of the legal system." McNeeley goes further in her analysis of television's bias in representing criminal justice generally, and, by implication, its support of the various Supreme Court rulings which have so deeply eroded the rights of convicted as well as merely suspected offenders. In a typical scenario of police shows, she notes, for example, that "the viewer sees the crime being committed and knows the identity of the criminal. Thus, when the police conduct an illegal search, it seems more 'acceptable' . . . than it might otherwise, since guilt has been established in the eyes of the viewer."[23]

McNeeley is certainly right about the way in which television portrayals of crime and criminal justice have traditionally tended to support the existing social order and the laws and policies that underpin it. Repression of crime and the rights of law enforcers to catch and convict "criminals" by any means necessary often clearly go beyond what the law allows. Thus, in series like *Law and Order* and *Homicide* it is all too common to see police officers—always the heroes, of course—brutalize confessions out of suspects and ignore Fourth Amendment restrictions on searches and seizures, among other things, with no hint that such behavior is both illegal and immoral. Until recently, as McNeeley suggests, such representations were sufficient to reinforce existing ideas about the need for *repression* of crime, within the communities in which viewers live. The implicit imprisonment of such apprehended and convicted offenders needed only to be assumed, since there was little interest in or need for graphic depictions of prison life itself. Traditional crime drama, as analysts from Raymond Chandler to Stuart Hall have taught us, has always focused on the removal of the dangerous individual from the community and the return to its peace and security that such narrative closure symbolized.[24]

But these authors were writing about a time when liberal democratic theories about prisons as sites of "correction" and even rehabilitation were dominant. The actual nature of that "correction" was not of as much interest—or concern—as it has become in these more moralistic, punishment-oriented times. For today's political leaders and the media producers who tend, by and large, to reflect and reinforce their messages, successful crime fighting involves more than mere apprehension and conviction. It demands that we see, with our own eyes, that those who break the laws that represent community values are not merely sent away, but punished. Incapacitation and retribution have replaced deterrence and, certainly, rehabilitation as the penal theories of choice.

And so we get *Oz*, as big, if not bigger, than life in its graphic portrayal of the "just deserts" that retributive penal theory requires. Does this series and its emphasis on punishment rather than repression contradict McNeeley? I don't think so. In fact, no previous series has made quite so eloquent a dramatic argument for the need to repress criminal conduct, by any means necessary, in order to preserve the social order. For these are times in which such repression is required. A public saturated with terrifying news and images of "superpredators" and twisted "natural born killers" demands to see for itself that they are appropriately punished and securely locked away.

Interestingly enough, the producers of the series don't quite see it that way. This is a sign of the political and ideological confusion of even intellectuals in these days of "compassionate conservatives" and "New Democrats." In fact, for the man who created the series, Tom Fontana, the series is an example of high tragedy inspired by the works of Aeschylus and Sophocles. He is so far from acknowledging, or even apparently understanding, the larger political meaning of the series that, in a *New York Times* interview, he equates the message of the series with that of the recent report issued by Amnesty International that cited the American prison system for heinous human rights abuses. "Insisting that *Oz* presents a true picture of American prison life," says the *Times* reporter, "Fontana cited a 1998 Amnesty International report critical of the criminal justice system in the United States." The report, he is quoted as saying, "had even given him ideas for the show. 'Throw rats in the cell?' Fontana said. 'I'm going to do that. The idea of a rat in a pod—oh man!' he said, wiping his brow with a sweep of his hand."[25]

But the politically astute will recognize a slight problem here, which the claim that the series is high tragedy rather than political agitprop nicely obscures: it is not the prison staff who are shown committing the atrocities cited by Amnesty International; it is the inmates themselves. Of course, it is a fact (although not the fact the Amnesty observers were concerned with) that most prison violence is indeed prisoner-on-prisoner.[26] But as is made clear by the insights of the prisoners and psychologists cited above and rare films like *Murder in the First*, this violence is not *inherent* in the men and women who come into the system, but is actually more likely to be bred into them by the conditions of incarceration itself.

Perhaps Charles Dickens said it best back in the nineteenth century when he wrote of his experiences in visiting prisons:

> I am persuaded that those who devised the [prison] system and those benevolent gentlemen who carry it into execution do not know what it is that they are doing. I believe that few men are capable of estimating the immense amount of torture and agony which this dreadful punishment [incarceration], prolonged for years, inflicts upon its sufferers; and, in guessing at it myself, and in reasoning from what I have seen written upon their faces, and what to my certain knowledge they feel within, I am only the more convinced that there is a depth of terrible endurance in it which none but the sufferers themselves can fathom, and which no man has a right to inflict upon his fellow creature.[27]

What Dickens implies is made dramatically visible in the powerfully filmed story of Henri Young: that such conditions themselves make inmate violence a likely if not inevitable occurrence. For it is only after Henri, a decent and caring young man when he enters Alcatraz, has suffered three years of extraordinary torture that he is transformed into a barbaric killer. But if Dickens and the Amnesty observers understood this point, the producers of *Oz* seem to have missed it entirely. For in this prison series, it is the prisoners themselves, and not the do-gooder liberal staff, who seem hell bent on torturing one another. And since the institutional environment and personnel are clearly not responsible, and no hint of what the backgrounds or experiences of the inmates were before entering Oz, the only conclusion the series suggests to viewers is the one the supporters of such institutions and their rules and policies preach: that these men are incorrigibly evil and unfit to be anywhere except where they are, and where they can only do damage to each other and not to decent citizens.

Before we look more closely at the series itself, it is worth taking a brief detour to examine the way it makes a perfect segué—rhetorically, stylistically, and ideologically—to the equally popular, if less critically acclaimed, tabloid police shows like *Cops* and *America's Most Wanted*. In *AMW*, for example, we see vivid, B-movie-style "reenactments" of the crimes of still-on-the-loose murderers and rapists. Most involve monstrous assaults on decent families in which women and children are most often the targets of unbearably bestial acts of violence. And on *Cops*, we see an actual police officer on his nightly rounds through poor, dilapidated communities in which drug addicts, drunks, prostitutes, and newly ar-rived immigrants, not yet acclimated to American society, are shown in various states of deranged, violent, or seemingly irrational behavior. Since the producers choose carefully from the hours of footage at their disposal, what we see in each twenty-two minute segment is a world of apparently out-of-control, primitive, and subhuman lawbreakers, incapable of rea-soning, abiding by law, or maintaining family ties. The heroic, clean-cut police officers must struggle to apprehend, cuff, and take them away. These offenders are thus represented as the dregs of society. But rather than present any cultural, political, or social context that might explain their deplorable state of life or suggest ways to remedy it, these shows represent the people as alien, depraved, and inferior, and therefore only the most repressive policies are appropriate for them.

If one corrects for the trashy settings, illiterate speech, and B-movie production values, it is not hard to see the link between the horrific, bes-tial images of lawbreakers on these tabloids and the equally vicious and depraved—if far more literate, rational, and intentionally malicious—convicts on *Oz*. *Oz* is set in a maximum-security prison whose name has been changed from the Oswald Correctional Facility to the Oswald Pen-itentiary because—according to the musings of the black dreadlocked, wheelchair-bound inmate who serves as a kind of Greek chorus (one of many nods to the high-art tradition of Greek tragedy)—"Nobody's pen-itent, nor are they sorry. Nobody." The population of this prison is ex-clusively male and, not surprisingly, a large number are black. Statisti-cally speaking, however, there are not nearly as many blacks as in the real prisons upon which *Oz* is based. This distortion of the racial truths about prison populations is not surprising. A series meant for the broad, up-scale audience that HBO, a subscription-based network, targets would, like other "quality" series, while always adhering to the politically cor-rect incorporation of a variety of racial, ethnic, and gendered characters, still tend to feature a cast of largely white stars. *Oz* is no different. Its prison staff is multigendered and multicultural although its chief is a white male. And while the prisoners themselves are culturally and racially diverse, the majority of major players are still white males. Here is where we see the less realistic aspects of fictional drama as compared to reality-based series.

The near-total absence of female inmates in an age in which, accord-ing to Steven Donziger, women are the fastest-growing segment of the ac-tual prison population is noteworthy.[28] Based on the trends I am following in this book, we can eventually expect to see prison dramas set in women's prisons, and women prisoners portrayed as every bit as vicious as these men. However, *Oz* is probably already ahead of the curve in even presenting the inside of prison life on a national, fictional series. So far the commercial networks have not chosen to follow in its footsteps and create their own prison dramas. It is therefore no more surprising that women do not appear as inmates on *Oz* than it is that the prison is unrealistically overpopulated with leading characters who are white.

What is realistic about *Oz* is its physical setting. The prison, like the real maximum-security prisons on which it is based, is equipped with a high-tech, state-of-the-art area nicknamed Emerald City, which supposedly supports the most liberal theories of correction, and to which it is a privilege to be admitted. The staff of this prison is made up of the kind of well-meaning liberals never seen in the prison movies analyzed above. (The only exception is a vicious, corrupt, racist guard who is quickly killed off in gorily brutal fashion by an inmate.) There is an Asian priest, a Latina nun, an African American doctor, and a white liberal male named McManus who runs the operation. All of these decent folk try hard to fight the system that—true to contemporary political reality—continues to reduce budgets for such necessities as medical care.

Certainly these characters and their all-too-realistic plight in an era prone to cut social services and favor punishment and shaming over compassion or rehabilitation provide the kind of ideological contradiction and ambiguity that make this series more intelligent, challenging, and complex than series like *Cops*. In fact, they serve to preserve the element of "quality" programming that viewers of series like *Homicide* and *Law and Order* are used to seeing, and redeem the series from potentially flirting with intellectual and dramatic simpleminded crassness. These characters really do try hard to do the right thing. They have taken these jobs because they believe in the old model of rehabilitation and redemption that overlaps intriguingly with its stronger push toward a far harsher view of prison authorities and policies.

Still, they are hopelessly impotent not only in confronting the bureaucracy they serve but also in their interactions with the prisoners themselves. In fact, as we look at this series in its chronological position, following *Law and Order* which is itself followed by *The Practice*, we can see that these series reflect an increasing diminishment of the power of liberal thinking. Rather, as important if not monolithic symbols of current trends, they reflect a rise in the sense of hopelessness that liberal thinking about criminal justice policy seems to imply—in actual legal circles as well as on television.

Violence, especially extremely brutal violence, does not often enter the picture in the more civilized of these series such as *Law and Order*. It does enter the picture in the more recent *The Practice*, where brutish clients are allowed to be abused and brutalized by the attorneys who revile their roles as defenders of beasts. And while the violent attorneys who scream at and attack their clients in the courtroom may be held in contempt, they are not taken out of the game or out of commission—as they would be in a real courtroom—for their actions. Instead, they are meant to arouse our sympathies, so distasteful are the criminals they attack in their outbursts of emotionally melodramatic spontaneity. Not so in *Oz*. Here the violence is performed only by the prisoners themselves and the often corrupt and equally brutal guards, while the liberal bureaucrats appear powerless to do anything more than express defeat as they wearily enter the prison each day and meet with the usual series of failures in their often noble efforts.

There is some plausibility in this situation. As prison budgets are cut and prisoner privileges reduced, even the most liberal and well-meaning of officials may well feel increasingly helpless. Similarly, the guards themselves, even those who start out with the best of intentions, finding themselves faced with a prison population increasingly angry and rebellious at the conditions in which they are forced to live, may well feel increasingly angry and prone to violence themselves as they live in frustration with, and fear of, those they must oversee. It is possible for progressive, informed viewers to "read" some of the violence as grounded in the atrocious conditions in which those who live and work in these places are placed. Nonetheless, there is little effort, in the series itself, to bring out these nuances of psychological and political reality about prison life and its effects on all those who must live and work in its current environment.

Thus, the central liberal characters are presented as essentially impotent in their goodness. And their impotence is presented in an interestingly contradictory way. For while these are clearly decent souls, it is obvious from the first frame, and the first oracular pronouncement of the cynical narrator, that the men they work to save are, like the criminals on *Cops*, unsalvageable. And there is no sense of why or how they became that way, since, as in *Cops*, we only meet them when they have reached the state of incorrigibility which their lives (and the prison system itself) have brought them to. The liberal lip service paid by the series is thus undercut seriously by the very strong implication that these guys are really wimps, living in some sort of time warp in which the decency of human nature is still taken seriously. In this, *Oz* resembles *The Practice* quite closely, if it is more viciously dramatized than the more sanitized commercial networks permit on their fictional series. For here again we have a set of decent, liberal "heroes" who are driven to the point of loathing and even violence against those they try so hard to help, as their "clients" prove, again and again, to be too incorrigible and depraved to be saved, even by those with the best of intentions.

This subversion of the strands of liberal sentiment is accomplished in sledgehammer fashion by the extremely one-dimensional representation of the inmates, who are not only brutal to each other and their keepers, but openly brag about the horrendous acts that got them sent to Oz in the first place. "I killed a cop," brags one white inmate to the others sitting in the prison barber shop. To this, another inmate, also white, replies while ominously shaving the disabled narrator with a straight razor that is poised threateningly: "I got ya beat. I whacked a whole family." He goes on gleefully and graphically to describe butchering and raping the mother and her "two sweet little kids." And when asked, "Why?" he leeringly replies "For fun!" Other inmates—black, white, and Latino—have committed such acts as gouging out the eye of a correctional officer and casually and indiscriminately pricking other inmates they passed in a corridor with a hypodermic syringe filled with the blood of an AIDS victim.

Unlike Henri Young's similar act of savage violence, these acts are in no way portrayed as spontaneous outbursts of rage resulting from long-term abuse by prison officials. On the contrary; no such official torture is shown. But there is certainly a lot of torture, all of it committed by inmates upon one another. But again, there is no sense that any of this violence results from the kind of treatment these men are subjected to. Nor do we ever see a trace of the economic or social environments that produced such brutal criminals in the first place. Of course, we did not see that in *Birdman of Alcatraz*, either. But we did see a radical and inspiring transformation of the hero of that film, something which *Oz* never portrays. Indeed, these men are almost wholly lacking in human qualities of any kind, not capable of the human bonding—among inmates, between attorneys and inmates, and even, in *Birdman*, between a kindly guard and an inmate—that is such a prominent feature of the prison movie genre. What this series shows is a total lack of human connection that is not based on self-interest and infused with (justified) mistrust. Gangs are the only bonding formations in this prison, and they are rooted entirely on race identity and hatred and nothing else. The only portrayal of "love," to my knowledge, was the unrequited sexual "love" of one cell mate for another. And that emotion, or desire, was repaid with vicious, eerily self-satisfied, betrayal.

In the midst of all this human bestiality and ugliness, occasional nods are given to actual prison indignities. But they are rarely presented in their actual political context, and, worse yet, are invariably portrayed in ways that call their legitimacy into question. For example, in one episode a class action suit is brought by inmates who were treated violently during a riot, but we never see the riot or the conditions that produced them. Instead, we see the Muslim leader who has instigated it engaging in a sexual flirtation with a white woman whose brother was killed during the incident. Not only does this situation create extreme friction and mistrust within his Muslim following, but it is also made even more distasteful because one woman, who is not an inmate but a relative, at first refuses to join the suit because, she says of the dead inmate, "He was a mean boy and he grew up a mean man. He probably deserved to be killed by that guard." Why does she return to join the suit? Because she is infatuated with the black man, as is he with her.

In another reference to the laws now being passed that infringe upon the civil rights and privileges of inmates, we see a woman on death row for what she describes as "a horrible accident" in which both her children were drowned (à la Susan Smith, of course). When her attorney comes to tell her that he can no longer afford to take her appeal case because federal funds have been discontinued for such work, she too—in the kind of stereotypically misogynist portrayals of women that typify the series—tries to persuade him with sexually suggestive advances not to desert her. In fact, so misogynist is the series that only a prison doctor and a nun are portrayed positively and without sexual innuendo. One guard is portrayed as a jealous harridan who, when McManus ends their sexual liaison, goes berserk and trashes his office, an act for which she is not even dismissed. Similarly, McManus himself tries to thwart the class action suit because another female guard with whom he has had a sexual relationship is actually guilty of the murder of the inmate mentioned earlier. But we, the audience, are apparently meant to sympathize, or at least empathize, with these two because they are, by some strange logic, the "good guys" of the series.

So much for the gory details of prison life, as seen on high-class TV. What is most interesting about the series' relationship to current political realities is its fit with a real political system that has taken to building more and more maximum-security prisons on the grounds that criminals such as those seen on *Oz* and elsewhere are all around us, creating an epidemically massive threat to decent citizens everywhere. As the warden of Oz tells a young guard who begs to be assigned to work in the cellblocks instead of his current office job, "These are the most dangerous men in the States." And indeed, when the young man finally gets his wish, he is almost immediately subjected to a violent attack.

If we look at other, less entertaining and hard-to-find presentations of these prisons and of the actual conditions of the prisoners who are—at increasingly young ages—being sent there to live out their lives, the picture we get is much different. Maximum-security prisons, as they exist today, combine a bizarre set of practices and regimes in which disciplinary "control" merges indistinguishably with outright physical torture in ways that make the use of prison terminology almost meaninglessly Orwellian. Prisoners in these facilities are subjected to virtual isolation, control, and behavior-modification techniques involving twenty-three-hour lockdown in steel-walled single cells that allow no communication with other prisoners and almost no physical activity of any kind. Reading materials are censored and education via correspondence courses is severely restricted if not forbidden.[29] But far from achieving the desired result of keeping them controlled or helping them to find more productive outlets for their energies and brains, these facilities in fact create inmates so rebelliously violent that physical repression and torture become unavoidable.

Thus we have the cycle of violence that our supposedly antiviolence regime produces. Marion State Prison in Ohio, for example—which opened in 1963, the same year that Alcatraz closed down—was designed to provide a kind of high-tech, non-violent or brutal disciplinary control mechanisms. But in practice the increasing difficulty of maintaining tight control in an environment that is obviously if inadvertently set up to create its opposite—i.e., instinctive, often psychotic acts of violent rebellion—has made old-fashioned techniques of physical repression and torture inevitable. For what passes as "discipline" on paper is in practice a severe form of punishment that breeds extreme mental distress and violent acting-out. As the Supreme Court itself understood, as early as 1890, "extended solitary confinement" of the kind these facilities are built to maintain as a permanent regime is not "discipline" at all but rather "infamous punishment."[30] More recent psychiatric studies of those subjected to such conditions have verified this truth, finding high incidences of acute anxiety, failed impulse control, and self-mutilation.[31] Permanent lockdown is thus a time bomb waiting to explode. And when it does, prison staff are forced to resort to more and more extreme forms of physical punishment and torture, from fire hosing and stun gunning to the calling in of "cell extraction teams" of guards in full riot gear, equipped with mace and steel-tipped rib spreaders to subdue individual prisoners.[32]

The need for such physical torment and repression is clearly created by the physically and psychologically brutalizing conditions of the "disciplinary" treatment itself, thus the meaningless distinction without a difference between what counts as discipline and what is in fact physical punishment. The Pelican Bay Maximum Security Prison in California, for example, built on the Marion model but with even more extreme control measures, has been described as "the prototype of the prison of the future." But as those who have studied it report, it is actually in many ways a throwback to the pretreatment era of penology in which physical torture was the accepted norm. For "its misguided efforts" to control violence has instead, according to one observer, made Pelican Bay "an extraordinarily violent place" in which inmates and guards alike are reduced to the most brutish of human behavior.

From Sophocles to Sophistry: Locating the Real Tragedy of the Prison System

We return now to *Oz* and its fictionalized masking of, and apologia for, the popularity of the new high-tech dungeons of discipline and control. Tom Fontana would have us believe that in creating his political imaginary, he is following in the tradition of the great Greek tragedians. His land of Oz, he insists, while reflecting, the realities of prison life today, is at the same time, in literary and dramatic terms, a classic example of tragic art. But in what sense is this series tragic? Or more to the point, in what sense does it present prison life as a tragic vision? To answer that we might actually look at some standard definitions and analyses of what constitutes tragedy. First, of course, is the portrayal of the tragic hero himself, a being "threatened by the beast world pushing up from below, but also illuminated by the radiance of the Olympian gods above," according to classicist Charles Segal. But he is also one who has a specific relation to "the moral and intellectual capacities of man in general, his relation to the natural and divine order, his rationality and unreason, his capacity for autonomy as well as his dependence on society."[33] Thus,

> if the hero belongs in part to the "raw" world outside the polis, he also has by, virtue of his energy, intelligence, and capacity for loyalty and love, a place of honor within the polis. Breaking the moral laws that give our lives meaning and security and bypassing the usual mediation between god and beast that constitutes for greatness or proneness to excess, possess as a given of their humanness. The hero has to reconstruct his humanness on new terms.[34]

In classic tragedy, then, there is much expected of any protagonist worthy of the role of "hero," not only in the complexity and nuance of characterization, but also in the responsibility to struggle with and find a proper relationship to the moral and civil order of society. Indeed, as Jean-Pierre Varnant has argued, "[Athenian] tragedy is contemporary with the City [Athens] and with its legal system." Tragedy, he writes, is "about the audience on the benches, but first of all it is the City . . . which puts itself on the stage and plays itself," putting into "question its own internal contradictions" and "revealing that [its] true subject matter . . . is social thought . . . in the very process of elaboration."[35] Thus there can be no tragedy without a serious engagement with the most pressing social, moral, and legal issues of the day. And that, as Joan Copjec argues, is what makes Greek tragedy still relevant to every age in which it is produced and read.[36]

Tragedy, then, is a narrative form in which the disastrous ends to which heroes come, and the horrendous acts to which they are driven, are presented in the context of a profound statement about the human condition, its soaring aspirations to transcendence, and its inevitable inability to fully live up to its highest goals and values. This is as true of Shakespeare as of Sophocles and his contemporaries. But this statement is always placed in the context of man's relation to his society and to its laws and values. Moderation, the Greeks believed, was the proper goal of mankind. And tragedy—which centers upon the "irreconcilable polarity between bestiality and divinity in defining moral and civic virtue"[37]—presents us with a dramatic message about the wages of excess in all areas of human experience and activity. "Nothing in excess," "seek not to become

Zeus," and "measure is best" are common themes of tragedy. In portraying the difficulty of maintaining such balance, especially for those blessed with the most privileged of positions and qualities, it provides a kind of explanation for the most troubling and inexplicable of human dilemmas: why bad things happen to good people.

In such a context, violence itself plays a symbolic, ritualistic, role, for Greek tragedy was a highly ritualized, rather than realistic, form. For that reason, its dramatized violence was understood by its audience to be symbolically emblematic of man's heroic but doomed struggle to defeat the urge to both hubris and bestiality. The audience was meant to leave the theater in a state of catharsis, purged of the intense pity and fear the drama produced, and enjoying a state of deeper understanding and acceptance of the human condition. This is hardly the goal or the effect of a series like *Oz*, in which extremely naturalistic conventions are employed in ways meant—according to the producers themselves—to mirror rather than ritualistically symbolize the human condition. Thus the series and the network disingenuously attempt to have it both ways. On the one hand, they insist, the series represents the reality of prison life and, one assumes by extension, human—or at least criminal—nature. But on the other hand, in an effort to justify the extreme brutality and suffering they portray as "art" rather than mere exploitation, they incorporate elements of classic Greek tragedy in order to justify the cruel and brutal acts of violence as "high art."

So which is it? Is *Oz* "realistic" drama or is it ritualistically symbolic and metaphoric, as in classic Greek tragedy? Certainly the violence and hubris of its damned protagonists, and their often shockingly brutal deaths, are similar to what one finds in Greek tragedy. But the resemblance ends there. For far from offering catharsis or eliciting pity for his characters, the series, if anything, creates a kind of anxiety-ridden tension that never abates. Indeed, its efforts to link itself to the lofty tradition of Sophocles and his ilk is most questionable when one compares this series' view of human nature with that of the classic Greeks. For it almost goes without saying that Oz's inmates have no link to the lofty goals and aspirations that true tragedy requires. There is no catharsis in any of the bad and bloody endings to which character after character comes in this series, because there is no suggestion that these endings are the result of a tragic struggle to transcend their lower natures and approach the status of the gods. On the contrary, they are portrayed as bestial in essence—and proud of it. Indeed, "I was raised by the system and I'm proud of it," says one lifer who has been incarcerated in a variety of detention centers, ending up in this supermax prison, since childhood. But what that childhood was like is never hinted at. Nor is there even a hint of a possibility that he, or any of his fellows, might ever have strived for, or even vaguely considered the notions of, human transcendence or moral virtue. For these are men who exist in a political and moral universe that men like Oedipus, Macbeth, or even Michael Corleone—all of whom struggled valiantly against their worse natures and were portrayed in many ways as admirable and potentially heroic in nature—could not conceivably fit into. The inmates of Oz are far closer in nature to the brute creatures of tabloid TV than to any of these memorable characters. And the "good guy" nuns, priests, medics, and administrators of the series are so flatly drawn and so impotent and pathetic in their face-offs with, or hapless efforts to help the evil inmates, that they make even poorer subjects for tragedy.

But of course Oz is not a body politic in the sense that Sophocles' Athens, Shakespeare's Scotland, or Coppola's crime family are. It has no code of honor; no sense of civic pride or family loyalty; no level of grace from which any character could conceivably fall. What is perhaps "tragic" is the way the series seems to justify and rationalize, rather than interrogate or expose, the stupidity and inhumanity—not to mention exorbitant expense—of current penal theories and policies. At best, these are making matters worse, and at worst they are depriving society of potentially worthwhile citizens whose social contributions—as the histories of even such brutal killers as Robert Stroud and Nathan Leopold reveal— might well do more to improve the quality of life on earth than the producers of television programs like Oz are doing.

PART II

News and Documentary Genres

4

Cameras, Court TV, and the Rise of the Criminal Trial as Major Media Event

Every trial in America is a political trial.   —Abbie Hoffman

Having looked at the entertainment forms spawned by the interest in legal and criminal justice issues in the public realm, and the ideological direction they have generally taken, we can now look more closely at the seminal genre whose popularity and influence did so much to spawn this interest in the first place. The coming of cameras in the courtroom allowed the televising of criminal trials and made Court TV, the twenty-four-hour cable network devoted entirely to such matters, a going concern. Arguably, there would be no *Law and Order*, no *Practice*, no *Oz*, and none of the dozens of other series that have come—and often gone—if Court TV had not first made trial watching a major national pastime and focus of public interest and debate.

It is not an exaggeration to say that when Court TV burst upon the scene in 1991—at a time when cable TV networks were proliferating at a rate that made the need to fill up airtime difficult and the rise of a new hot topic was a boon to networks hurting for product—it signaled the beginning of a radical transformation not only of what American audiences would be watching for entertainment, but what we would be seeing and hearing in all television formats. Twenty-four networks, news networks, narrowcasting networks like A&E, Discovery, FX, Lifetime, and even the E! Entertainment network, among others, began featuring a variety of programs, from serious documentaries to tabloid exploitation series and delvings into the occult possibilities of *Unsolved Mysteries*. All of them were attempting to cash in on the hot new media sensation. Indeed, even the broadcast networks soon followed suit, devoting more and more of their magazine format series to criminal and legal topics.

Suddenly, the first of the "major media event" trials began. First there were the Menendez brothers, who had admittedly killed their wealthy parents but whose defense rested upon the argument that they had been so thoroughly terrorized and abused that they feared for their lives. Then came O. J. Simpson, the African American football hero and sometime movie and TV actor, accused of the murder of his beautiful blonde wife. DNA technology, Fourth Amendment rights, the "abuse excuse," and legal jargon became household words, and trial watching became a national pastime as popular as football or video rentals.

"Soap opera," moaned the chattering classes, indignant at the elevation of such sensational events to the level of high social and political significance, and at the sensation-seeking Americans who sat enthralled in front of the TV for long hours, watching the high drama of these trials. The high-tempered attorneys, the parade of sinister, quirky, sleazy and melodramatic witnesses, the teams of forensic and psychological experts, the sometimes amusing but often horrifying testimony of those involved in the most trivial or intimate ways with these cases, and the media-ready judges trying lamely to be amusing enough to become, perhaps, the next Judge Judy: all these made for better entertainment than most of what was offered elsewhere on TV. Careers were made and destroyed in these trials as many participants did in fact go on to become regular TV celebrities. And, as is true of daytime soap operas, Internet chat groups focusing on everything from the actual issues involved to the roles and lives of the most minor characters sprung up like wildflowers as Americans gossiped and argued and fantasized.

But were these trials "mere" soap opera, with no redeeming social value or significance? The pundits—hypocritically deploring the attention drawn by these trials, even as they fanned the flames with their endless discussions of the case and the endless reruns of the most sensational video clips—insisted they were. Of course, on one level they certainly were: there was high melodrama every day. There were exposures of unsavory but titillating sexual and family secrets; there were glimpses into the homes and habits of the wealthy, glamorous, and powerful; and there was violence and intrigue of the highest order in the highest places. Many of those who denied interest were probably at least a bit untruthful. It was all so irresistible that friends and acquaintances of mine admitted to O. J. or Menendez "withdrawal symptoms" when the trials ended.

As someone who happens to like soap operas for reasons which, I am on record as arguing, go far beyond mere sensationalism,[1] I felt no shame for the almost addictive effects these trials had on me personally. For despite the lofty disdain of the "serious" media, these trials dealt, if always in an overly melodramatic and stylized way, with some of the most serious social and personal issues of our day. Racism, gender violence, incest and child abuse, corrupt law enforcement institutions, and the material inequalities that, as Scott Fitzgerald famously noted, render "the rich . . . different from you and me," were too socially, legally, and politically important to ignore. All these issues, and the warring positions on them that divide our nation in ways made dramatically if painfully clear in the aftermath of the trials, were raised and feverishly debated as a result of these heady courtroom dramas.

But was the courtroom—particularly one with cameras glaring and reporters hovering in droves—the appropriate arena within which to hold such important national debates? I think not. In fact, one of the major themes of this book is the effect on the American political and legal environment of reducing every major social issue of the day to a matter of law, especially criminal law. Still, it is understandable that television should have chosen this arena within which to negotiate such issues. For trials, like so many other dramatic rituals of Western societies, are filled with drama and suspense. On the stage, on the movie screen, and more recently in the made-for-TV movie, courtroom drama has been a popular genre for these very reasons. It has moral conflict, an adversarial setup in which good guys and bad guys duke it out, and, quite often, twists, turns, and surprise endings that keep viewers riveted. "Who (really) dunnit?" is the most usual question, of course. But even when that is a given, there is still the drama of the verdict, what the jury will ultimately decide about the case. The verdict rides on the performances, the witnesses, and the evidence that the opposing attorneys manage to pull out of their hats as the trial proceeds.

The best of the genre—whether it is on stage or on the big or small screen—is one in which more is at stake than mere guilt or innocence. Sidney Lumet's *The Verdict*, for example, one of the best of the genre, raised issues of medical malpractice and class inequity. *Jagged Edge* was, at root, an exercise in gender politics[2]—at a time when feminist concern about such issues was just becoming a national issue—in which the female attorney's vulnerability to the charms of her psychopathic client was the real issue.

And so it was understandable that the coming of cameras into the courtroom opened a door through which the lure of ratings, especially for cable networks starved for "product," loomed enticingly. The televised trials satisfied not just the financial interests of the media industry, or the lust for sensation and drama of the public, at a time when Bruce Springsteen's "57 Channels (And Nothin' On)" was popular. They also provided television with a way to present issues of social and political significance in a form that would awaken and impassion audiences rather than put them to sleep, not done since the heyday of the sixties. Issues of race, gender, sexuality, economic inequality, and more, while not salient factors in every criminal or civil trial,[3] are blatant, highly charged issues in enough trials to fill the airtime of an entire cable network. They produce, as an almost equally watchable by-product, enough dramatic material for the pundits, whose numbers would soon be filled with more criminal prosecutors, judges, and defense attorneys than Americans—most of whom have never been in a courtroom at all—knew existed.

Nor is it insignificant—as I shall discuss in greater detail below—that, in the aftermath of the September 11, 2001, attack on the World Trade Center and the ensuing, now global "war on terrorism," issues of law and courtroom procedures have again come to dominate much media and popular discussion of the issues involved. How should we try the young American-turned-Taliban warrior John Walker Lindh for his "crimes?" Is it appropriate to use secret military tribunals to try suspected terrorists on American soil? What are the legal rights of the many detained Afghan immigrants being held in detention camps in Guantanamo Bay? And what of the civil liberties of civilians, now that fears of terrorism and the need for "heightened security" pervade virtually every aspect of our daily lives? These issues are discussed virtually every night across the spectrum of television networks.

Television and the Law

This book argues that the televised courtroom and its generic dependents—the endlessly proliferating talk shows, reality tabloid shows, legal dramatic series coming "straight from the headlines"—have become the major arenas through which Americans now come to understand and debate charged social issues of every stripe. I also consider how this has happened and what it has meant for the functioning of a democratic state.

Perhaps most importantly, I discuss the way in which this media phenomenon has worked to further a right-wing political agenda, driven by the increasingly punitive legal policies that now dominate the thinking of those who make and enforce the laws governing criminal justice institutions and procedures.

While televised trials and the many fictional and nonfictional genres that have risen to prominence in the wake of this phenomenon now seem to be a part of daily life, they are in fact a relatively new phenomenon, as are the many other television forms they have influenced. Cameras entered the courtroom officially, on a large national scale, only in 1981, when the Supreme Court, after decades of resisting the arguments favoring televised trials, suddenly did a dramatically unexpected turnaround on the issue. To many it may seem that this was simply a matter of "keeping up with times" and accepting the inevitable, but it was anything but that. In fact, there is no question that the justices who formed the majority on this decision had politics on their minds. If they did not foresee the larger political implications of their decision, they still had an agenda in mind that was explicitly political in its reasoning and, in the long run, in its effects.

This agenda was not explicit in the various rulings that ultimately made way for the wide-scale televising of high-profile trials. But it is intriguing to follow the snakelike route by which the political interests of the state, the economic interests of the media industry, and the public's general interest in entertainment and high drama came together at a time when both national and international affairs offered little to engross the average citizen beyond White House and Hollywood scandals.[4]

Talk of television trials had been going on since television itself became a national "public sphere." State legislatures had individually dabbled with the idea of allowing cameras in courtrooms for just as long. It was Florida that provided the legal precedent by which the Supreme Court justices validated their own 1981 decision. For in 1977 the Florida Supreme Court, after seeing the results of a year-long study that concluded that the effect of cameras in court was insignificant if not nonexistent, ruled that cameras could be present in all state trials in which the sitting judge agreed to allow them.[5] The U.S. Supreme Court used this study and the subsequent guidelines established by the Florida court as the basis for its abrupt turnaround. But beneath the surface of this apparently purely legal decision, one finds more complicated strands of cause and effect.

To understand what the justices were primarily concerned about and what they really hoped to accomplish by allowing the general public into the previously hidden arena of civil and criminal justice, it is important to see the decision in historical context. In the decade or so preceding the Supreme Court ruling, the country went through a period of extreme political and social upheaval, from which the legal system was not exempt. The era referred to as "the sixties" was one of earth-shattering social protest and the questioning of all national institutions. When it was over, the nation began drifting slowly but ultimately radically rightward. The left-leaning idealism of the sixties may have died, but the skepticism about national institutions—not least the courts—certainly did not. Ironically, however, in the far more conservative eighties and nineties, the skepticism about national values and institutions bred by the sixties led to a questioning of the legal system from a perspective diametrically opposed to the left-leaning idealism of the sixties' social activists. For now the rulings of the notoriously liberal Warren Court, which tended to favor the rights of defendants and civil liberties generally, were being challenged as our nation turned fearful as well as conservative, worried about a legal system it saw as "soft on crime."[6]

The 1960s Warren Court had, as noted in the Introduction, brought with it dramatic changes in legal policy. A number of new rulings recognized the importance of the individual rights of those accused or suspected of crimes. After *Miranda v. Arizona*, alleged criminals would be read their rights before interrogation. After *Gideon v. Wainwright*, the government would provide legal counsel to the indigent; and after *Weeks v. the United States* illegal searches and seizures were forbidden. These rulings represented a dramatic shift in the focus of criminal justice law toward the rights of defendants and, implicitly, away from a central concern for the crime itself and especially for the suffering of victims. Now, it seemed to many, it was the criminal who had become the "victim" in the eyes of society and the courts. "Personal responsibility" for one's actions and concern for the pain and suffering of the "real" victims and their loved ones were lost in the rise of sympathy for those who broke society's laws and rules. Many were baffled that alleged criminals were treated with kid gloves by a system which, through the acceptance of a plethora of "legal technicalities," hampered police and prosecutors in their efforts to bring them to justice.

It was not only the Warren Court's rulings about criminal defendants' rights that created public anxiety about the ability of the courts to render justice. For, as I mentioned briefly in the Introduction, the sixties and its many social movements—for civil rights, gay rights, women's rights—had left a legacy that affected the legal system in far more complicated ways. These movements and the generation of young attorneys influenced by them created a general questioning of *all* institutions for their allegedly inherent racist, sexist, and homophobic biases. Now suddenly the courts were filled with new defense strategies—often successful ones—which demanded that issues of gender, race, sexual orientation, and others be considered in weighing the actions of those on trial. Juries, also influenced by the national "consciousness raising" that sixties activists had achieved, were increasingly prone to take these issues seriously. During the reign of sixties' liberalism and radicalism, the media had presented audiences with dramatic images and narratives that tended, most emphatically, to legitimize the skepticism about public and private institutions. The haloed police officers of the *Dragnet* era had long ago been replaced by the more morally ambiguous cops of *Miami Vice* and *Hill Street Blues*. TV movies like *The Burning Bed* and *Silent Witness* made the battered woman syndrome and date rape commonly understood terms. And similar TV and theatrical films—*Something about Amelia*, about incest; *Consenting Adults* and *An Early Frost*, about homophobia; and *Serpico* and *Prince of the City*, about police corruption and racism, to name only a few—brought to the general public an awareness of institutional and family dysfunction and injustice that had been America's "dirty little secrets."

As a result of this cultural turn, long-held assumptions governing criminal trials were suddenly held suspect. Juries were asked to consider all sorts of possibilities: tainted evidence planted by corrupt and racist cops; the psychological effects on defendants of emotional and physical abuse by those more powerful; and so on. Acquittals based on suspicion of the police and acquittal of murderers based on "expert witness" testimony about state of mind were now becoming all too common—or so it seemed. This public assumption was highly exaggerated. For it is a little-known fact that of all the cases that actually go to trial (prosecutors may choose to try only those cases they think winnable and plea bargain out-of-court deals for the rest), a full 95 percent result in convictions.[7] But these everyday trials were, by definition, not "news"; only the most unusual or sensational trials and verdicts warranted that label. Thus came the growing anger of a public increasingly hungry for "law and order" and thirsty for vengeance and punishment. The system seemed—if one believed the media—to have gone haywire, accepting all sorts of "abuse excuses" and other "politically correct" defenses that allowed murderers to walk free, to kill and kill again.

It is in this cultural and historic context that the Supreme Court's decision to allow cameras in the courts must be understood. For it was the sudden hew and cry of a growing number of increasingly vocal members of a public grown weary of the reign of liberalism in general, and a legal system increasingly "soft on crime," that suddenly came to alarm those responsible for maintaining that system. If, as seemed increasingly true of the executive and legislative branches of government, the judiciary came to be widely viewed with cynicism, the rule of law itself, upon which social stability rose or fell, was in big trouble.

The members of the Supreme Court in 1981—the beginning of the Reagan-Bush years—heard these cries, and heeded them. This fact is at the root of the reasoning behind their decision to open the courts to public view. Charles Nesson and Andrew Koblenz, in their article "The Image of Justice,"[8] tracing the long path by which the Supreme Court was persuaded in 1981 to allow the televising of criminal trials without the defendant's consent, explain that the justices' decision was based largely on the Court's concern for "the *appearance* of justice" and its "preoccupation with judicial image." "In the Madison Avenue world of image," they write, "true damage is done to the image of justice and courts only if the specter of injustice strikes the public imagination and is widely communicated." These justices were concerned that just such a state of affairs had indeed become a reality. In an effort to correct the growing perception that the legal system, like the other major American institutions, was indeed "broken," that it was no longer dispensing justice but rather was exercising lax, irresponsible control over courtrooms in which slick defense attorneys and dangerous criminals were running the show, they turned in desperation to the very cameras they had so long feared would destroy the dignity and sanctity of the courts. Ironically, this dignity and sanctity had somehow fallen away of its own accord. In an almost humbling posture, the justices had nowhere to turn for help in reconstructing it—in putting the pieces of the juridical Humpty Dumpty together again—except through the glaring eye of the cameras.

According to Nesson and Koblenz, "Televising trials looked to some judges like a possible counter to [such] charges against the judiciary."[9] While public opinion seemed to think otherwise—given the number of apparently short sentences, soft plea bargains, and shockingly incomprehensible acquittals of the "obviously" guilty—in actuality, as the justices well knew, the truth about criminal trials was quite different. Showing actual trials would be far more reassuring to a public increasingly fearful of the rampant crime that was so exaggerated and sensationalized night after night, on televised news.

The media vision of criminal justice was and is entirely misleading, if not downright fictional. Indeed, as the justices knew, the system was already working very much as the public seemed to want it to. As they themselves put it, in reality "trials show the justice system at its best."[10] By this they meant of course in a light that—at least most of the time— revealed the system to be very hard on crime indeed, and almost overwhelmingly prone to convict alleged criminals, whether they had actually done what they were accused of or not. And so, they reasoned, if the public could be given access to the actual workings of criminal justice they would surely be reassured that, as they so fervently hoped, most accused criminals were convicted and put behind bars. And so, at last, in desperation, they agreed to open the courtroom doors to the public, to allow them to see the long arms of the law at work and justice being harshly meted out to the "guilty."

The Whole World Is Watching: The Law Goes on Trial

What happened next was far from what the justices had anticipated. At first, things seemed to go well enough for them and their conservative, law-and-order supporters. The first three highly publicized trials to be televised all ended in guilty verdicts, as the justices hoped. The 1981 trial and conviction of Claus von Bulow for the murder of his bedridden wife managed at once to "prove" the system worked even as it demonstrated that criminal trials also made for high television entertainment; that, in effect, melodramas of sex, violence, and family dysfunction were as enthralling to audiences—perhaps more enthralling—as those portrayed in fictional or "based on fact" dramas. We are, after all, living in times when reality—in both literature and television—has increasingly replaced fiction as a source of fascination and entertainment. Biographies and memoirs outsell novels; and talk and tabloid TV shows often outrate fictional drama because truth as presented by the media has indeed proven to be stranger and more interesting than fiction. The von Bulow case had it all: a debonair society hanger-on with no real means of support; an enormously wealthy, mysteriously bedridden wife, found dead of an overdose of insulin; and a pair of grown children bitterly hostile, angry, and out for the blood of the long-despised stepfather.

But it was the second of these 1981 trials that really brought home the potential political impact of televised trials on American social and political debate. The Big Dan's Tavern trial concerned a case in which three men were accused of gang raping a woman on a pool table in a local Massachusetts roadhouse. The Big Dan case was even more sensational than the von Bulow case. Not only were there sex and violence, but there were also several of the hot-button issues raised by sixties' activists: sexual violence as well as class and ethnic conflict. The alleged victim—played by Jodie Foster in *The Accused*, the movie version of the case for which she won an Oscar, and by Melissa Leo in the less well known docudrama *Silent Witness*—was a working-class white woman of allegedly "easy virtue," the kind of victim to whom feminists gave passionate support. The defendants were members of the Portuguese community in New Bedford, where the alleged rape took place. They had the equally avid support of that community, which, as a forerunner of the dramatic conflicts that made the O. J. Simpson case so compelling, charged that racism drove the prosecution. The details of the crime, as reported by witnesses, were indeed gory and dramatic, and the attorneys were predictably dramatic in their openings, closings, and direct and cross examinations.[11] CNN had found a new "major media event," and a new television genre was invented, one which not many could have predicted would become one of the most popular and influential genres of the cable age.

Other trials similarly caught the attention of audiences by offering a steamy, provocative mix of sensationalism along with serious social issues of the day. The most notable was probably the 1987 trial of attorney Joel Steinberg for the murder of his seven-year-old, illegally adopted, and seriously abused and neglected daughter, Lisa. Here, drugs, domestic abuse of the most shocking kind, and a behind-closed-doors peek at the squalid and decadent lives of an apparently "normal" professional middle-class family figured dramatically. It was not long before Steven Brill, a media-savvy lawyer with a nose for the next big thing, decided there was money to be made in the wide-open field of cable television, where airtime was easy to get but harder to fill. He formed a new network, Court TV, devoted to twenty-four-hour-a-day coverage and commentary of criminal and civil trials. Brill's idea was on the money, literally. He saw the potential in airing trials that admittedly combined the lure of sensationalism and melodrama with a serious look at the workings of a system—the legal system—which had, with the demise of 1960s activism, become the major arena within which contested social issues were now being negotiated and debated.

The von Bulow verdict was successfully appealed, of course, but millions watched the drama in which the villainous husband and stepfather was harshly and swiftly judged guilty. The Big Dan case, while it pitted gender issues against ethnic ones, rarely was presented in those terms by the media. In fact, the victim herself was, surprisingly, not pilloried by the press for her less-than-savory sexual past; rather, she was sympathetically presented, most often simply as a "mother of two."[12] The Steinberg case especially proved a godsend to the law-and-order forces: the defendant was a shockingly scary character, and his deeds—as graphically shown in the footage of his sordid home and the horrifyingly disfigured face of his battered common-law wife—were as unbelievably vicious as any horror movie villain's. His sentence to life in prison could hardly have been less controversial.

Trouble in Paradise

And then came trouble. Court TV began operations with little fanfare in 1991. Within a mere two years, it became a major player in the cable TV sweepstakes with its coverage of the highly sensational and—for many—addictive case of *California v. Menendez*. That trial, which ran from July 1993 to January 1994, gave viewers a peek inside one of the more lurid examples of life among the rich and famous, Beverly Hills style. Those who tuned in for the gavel-to-gavel coverage had already had a lurid televised glimpse of the two young defendants, Erik Menendez and his slightly older brother, Lyle, by the time the actual trial began. First came the much rerun footage, in August 1989, of the Los Angeles Police Department taking the bagged bodies of the parents, Mary (Kitty) and Jose, from their palatial home. Lyle had called the LAPD, reporting that his parents had been shot. By May 1990, we saw the two young men arrested and then arraigned. The images of the "swaggering" and "smirking" duo (to use the media's favorite adjectives), dressed in expensive Armani suits, were already enough to convict the brothers in the public's mind. So consistent and negative were the media reports of the crime and the arraignment that, as one juror in the first trial, a telephone company employee named Hazel Thornton, put it when describing the first day of jury selection:

"Even I knew that Erik and Lyle Menendez were the Beverly Hills teenagers who shotgunned their parents to death in their home because they were greedy for their inheritance. When Erik walked into the courtroom my blood ran cold."[13]

I will quote liberally from Thornton's fascinating diary because it is a firsthand account of what was experienced by many of those who watched the trial unfold, whether they did so regularly or only in snippets of trial highlights on the nightly news. Thornton was one of the women jurors who, like me, came to see—and *see* is the operative word here because the trial was so visually and dramatically arresting—the events very differently as the defense presented its case. That the trial resulted in a hung jury—most importantly, along gender lines—is significant. Those who did not watch the trial regularly, even women reporters, continued to be outraged by the jury's unexpected verdict. Those who did watch fairly regularly—especially women and college students[14]—came to see a situation that looked very different from the one they had originally assumed—once the issue of sexual child abuse became a central theme.

Thornton's diary is thus a document that reports the events of the trial from the point of view of a significant segment of the American public who had become sensitized to issues of gender and family violence over the years that feminists had made them public issues. Through her words, we can see most clearly what this significant element of Americans also saw as they watched the trial, in part or whole. The diary shows the power of television to present charged political issues in dramatically compelling ways in a culture in which, as already noted, *sight*, the ability to "see with one's own eyes," is the major earmark of credibility. Thornton's view makes clear why both the jury and the viewing public in general were split over the case as it was first presented. It also makes clear why, in the second trial, so much of what Thornton saw and heard was deleted by the same judge who again heard the case. This second trial was necessary because the first trial did not result in a verdict, giving the state the option to have another go at the defendants. In a high-profile case like this one, it could hardly say no. (Defendants can be tried for a single crime more than once as long as juries continue to fail to reach a clear verdict and the prosecution continues to believe the case is important and will yield a guilty verdict with the proper strategy.)[15]

Thornton's description of the opening statements of the opposing attorneys, in Erik's trial, is particularly relevant here.[16] It explains why the trial was about to become such a charged, disturbing, and conflicted intellectual and emotional process for the jurors and for the many Americans given entrée to the proceedings through the constant presence of Court TV's and CNN's cameras. Her words are worth quoting at length because they give a real sense of the drama of sensational trials as well as the ability of opposing attorneys, given a sufficiently complex and ambiguous case, to raise arguments powerful enough to call into question, and ultimately even alter, apparent "common sense" certainties about a case in the course of a trial:

> Opening statements were as riveting as anything I've seen on TV. I was glued to the edge of my seat. I think I forgot to breathe for an hour and a half. Prosecuting attorney Lester Kuriyama didn't have anything surprising to say. His comments were brief and to the point about how cold and calculating and greedy he intended to prove the defendants were. But defense attorney Leslie Abramson spelled it right out, saying, "The question isn't who murdered Jose and Mary Menendez, but why they were murdered." She proceeded to give us quite a detailed description of the years of mental, emotional, physical, and sexual abuse supposedly suffered by the boys (especially Erik, because we are Erik's jury) . . . for so many years that they felt they had no alternative in the end but to kill their parents in "self-defense." Erik cried, noticeably but unobtrusively, when Ms. Abramson talked about his mother. Her given name is Mary Louise, but everyone called her Kitty.[17]

And so the drama—filled with kinky sex, gruesome violence, financial and emotional intrigue and betrayal, family infighting and divisiveness, grisly photos of mutilated bodies and sexually suggestive images of small children, passionately rendered rhetoric, tears and muffled sobs, and a good bit of not necessarily intentional humor—began. It was indeed riveting television. Americans, I among them, were glued to the edges of their own front-row seats as a mind-boggling, and, to the prosecution, devastating sea change rocked the courtroom and the living rooms of a nation of real and vicarious "jurors."

What took the prosecutors—and the many increasingly intrigued television viewers—by surprise was the brilliance with which the two lead defense attorneys, Leslie Abramson for Erik and Jill Lansing for Lyle, managed to bring into the legal mix a whole potpourri of issues and emotionally loaded testimony. The prosecutors and journalists could never have anticipated this tactic, although—if they had been aware of the real impact of the ideas and issues raised by feminists in the sixties—especially the issues of domestic and sexual abuse within the male-dominated nuclear family—they certainly should have. But, to be fair, what most blindsided everyone in the legal and journalistic world was the gender of the defendants. Had the two brothers been sisters, accusing a powerful patriarchal father and a passive, submissive mother of the horrible crimes of child sexual abuse, the nation and the media might have felt more sympathy for the defendants from the start. After all, we had already been through the equally gruesome Steinberg case. Here jurors and journalists had no difficulty seeing Steinberg as a demon; his companion, Hedda Nussbaum, as both a victim and a facilitator; and the sweet-faced little Lisa Steinberg as a victim as innocent and compelling as Dickens's Little Nell.

The mounting evidence and testimony submitted by the Menendez defense teams of the abuse suffered by the defendants—in a household in which maternal neglect and abuse, sexual deviance, alcohol and drugs, and gay pornography all figured—clearly rocked the courtroom and shook the smug confidence of the lead prosecutors. Therefore it was not so difficult to convince at least half of the jurors in both trials that the defense case was valid. It rested on the feminist-inspired "battered woman defense" in its argument that long-term terror and abuse might so deeply affect the emotional state of the victim that she (or in this case, he) might well believe there is an imminent threat of death by the abuser's hand; and they might also feel so helplessly dependent upon and terrified of their abuser that they felt unable to leave the household for fear they would be hunted down and murdered by him, as often happens.

This sixties-born social issue—domestic abuse and its impact on its victims—formed the unexpected political core of the defense case. But it would not have been nearly so effective in convincing enough jurors of its validity and lead to two hung juries and two mistrials without the emotional power of the defense case itself. For it was a defense which, with less-talented attorneys and less money to support a lengthy and thorough presentation of the brothers' case, could easily have misfired.[18] Abramson and Lansing were not only brilliant attorneys, but they had the means to bring forth relatives, friends, teachers, expert witnesses, and others from far-flung places and, in some cases, for high fees. They kept the trial going for as long as the brothers could afford to pay their fees. Thus the jurors and the public witnessed an overwhelmingly dramatic and—given the amount of testimony—unusually persuasive case. All but the most ignorant and intolerant of jurors were forced to struggle hard to maintain their original assumptions—and those of the state—that this was a slam-dunk case in which evil, ungrateful children committed cold-blooded parricide for financial gain.

To read the Thornton diary is to see the impact of the dramatic presentation of the defense cases upon thoughtful but ultimately shocked and shaken jurors. As attested by Internet chatrooms and newsgroups that focused on the case during the trial, many of us reacted the same way. We invested long hours of our own, taping and watching the full gavel-to-gavel coverage. For as the case wended its long and twisted way toward a verdict, the prosecution, unprepared for a strong defense, appeared to jurors to be far from convincing in its efforts to meet its burden of proof "beyond a reasonable doubt." The defense, meanwhile, was absolutely dazzling in its ability to use the tools of trial law, which have always relied heavily on performance and drama, whether televised or not. It created a counternarrative to the prosecution version in which the defendants became the real victims while the dead parents emerged as horrifying, neglectful, and abusive monsters. In fact, the number of colorful, intriguing, and emotionally moving moments and characters in the trial, most brought by the defense, made for such an engrossing experience for jurors that Thornton remarks in her diary that she "can't believe I've had Court TV all this time and never watched it!" Such is the power of good lawyering in cases in which real issues of social and political as well as moral and human concerns are brought to the fore. Those who were willing to keep an open mind and to take seriously some of the most contested issues raised by sixties activists found the trial more than merely engrossing or entertaining: it was an experience during which consciousness-raising and dramatic changes in perceptions of what constitutes a crime, a criminal, and a victim actually occurred. For a criminal trial, after all, is never really about "truth." It is about two versions of "truth" and which one will appear most convincing to a jury.

The shifting attitudes of Hazel Thornton show the skill, and political savvy, of the defense attorneys. In fact, very early in the trial, after the prosecution's case had been presented and the defense began to present its own witnesses, Thornton remarks on a dramatic shift in her own feelings, which at first, as she admitted, were firmly informed by the media's biased pretrial reporting. As witness after witness—from cousins and aunts to tennis coaches and close friends of the victims—testified dramatically about the abuse and neglect to which the boys had been publicly subjected as small children, and of their growing terror of their father and their often out-of-control, alcoholic mother, Thornton, in her intermittent summing-up of her changing attitudes—remarks that while she is not yet sure of her ultimate opinion, "I am no longer afraid of [the brothers] and even feel very sorry for them." As the trial proceeded over a period of months, this shift in attitude grew more dramatic. The testimony of Lyle Menendez, for example, of which most American saw only sound bites accompanied by the most cynical and callous media commentary, was for Thornton (as it was for me) more than convincing. "All I can say," she writes, "is either that boy is the best actor I've ever seen in my life or he's telling the utter truth."[19]

Even the prosecution's own witnesses were, for the jurors, not only unconvincing but, by the time the defense got through with them, virtually reconstructed as defense witnesses. For example, the prosecution's main witness, the defendants' therapist, Dr. Oziel, who had taped a session in which one defendant confessed to the crimes, was called "Dr. Weasel" by the time the defense had finished cross-examining him and presented its own witnesses—including his former lover, who had been present at the taping. As a former housekeeper, flown in to testify briefly, put it, he was "the most dishonest man [she] had ever met." But even in less shaky instances of the state's case, Thornton was less than impressed with the skill of the prosecutors, who have, quite obviously, underestimated the textured tale that their opponents were preparing to present. "[Pamela] Bozanich (lead prosecutor against Lyle) is trying to make a black and white issue out of one which appears to me to made up many shades of gray."[20] But of course Bozanich, like the rest of the nation, had not considered that this trial was about much more than parricide. That the defense realized the case was about a hot social issue was a powerful ace in the hole for the jury. As the defense was betting, the jurors were at least aware of the issues of domestic and sexual abuse within families. Hopefully they were even sympathetic to the victims of acts which, because of second-wave feminism, had become a hotly contested issue. Many Americans were now prepared to see them as serious breaches of human conduct, if not horrific crimes.

Another of Thornton's comments on Bozanich's poor lawyering indicates that the defense's hunch was right. When arguing in Kitty's defense, for example, Bozanich used the very arguments about the profound impact of Jose's abusive behavior that she has refused to accept about her sons. "She [Bozanich] is using the same arguments to justify Kitty's suicidal feelings, depression, isolation, nowhere to go, etc) that she finds so ludicrous when the defense uses it to explain Erik's and Lyle's states of mind. I feel like asking her: So why didn't Kitty 'just leave'—she was a grown woman wasn't she?"[21]

The most fascinating part of Thornton's diary is her account, not seen on TV, of course, of the jury's deliberation. For here is where the real power of the progressive ideas presented so powerfully to Americans by sixties activists can be seen to have determined the outcome of the trial—an outcome which seemed so unbelievable to the media and the general public. There was no chance of an out-and-out acquittal (although Thornton at one point admits to having seriously considered it). A murder had been committed and only the most unified, sympathetic jury could possibly have determined that no punishment was necessary. Nonetheless, the breakdown in the ultimate vote was dramatically split along gender lines, with all the women on the side of leniency and all the men on the side of the harshest punishment. In fact, the entire deliberative process revealed a sometimes hilarious example of the very heated and contested debates about issues of gender and sexuality that had—since the rise of second-wave feminism—rocked the nation as a whole.

First was the issue of sexism within the jury itself. The women became increasingly incensed at the way in which the men consistently interrupted them or dismissed their arguments as silly. "These guys (I hate to lump them together . . . but they're all driving me crazy)," she notes more than once, and with increasing irritation, "can't even let us get to our point without jumping in and interrupting."[22] But most amazing was the consistency with which the men expressed (to the women) bizarre opinions about family values and homosexuality. "Rocky thinks this society would be better if more parents raised their kids like Jose and Kitty!!!" she notes at one point. And the male terror and hatred of homosexuality seemed virtually to permeate the deliberations, as one man after another insisted that the defendants must be gay for any number of nutty reasons, and therefore, by some circuitous reasoning processes, must be guilty. One man believed that "Erik and Lyle must have been 'doing each other.'" Another thought that Erik could only have concocted his tales of sexual abuse because he himself was gay and so, it seemed to follow, familiar with the most extreme forms of S and M practice. And still another believed that once he turned eighteen, Erik's participation in sexual relations with his father had to be consensual since "he was a man." Thus, now, he was himself a homosexual who would automatically—the day after his birthday—take pleasure in his father's treatment.

This intense battle of the sexes formed the heart of the deliberations and made it impossible to reach a verdict. And so the jury was hopelessly hung and a mistrial was declared. At this point, which was particularly infuriating to Thornton, the media began to berate the women jurors for their "stupidity" in not reaching the obvious conclusion that the brothers were guilty of murder in the first degree. In fact, in my own survey of press coverage—print and electronic, reportage and commentary—I could not find a single example of any report or column, by a male or female, "liberal" or conservative, that didn't take this position. And so the trial was considered by consensus to have been a disastrous miscarriage of justice in which a flaky female jury was bamboozled by a couple of slick and sleazy attorneys.

What is interesting here is of course the dramatic difference in opinion between those of us—especially the jurors themselves—who had the time and inclination to tape and watch the entire trial, and those who merely caught snippets, shown out of the context of the entire day's events, much less the entire trial, of the sensational moments. Unfortunately, most Americans could not do this or had no interest in doing so. For them, it was the media—both print and electronic—that provided the "official" version of the trial. Thus, the important issues remained the same: these kids were demonic liars and butchers, and their defense attorneys were the kind who could sleazily manipulate any situation to get their guilty clients off. Fear of teenagers, perhaps especially our own in too many cases, as will be discussed later in the book, was another factor in the case. Juvenile crime has been a media bugaboo with a powerful emotional pull since the 1950s, when family dysfunction and youthful alienation became national issues.

Television and the Dilemma of the Rising Right Wing

This split between the experiences and judgments of the jurors and those in the general population who actually took advantage of the televised coverage, and those who merely watched, reported, and heard only snippets that reinforced existing prejudices against male youth, wealthy defendants, and attorneys who had already created the always false impression that the system was "soft on crime" is at the heart of what has happened to criminal trials, televised or not, since the Menendez and Simpson cases. For the justices who had hoped that TV would show the system "working," these first highly rated television trials were a body blow. In the trials' aftermath, those who preside over criminal trials and made the rules by which they proceeded became very cautious about what would and would not be allowed to occur in criminal courtrooms. Though the number of Americans who watched both trials may not have been a majority, there is no question that the trials raised an interest in the trial process and legal system that affected public and private debate across the nation. Television reporters, as well as my own acquaintances and students, were suddenly talking about "probable cause," "Fourth Amendment protection," and other legal issues that had suddenly become as much a part of everyday conversation as football or *Seinfeld*. Indeed, there are many Americans who might not have known, for example, that defendants are often tried several times for the same crime, or that the same defendant often is tried twice for the same crime even when acquitted if someone brings a civil suit of wrongful death against him or her. In fact, the very existence of so many legal series and documentaries makes clear that whether one watched the trials in full or not, the issues they raised became national concerns of the most common and popular order, and the language of law became a much greater part of our common vocabulary than ever before.

In the retrial of the Menendez brothers, things were handled very differently by the judge, the same man who had presided over the first trial. But before discussing it we need to take a thorough look at the first Simpson trial, in which an amazingly similar pattern of events took place. Once more we had a wealthy defendant who could afford the best possible defense, which all defendants are, by law, entitled to. Once more there were hot issues of gender and race which reflected, as in the Menendez case, vexed and contested social and political issues put on the national agenda by 1960s activists. And once more a group of women jurors, this time forming a majority with none of the gender-baiting or sexist ignorance that brought the Menendez trials to such hopelessly unresolvable stalemates, presented a verdict that most (white) commentators and citizens considered hopelessly stupid and erroneous.

In the case of the Menendez brothers, a kind of reverse sexism, laced with homophobia and a healthy pinch of youth hatred, made the social issues raised by the defense teams so provocative that even progressive Americans found it difficult to sympathize with the defendants or the juries' verdicts. In the case of O. J. Simpson, the social-issue conflicts were far less subtle and more divisive. In the Menendez case, sexual abuse of male children, especially as they became teenagers, was difficult for even feminists to respond to sympathetically unless they had witnessed the entire trial and saw the defendants as more than media sound bites.[23] In the Simpson case, the issues at stake—violence against women and systemic institutionalized racism—were all too clearly understood. Indeed, the passion American women and minorities had come to feel about these matters since the 1960s was at the heart of the divisive impact of the entire trial on the general public.

Moreover, while the Menendez trial was a ratings success for the fledgling Court TV, and certainly the case itself drew enormous media attention, the number of people who actually watched the trial religiously and knew its various players, legal ploys, and issues in detail was minor compared to the attention paid to the Simpson trial. For one thing, O. J. Simpson was a real celebrity and a hero to many, especially in the African American community. The Menendez brothers were widely hated and feared by Americans well before the trial even began. But Simpson, even from the start, received enormous sympathy. And what a start it was. The Menendez case had a brief media moment when the murders occurred and another when the defendants were arraigned, but in the Simpson case there was that amazingly unforgettable and long car chase. Who can possibly forget the experience of turning on the TV on that bizarre summer evening in 1994 and blinking in confusion at what seemed to be an unbelievable television "program." For hours on end, a white Ford Bronco, followed by a group of police cars, made its way across the Los Angeles freeways. It was impossible to figure out what was going on. Then it became clear that it was the Heisman trophy winner, Hertz Rental Car pitch man, football hero, and sometime movie star O. J. Simpson—the "Juice"—in the car, and that he was fleeing the police because he was suspected of brutally murdering his gorgeous blonde wife. The pull of the TV screen became irresistible. For hours, American audiences watched the car weave along as TV reporters struggled to find small changes to fill the time; Simpson fans gathered along the freeways yelling and waving placards in support of their hero; and snippets of rumors—that O. J. had a gun to his head and was about to commit suicide—combined to create one of the most amazing live media events in television history.

As the chase ended and O. J. was seen surrendering to police and being cuffed and taken away, more and more of the details of the case trickled in. At first, domestic violence dominated the coverage. We learned that

Simpson had a long history of wife battering, that he had even pleaded *no contendere* (no contest) to a previous charge and had been given a suspended sentence; as punishment he only had to speak on the phone now and then with a friendly psychiatrist—rather than attend the group therapy sessions that other batterers must attend. We learned that there was a police tape of Nicole Brown Simpson screaming in fear, insisting that the police "knew" her ex-husband's record and ominously warning that if nothing were done he would surely kill her.

During this stage of the seemingly endless media saga, it was the feminists who dominated the talk shows and news conferences. In fact, many ex-wives of well-known athletes came forth to testify to their own experiences with domestic violence. Feminist authors and spokeswomen attested to the prevalence and horror of domestic violence in America, and in particular they spoke of the startling statistics correlating such abuse with major sports figures and their most ardent fans. The soap opera elements added to the feminist slant of the pretrial media coverage. After all, it was an all too common story, wasn't it? A beautiful, abused wife leaves her husband. She begins seeing other men. Her possessive husband, typical of scorned batterers, begins stalking her, peering through her windows, and growing more and more enraged as he sees her in intimate moments with new lovers. And finally, one night, after being snubbed by her and her family at their daughter's dance recital, he lurks outside her home, sees her with a handsome young companion, and goes berserk with murderous rage. We women had all seen at least one TV docudrama or soap opera featuring this story, hadn't we?

The issue of race was a factor in the story as well, and one which was already at least subtly troubling. For the issue of interracial sex, and the undercurrents of anxiety and fear generated by images of strong, virile black men and fair-haired, beautiful white women, were as old as the old South. In fact, the Othello/Desdemona story was impossible to avoid in the first, pretrial version of the story. No wonder the prosecution—as in the Menendez case—was overly confident. Marcia Clark, a white woman known to be tough on crime, especially on gender-related crime, was chosen as lead prosecutor, and a black male, Christopher Darden, was chosen as second chair, just, many commentators believed, to make sure the racial issue was covered.

But once agin, the state missed the seriousness and complexity of the social issues the case would raise. For once again, a defendant with almost unlimited resources hired a legal team with the ability to track down and fly in any number of unexpected witnesses and experts who were able to shift the emphasis of the trial away from the slam-dunk assumptions of the prosecutions: that this was a murder based on sexual jealousy and obsession. They used an entirely different and unexpected defense: racial bias and corruption within the police department. And so, again, we had a televised trial, this one really *viewed* rather than merely followed in the press. The criminal act itself was overshadowed by the circumstances surrounding it, and the villain—as the powerful defense team was able to convince jurors—was not the defendant but the supposed "good guys"— the policemen who brought him in.

Because of the constant attention of TV audiences, the importance of television and its inherent generic conventions and powers were even more important a factor here than in the Menendez trials. For if the latter trials made judges and the public generally anxious about the effects of allowing cameras into courtrooms where verdicts might not be as predictable, slick, and reassuring as those on other television dramas, the O. J. trial made them truly and openly hostile. But what is interesting here is that television—the villain of choice for virtually all commentators—was actually not responsible for the surprising outcome of these two trials. Rather, it was what television allowed us to see happen when criminal defendants have access to the best counsel. These men had lawyers with the *political* savvy to construct counternarratives to apparent slam-dunk murder trials in which social and political factors were allowed to enter the courtroom and give texture and color to the states' preferred "just the facts, ma'am" style of proceeding. If television drew audiences, or at least attention, to these high-profile cases, it was because good lawyering, as long as it is well funded, makes good television. Even the best attorneys could not have done what the Menendez and Simpson defense teams did without the resources that very few defendants can afford.

Thus, the Simpson trial, like the Menendez trials, made very good television largely because the defense teams were able to employ, to their very best effects, the tools that bring both courtroom drama and television drama to life—melodrama, pathos, humor, suspense, and surprise. As George Lipsitz has noted, the Simpson case was "made for TV." And television was ready for it. It ran for 631 hours on CNN and put Court TV, which at that time was available in only 24 million homes, definitively on the map, making its coverage among the three most watched television "programs" of 1995.[24] As in the Menendez case, the drama was powerful, even without the added attraction of celebrity. There was wealth and glamor; there were issues of conflicted family loyalties; and there was sex and violence. In fact, the theme of sexual desire gone berserk and ending in brutal violence would be an irresistible story for any producer. Indeed, the elements of the Simpson trial were the very elements that made *Dallas* and *Dynasty* the most popular shows of the 1980s.

The prosecution case had all of this to begin with, of course. The pictures of Nicole's bruised face and body, the tales of Simpson's rages, his public abuse of his wife, his womanizing—all were there. And the Brown family, especially Nicole's equally beautiful and glamorous sister Denise, who gave dramatic testimony, filled with sobs of grief and outbursts of rage, were constant reminders of the family tragedy at the heart of the case. And of course there were also the Goldmans—the father, step-mother, and equally melodramatic sister of the other victim, Nicole's young friend Ron Goldman, who had apparently inadvertently arrived upon the scene to return some glasses to Nicole and was bludgeoned to death along with her. Like the Browns, they appeared in court every day, and the cameras loved to pan to their made-for-television expressions and movements as witness upon witness recounted the bloody scene and the outrageous history of the Simpson marriage.

But what turned the tide of American sympathies—split them wide open, actually—was the defense case, which opened what became a can of worms more deadly than the most gruesome horror movie creatures. What was called "the race card" by those who supported the prosecution was, as Judge A. Leon Higginbotham, Jr., eloquently explains in his own postmortem of the case, not a trick "card" made up by some slick lawyers. It was a perfectly legitimate issue in a case in which—as in all criminal cases—the burden of proof is on the state. The very suggestion that racial prejudice on the part of the LAPD might have led to false testimony, tainted evidence, and/or deliberate mishandling of the case itself was important enough to constitute the "reasonable doubt" that is all that is necessary for a jury to acquit.[25] For as one juror herself explained, in defending her vote to acquit, her vote did not signify her certainty of Simpson's innocence, but only the "reasonable doubt" that the court considers serious enough to find a defendant "not guilty." Which is not the same as "innocent." As this woman insisted, "I did not find him innocent!"[26]

There were two factors in the case that turned the trial away from its focus on domestic violence and toward the issue of racism that ultimately led to Simpson's acquittal. The first was the DNA evidence skillfully explained by Barry Scheck, which cast doubt on the handling of the blood evidence found at the scene of the crime and suggested that that evidence might indeed have been planted by the police. The second, of course, was the evidence brought *against* the lead detective in the case, Mark Fuhrman. The defense luckily had the resources to go all the way across the country to dig up tapes held by a screenwriting teacher who had consulted with Fuhrman on a crime-movie script she was writing. But having such financial resources did not make the story less compelling. It only showed how important it is that defendants—especially those accused of murder—have the ability to locate and bring forward every bit of evidence that might be relevant to her or his case. Few have it, of course, but O. J. did. And once Mark Fuhrman was revealed to have been guilty of truly odious racist views and actions, the possibility that evidence was planted or tainted was hard to deny.

Unless, of course, you chose to ignore the evidence because you were so convinced of Simpson's guilt, and so enraged by his actions, that you simply wanted what many people called "justice": to see the man put away for life, or dead. That "unless" was the knife that cut through American society, pitting blacks against whites in a public forum about race and gender so ugly and heated at times that one feared that more blood might flow, no matter what the verdict.

Most (white) feminists were outraged at the outcome of the trial; blacks—even black women—were largely overjoyed. This is indicative of the powerful, at times dangerous, passions that were raised by the heated social movements of the sixties. But it is also indicative of the complicated tensions that arise when the criminal justice system is made to substitute for the larger public forums and political processes of deliberation and debate within which such issues should be debated. It was not the job of the criminal justice system to solve problems of racism and sexism in America. And yet, by 1995, with the rise of televised trials, it had unfortunately become the only public arena capable of engaging the entire nation in such debates and deliberations. Because of this unfortunate state of affairs, the very meaning of the process itself was lost, at least to many of those who, one would assume, would be most informed and rational about the legal system: educated, middle-class whites. For wasn't it TV that has educated most white people about race in America? Educated and liberal as we may be, in the abstract, what this trial proved, beyond a reasonable doubt to many, was that for most of us, black men can play only two possible roles: that of Bill Cosby, or that of some thug on the local news or in *America's Most Wanted*.[27] One of the most fascinating aspects of this case was the way in which, as the whole world watched, O. J. Simpson morphed before our very eyes from his long standing role as a "Cosby" guy to the dark-skinned "thug" pictured in the infamous, darkened mug shot that was on the cover of *Time* magazine.

And so, as it turned out, African Americans had the experience and knowledge of the workings of the legal system that made them far more able to understand what "reasonable doubt" means and how important it can be in a trial in which primarily white police officers and prosecutors are accusing a black man—any black man—of a serious crime. In fact, one of the saddest aspects of the entire event was the way in which the women jurors—this time primarily educated, professional women of color—were pilloried and demeaned by a public out for blood in a confusing case. The actual rules of the system—on the streets as well as in the courtroom—were poorly understood, or understood erroneously because of the subtle influence of television news and drama.[28] For in our particular system, it has always been assumed that it is better to err on the side of caution and acquittal, especially when a life is on the line.

Were these black women jurors really as dense or prejudiced as so many white people charged? Did they decide, with barely an hour of deliberation, to acquit a clearly guilty man because of racial loyalty? Three of these jurors have written their own account of the trial and of their processes of thought in an attempt to defend themselves.[29] And like Hazel Thornton's book, theirs is filled with important information which very few people will ever read. For one thing, far from being ignorant or uneducated, all the women were government employees with college degrees. And their reasons for acquitting so quickly were sound enough: the possibility of tainted evidence, the hard-to-believe stories told by the police witnesses, and a clear understanding of their charge—to find guilt "beyond a reasonable doubt." As for the brevity of their deliberations, they explained it quite sensibly: they had already been in that courtroom for nine months "deliberating."

What was really at issue here was the realization—still largely ignored by public figures and many white people—that most people of color live in a different world from white people, one in which institutionalized racism, across the national board, is never far from their experiences or consciences. As for the feminist response, it too was understandable if not, in my own view, reasonable. For we too have suffered for ages in a system in which violence against women, like racism, is still largely ignored or underestimated by those who have not experienced it. And so, in a far more socially destructive way than in the Menendez case, this trial ended with a "soft on crime" verdict that left many Americans outraged at the criminal justice system and opened some socially divisive and painful wounds in the body politic that it was not able to heal. Perry Mason was indeed dead; Ben Matlock was in syndication on the back burners of cable TV; and the hope of the justices that televising trials would—like these old TV series—reassure America that the system worked, that the guilty went to prison and that the innocent went free, was irrevocably dashed, or so it seemed. For, as Steven Russell has noted, "In high profile criminal trials judicial concern is with what kind of story the camera will tell . . . about the criminal justice system. Will it be a hegemonic narrative ('The system works') or a subversive narrative ('The system is broken')?"[30] Most commentators agreed that the messages of the Menendez and Simpson trials are anything but hegemonic; in fact, they were exactly what the justices hoped to counter: subversive narratives that upheld the popular perception that the system was indeed broken.

Televison indeed became a major player in projecting the image of a "soft on crime" legal system, dashing the expectations of the justices who had allowed the camera in as an assumed corrective to such apparent legal atrocities. Once the power of the medium to do such damage to their cause was made apparent by these two really aberrant cases, the nation at large, and certainly those involved in determining the rules by which trials would be conducted, became even more determined to change the image of the system to ensure that never again would such an unexpected and drastic upset for their side occur on television.

Damage Control and Finally Getting It Right

What to do? For most Americans, unhappy with these two verdicts, the answer was simple. Get rid of the cameras. And in the next Menendez and Simpson trials—the first a retrial in the criminal court, the second a civil suit brought by the Brown family—that is exactly what the nervous judges decided to do. But that strategy, ironically, also backfired. For the real issue was never television itself, but what television might reveal about American life if all the complex issues of race, gender, family dysfunction were allowed to be shown on television, unedited, uncensored, in the raw. And so, the second trials of all three defendants were handled by judges and prosecutors—in Simpson's case, by a defense attorney—in a radically different manner. In these trials as much as was legally possible was done to insure that this time viewers concerned about a legal system frighteningly "soft" on crime would be properly reassured that the system could be made to "work." Justice, in the form of some kind of severe punishment, would at last be meted out to these "monstrous" offenders.

How did the legal system manage this? It made sure that the issues that had made such a botch of the first trials—the inclusion of too much and too dramatically powerful testimony about highly vexed political and social issues—were curbed. The judge in the Menendez retrial—the same former prosecutor who, as the cameras revealed quite clearly, found the brothers' attorneys, especially Ms. Abramson, so annoying—this time made sure that their power would be reined in.

While expert testimony about sexual abuse of children was still allowed to be included, the dramatic power of that testimony was severely diminished this time by the judge's decision to disallow the vast majority of personal testimony by those who had witnessed Jose's and Kitty's treatment of their sons and its effects on them since earliest childhood. And what good was a lot of "psychobabble"—as the prosecutors put it—without the concrete details that gave it life and blood? For criminal trials, whether televised or not, do indeed depend, like any good drama, on the emotional impact of the narratives being offered: the human elements of pain, grief, suffering, and scars that either side can demonstrate in the interest of persuading juries to vote with them. All the psychological theory and DNA evidence in the world cannot make up for what is lost when human beings, with their human experiences and feelings, are absent.

The second trials, then, were much shorter than the first, and far less emotionally vivid. The verdicts this time came much more quickly from jurors whose deliberations involved far less impassioned struggle than the first trial engendered. Both Menendez brothers, to the great relief of most Americans, are now safely ensconced for life in maximum security prisons.[31] Nothing in the prosecution's cases ever hinted even mildly that there was reason to think the brothers, let loose upon society at some point in their lives, would actually have reason to kill again.

As for O. J. Simpson, his second trial was also carefully staged and orchestrated to insure, as far as possible, that the "correct" story would win out and the killer would at least be made to pay some sort of debt, if not to society than at least to the families' of his alleged victims. Of course, in every retrial of a case in which prosecutors have made serious errors in planning their strategies, they have the great advantage the second time around of knowing what to expect. This was as true in the Menendez case as in the Simpson. But where, in the Menendez case, the state (and the clearly biased judge himself) needed only to eliminate the emotionally and politically charged aspects of the case entirely, with the Simpson case the problem was trickier. For here, as we have seen, competing narratives were at war. In the criminal trial the defense team managed to push the issue of domestic violence to the back burners, and—with the help of the all-too-well-cast villain of their piece, Mark Fuhrman—it made institutionalized racism the key factor. This time around, the attorneys hired to "prosecute" Simpson knew exactly how to turn the tables and make the issue of racism far less prominent and moving than that of sexism. For one thing, the trial itself was moved out of downtown Los Angeles— where the jury pool was made up, primarily, of poor minorities, especially blacks and Latinos—to Santa Monica, an upscale, largely white community.

But more importantly, perhaps, the jurors' heart strings were now pulled far more powerfully by the sufferings of the victims than the sufferings of those for whom racial discrimination and harassment were painful daily realities. In this trial we see the beginnings of a learning curve whereby prosecutors have steadily acquired an expertise in how to prepare cases for television. Jurors were made to look at a larger-than-life-size photograph of the bruised and battered face of Nicole Brown Simpson. Every witness was made to sit in front of that horrific, overpowering iconic image, and for O. J. Simpson in particular this visual device was as devastating as any "evidence" introduced. Forcing him to appear in that setting, so diminished in stature, both in relative size and in "star power," was a brilliant legal tactic, especially since those in the new jury pool were so much more likely to identify with the beautiful, brutalized blonde than the first group. Because in this trial the plaintiffs were the victims rather than the accused, the presence of the Browns and Goldmans was far more likely to win sympathy from this jury than the first. Each one of them could easily have been cast in a high-budget "Movie of the Week" version of the story, so "made for TV" were they as images of prime-time-style melodramatic suffering.

This trial was lesson 1 in producing made-for-TV criminal trials in which the "good guys" win and the "bad guys" pay. Too bad we never got a chance to see it. But never mind. We would, soon enough, see versions of it played out with equally skillful dramatic slickness on the many televised trials to come. Unfortunately, however, not soon enough for the trial of all late-century trials: that of *Oklahoma v. Timothy McVeigh*, the man accused of the murder of 168 people in the planned bombing of the Murrah Federal Building in Oklahoma City in April 1995. If ever there was a trial in which a villain was as apparently evil as any monster devised by Hollywood horror-movie producers, it was this one.

Because the trial was not televised, its inclusion here may seem confusing. On one level, I am arguing that the lessons learned by prosecutors from this trial set a precedent that made future *televised* trials more likely to avoid the unsettling confusion of the first Menendez and Simpson trials. But I am also suggesting that in a real sense much of the substance of the trials was in fact televised. In fact, the interest in this case garnered it more media and public attention than either of the two cases discussed above. Like the events of September 11, 2001, it was a case that raised fear in the public in general. It is fair to assume that at least as many Americans watched the extensive nightly coverage of the trial as watched the other two. Because cameras were not allowed into the courtroom, the nightly news coverage and press conferences held by victims and witnesses became the only televised version of events to which viewers had access.

The reason this is relevant to a discussion of *televised* trials is that so much of what actually happened in the courtroom was in fact repeated in these nightly televised press conferences. For this was a case in which almost all the "evidence" presented by the successful prosecutors was in the form of testimony given by those who were not in fact "victims" (although they were referred to as such and considered themselves such) but whose lives were deeply and harshly affected because they had lost loved ones in the bombing. In a real sense, therefore, the "testimony" given each night by the "victims" reflected much of what we would actually have seen and heard had we been permitted to view the actual proceedings.

We thus had a trial that became a case study in how to do what prosecutors, and prosecution witnesses, needed to do to win the hearts and minds not only of jurors but of audiences in future cases. The reasons were obvious. So hideous was the crime itself in the American mind, so powerful was the fear and hatred it engendered in a nation not prepared to experience the tragic effects of warfare and terrorism on its own soil, that the prosecutors, and the judge himself, were understandably determined to make sure that this one went well. This time, no one would be able to complain that some slick defense team or legal technicality would allow this devilish defendant to slip through the vice of true justice through any kind of lawyerly loopholes. It was crucial that the "appearance" of justice insure that McVeigh was represented by a qualified, talented defense attorney. But there was really no way that even a modern-day Clarence Darrow could have battled the forces brought to bear against this defendant and won. For one thing, McVeigh himself was a particularly unattractive defendant: emotionless, apparently remorseless, and unaffected, as far as anyone could tell, by the voluminous verbal and visual "evidence" brought forth by the state. The victims' tearful tales of horror and graphic photographs of the sufferings of the innocent, many of them mere babies, caught by a bomb as they played in a state-run day-care center, left him cold. He was, as his later statements revealed, indeed guilty, even proudly and arrogantly guilty, of a crime which did indeed, and understandably so, ignite the fires of horror and indignation in most of us. In his later statement, for example, he referred to the many victims as "collateral damage," including the children. Those for whom crime and criminality are viewed as the acts of inherently "evil," even "inhuman," beings, craved for the stiffest punishment.[32]

I put the word "evidence" in quotation marks above because what the prosecution presented, and the judge allowed, was not, for the most part, real evidence of McVeigh's guilt,[33] but rather the endless testimony of those affected by the bombing itself. The stories would have been the same no matter who had constructed and detonated the bomb. It is in fact questionable if it was even legally appropriate to allow the families of the victims to be present in the courtroom during the trial. The reason was that, if McVeigh were to be found guilty, many of them were to be witnesses in the penalty phase of the trial. This process allows "victim impact statements," now permitted in death penalty cases, in which those affected by the crime are allowed to speak of their losses, of the virtues of those now dead, and of their own often passionate desire or need to see the defendant punished in the harshest possible way.

But the potential witnesses were indeed allowed into the courtroom. In fact, they were allowed to testify as the main witnesses for the prosecution, thereby, in effect, giving their victim impact statements in the trial itself. So unorthodox was this procedure that, had it been any other crime or any other defendant, there would surely have been an appeal or at least some media discussion about the judge's decision to allow it. In fact, if one takes the doer and the deed out of the equation, the whole procedure takes on a kind of *Alice in Wonderland*, "off with their heads," quality of absurdity. For if ever there was a case in the United States in which the presumption of innocence was never even a consideration in most minds, it was this one. But then, the McVeigh trial was a spectacle of judgment and punishment made to order for a nation struck dumb by the unique horror of the crime itself. McVeigh was a poster child for the arguments favoring not only the death penalty, but for the public's "right" to view the legal execution of one of its own citizens.

But was the crime really so unique? Certainly it seemed so from the point of view of those who could not remember or imagine a comparable event. As in the Menendez case, the symbolic impact of the crime itself was the major factor, I would argue, in the trial's impact on the nation. The pity and fear—to use the Aristotelian terms describing the emotions invoked by true tragedy—aroused by a child's murder of its parents, by the heartless, cold-blooded destruction of so many innocents by a person who seemed to personify the very term "un-American" in his openly avowed hatred for the American government, were clearly unparalleled in these two cases. Not since the witch hunts of McCarthyism has a person stood before a group of "real" Americans and been forced to answer to charges of treason of the most evil and unforgivable kind. But of course McVeigh's crime, like that of the Menendez brothers, was far more visually and symbolically troubling than anything McCarthy could come up with on his best day. The blood of innocent children, or of one's own family member, strikes at the very heart of what holds us together as a human community. And it was this kind of symbolism, especially in the McVeigh case, that was at the core of the spectacle.

In fact, McVeigh's evil, his made-for-TV casting as national scapegoat and sacrificial lamb, was far worse than that of the Menendez brothers, despite the equally horrifying symbolic nature of their crime. First, the brothers had friends, family, and other members of the community on their side. McVeigh had no one. He was a bitter, angry loner whose own parents did not appear in court until the penalty phase, and even then had little to say on his behalf. And second, the crime of incest had been put on the national agenda by the sixties activists, especially the feminists, and so it had the power to trouble and vex the jury. McVeigh, however, was guilty of a crime that even the most ardent of the 1960s activists found hard to empathize with.

I do not mean to make an excuse for McVeigh's horrifying, cruel, and brutal act. I only mean to suggest that certain causes have universal appeal; others have none at all; and still others have violently mixed meanings for Americans for reasons that often have little to do with the mere act for which one is judged and punished. The man who now sits as president of the United States, for example, is in a real sense responsible for the state-sanctioned "murders" of more people than McVeigh killed. As governor of Texas, he allowed more death row inmates to be executed than any governor in history.[34] Similarly, other presidents have been responsible, as McVeigh understood all too well, for the deaths of far more innocents in wars of aggression. But the symbols of patriotism and "law and order" made these deaths appear to most Americans to be heroic, while McVeigh's act—unforgivable as it was—had no such symbolically popular phrases or images upon which he could garner national sympathy.

To many readers I may have a perversely odd perspective on the McVeigh case, but I think it is important to understand the power of emotion-laden symbols, in courtroom dramas and television dramas alike, in swaying audiences and jurors to one position or another about guilt and innocence, evil and virtue, patriotism and treason. This point is at the heart of all three cases I am examining here. In all three, the ability of attorneys and judges to orchestrate their cases around a successful deployment of such emotion-laden symbols has meant the difference between success and failure, freedom and imprisonment, and, in McVeigh's case, life and death.

But it was the McVeigh case, more than the others, which made the most successful use of such images. Even if the cameras were not present to make the spectacle available to everyone, there were certainly many in the juridical realm who suddenly regretted their too hasty conclusion—on the basis of the Menendez and Simpson trials—to write television off as a tool for reassuring Americans that the system worked and reinforcing dominant political and social values.

Not surprisingly, the emotional heat of that courtroom was, according to those present, palpable. Andrew Cohen, a Denver lawyer and journalist who was present at the McVeigh trial, described it as a masterpiece of legal management of dramatic effect: "One day it was forensic experts telling the eerie tale of McVeigh's bombing plans. . . . Next it might be one of the many sad survivors of the bombing, come to tell her tale of woe. And if it wasn't the witnesses themselves, it was the way prosecutors arranged their order. If the jurors appeared to be getting sleepy . . . a survivor whose testimony woke everyone up and got them good and sad" was brought on. "Lawyers are convinced they need drama and entertainment in an age when attention spans have been diminished by television," Cohen argues, and the McVeigh trial, with its plethora of victims and tales of loss and suffering, bloodshed and gore, was a model of how such drama and entertainment could be most effectively provided.[35] Indeed, it is worth noting that when, in February 2001, McVeigh requested that his execution be nationally televised, his request was quietly denied. For the spectacle of a state-sanctioned "murder," which McVeigh no doubt had in mind when he made his request, would surely have raised the social debates the courts did not want to risk arousing. This was especially true since the death penalty itself had already become something of a vexed issue in some quarters. The publicity in the wake of a spate of death row inmates who were, with the help of DNA testing, found innocent and released in the two or three years preceding McVeigh's request added to the concerns.

The McVeigh trial marked a turning point in the awareness among judges and prosecutors of the power of dramatic visual staging of criminal trials, the increasing adeptness at using the techniques described by Cohen, and the declining suspicion that television is an aid in doing what the justices, in 1981, predicted—creating the appearance of a system whose wheels whirred smoothly along toward the kind of closure that would most reassure the public. In fact, since that trial, there has been a notable rise in public confidence in the legal system. In March 1999, for example, the American Bar Association conducted a survey of public opinion about the workings of the justice system. It found that, indeed, in the last decade, Americans' opinion of the court system has risen significantly, while other institutions—especially the media and Congress—were deemed even more corrupt and ineffective than in previous years. The ABA's recommendation was that in order to further educate the public about the judicial system, and further improve its public image, the Supreme Court, so long adamantly opposed to being televised, should now allow cameras into its own proceedings.[36]

And so they have allowed more cameras in, with decreasing uneasiness about what those cameras might reveal about their system. There is, after all, a clear and present hunger these days—reflected in and reinforced by television—for an increasingly punitive and harsh system of justice in which the vagaries about what justice really is are put to rest once and for all. Americans want a return to the good old days, when crime was crime, plain and simple, and one knew it when one saw it and treated it accordingly. Even if the Menendez and Simpson trials made for terrific television, they did not make for the kind of television that those who most strongly longed for a return to a legal system wanted to see. They wanted right and wrong to be clear and simple, and bleeding-heart liberals, with their abuse excuses and cloying appeals for mercy, should be silenced and restrained.

In the following chapters, we will look at the way a variety of socially charged televised trials were resolved. Most aired after the Simpson and Menendez cases and then were condensed into mini-docudramas on Court TV's *Crime Stories* series. The issues raised—gender violence, youth crime, family dysfunction, the suffering of victims and their "right" to vengeance—are ones which, as we have seen, were also raised in the trials of the Menendez brothers, O. J. Simpson, and Timothy McVeigh. In these televised trials, and in the rise of the Victims' Rights movement, we will see how the legal system (with obvious exceptions, of course) now tends to deal with such issues. The perspective will be historical in terms of media as well as social and legal trends. For as we shall see, in a variety of television genres the media of more liberal eras treated these issues in ways that were pointedly and intriguingly different from the Court TV versions of more recent trials. The trials, especially those edited down to *Crime Stories* segments, clearly reflect the rightward drift of both criminal justice policy and television programming.

As I explained in my Introduction, the chapters that follow all deal with cases in which social issues have increasingly been "criminalized" in the legal system. That is, they have increasingly been handled as issues that should be viewed in the context of criminal justice rather than within the many other social contexts in which they had been primarily understood. Gender violence, for example, can and has been understood by feminists as a problem that should be addressed by changing the many sexist social institutions that socialize men to become violent. Today, however, such cases are largely understood as matters to be handled by the criminal courts. As a result, men who commit these "crimes," when convicted, are sent to prisons—places that are unlikely to do anything to end the sexism that is at the root of these violent behaviors. Similarly, family dysfunction and youth delinquency, issues that were previously handled by social service agencies and therapists, are increasingly being criminalized. Parents and troubled young people are, like the perpetrators of violence against women, increasingly finding themselves facing criminal proceedings and sentences rather than being offered the help they need to function in more healthy, productive ways. Finally, in discussing the rise of the Victims' Rights movement, I will address another major shift in criminal justice practices and the increasingly wide berth this movement is being given to handle all manner of troubles and sufferings that might more effectively and democratically be handled by other agencies.

In each chapter I use a similar strategy. I try to draw clear parallels between what is in fact happening in the realm of criminal justice and what is being portrayed on television. I also analyze the televised trials in which each of these issues is central. I compare them—as I did in the chapter on prisons—with earlier television and film formats that offered more liberal perspectives on these issues and more hopeful suggestions on handling them than the criminal justice system—with its single-minded approach to every issue as one in which punishment is the only option offered as a remedy—offers today.

5

The Politics of Representation
Gender Violence and Criminal Justice

From the trial of Socrates to the dozens of proceedings reported
daily in the press, the popular trial has been active as a rhetorical
form, a social practice and a symptom of historical change.
—Robert Hariman

Every man I meet wants to protect me. Can't figure out what from.
—Mae West

In 1977 an East Lansing, Michigan, woman named Francine
Hughes, having suffered seventeen years of domestic abuse, set her sleeping husband's bed on fire, took their three children, and fled. In a prece-
dent-setting case, she was, astoundingly, acquitted of murder and set free.
From this trial, in which the defense was not self-defense (she was clearly
in no immediate danger when she acted), but temporary insanity due to
years of psychological and physical abuse, came what is now widely
known as the "battered woman defense."

This trial was significant for a number of reasons. For one thing, it represented a major victory for feminists, who had coined the term—now
universally accepted as part of everyday parlance—"domestic violence."
Indeed, since the late 1960s, feminists had been agitating for recognition
of and redress from this all too common but largely hidden—or worse,
"naturalized"—form of gender oppression. "Domestic squabble" was
the term typically used by police to describe wife beating, which, because
it occurred within the private sphere, in which "a man's home is his cas-
tle," was not seen as "abnormal," much less criminal.

But it was not until seven or eight years later, when an independent
television producer named Robert Greenwald sold the story to a major

television network as a made-for-TV movie, or docudrama, that the issue of domestic violence dramatically entered public consciousness. It significantly came to influence lawmakers and other institutional authorities to legislate reform measures to address the problem. When *The Burning Bed*, which dramatized Hughes's experiences, her "crime," and the trial in which she was exonerated, aired to an audience of 75 million in 1984, the battered women's shelter movement gained momentum; police officers began taking "sensitivity training" for the handling of what was now recognized as a violent crime, punishable by law; women imprisoned for killing abusive partners were given clemency in significant numbers; talk shows, soap operas, police dramas and even sitcoms began regularly featuring story lines and segments addressing the issue; and Americans generally began seriously to confront and debate it.

In the early 1980s, then, network television was apt to present what I will argue were highly progressive, feminist-informed portrayals of the issue, its root causes, and its potential cures. But by the 1990s, as the nation moved politically and socially rightward, the representation of this highly charged issue shifted dramatically to reflect far less progressive approaches to the problem. The new approaches emphasized a "law and order" mentality favoring punishment of male violators rather than the earlier approach presented in movies like *The Burning Bed*, in which the liberation of women from the threat of violence was understood to involve a restructuring of social institutions in ways that empowered women to free themselves physically, economically, and psychologically from male control and violence. As I will further argue, this shift in ideological perspective was achieved primarily through the drastic revision of the classic social issue docudrama and the rise of a new genre invented by Court TV in which actual trials are condensed into one-hour docudramas. In these, the entire issue is presented and analyzed solely in terms of legal and criminal justice terminology and assumptions, rather than the broader social analyses provided by early docudramas.[1]

It is significant to note that in recent years, television has continued to air matters of gender violence—rape, date rape, sexual harassment, incest, and domestic abuse—regularly for a variety of reasons: it's sexy, it's violent, and it addresses serious issues. But it is not only television that seems to have selected this issue from the myriad others raised by feminists since the late 1960s—child care, health care, economic equity, employment discrimination, reproductive rights, lesbian rights, and so on. Especially in recent years, at a time when feminists have been suffering depressing losses in many other arenas of struggle, politicians of both the left and right, in their eagerness to win the "women's vote," have become ever more vocal in their proclaimed commitment to the battle against domestic and sexual violence.

It is hardly surprising that gender violence has continued to be a popular theme in both fictional and nonfictional television programming, given its sensational nature and its continued importance in public policy and criminal justice debates. But the dominant approach to the subject has shifted dramatically in the years since Robert Greenwald made his influential movie. Indeed, the docudramas and other made-for-TV movies about violence against women, which still come out in droves, are far less socially provocative and insightful than *The Burning Bed* or *Silent Witness*, another, more loosely based-on-fact movie about a gang rape that aired a year later. Most of these newer TV movies, in fact, appear on the woman-targeted Lifetime network. They are near nightly fodder for this network's audience of women for whom melodramatic "weepies," similar to those produced for a female audience by Hollywood in the 1930s and 1940s, are still favorites. But these Lifetime movies are really television's version of the "B movie" of earlier eras. They are not publicized as "major media events" as the earlier network versions were, nor do they garner the ratings or broad-based audiences of the classic docudramas. Largely for the sake of sensationalism, these movies exploit the issue of gender violence placed on the political agenda by feminists in the 1970s and early 1980s. But they also manage to declaw the form—and the issue—of all political significance by reducing it to a few endlessly repeated generic formulas, part melodrama, part horror, in which no social, political, or institutional context exists at all to explain the behavior of any of the major characters. As is typical of what Sarah Projansky sees as a "linear, historical postfeminism," which, "does not [bother] with a feminist perspective at all, now that feminism is supposedly 'over,'"[2] these movies simply assume we all "get it" by now. They proceed to give the merest skeleton versions of the now familiar arc of innocent passive woman, charmer-turned-monster male, and predictable dénouement in which, most typically, some form of law enforcement "saves" the woman from near certain death.

The television form that has emerged to take the place of the more serious 1980s movies is the live televised trial. The coming of cable has brought with it an onslaught of representation and discussion of violence against women, the likes of which Robert Greenwald, whose possible venues were only the three major networks, could only dream. Cable channels such as CNN, CNBC, MSNBC, and Court TV, which have the time and desire to give inordinate amounts of attention to an issue so gripping and dramatic—have made criminal and civil trials involving sexual violence mainstays of television fare. Court TV, which has had a particular interest in sensational trials, has run gavel-to-gavel coverage of a very large number of trials in which some kind of violence against or harassment of women or girls figures. Indeed, its nightly *Crime Stories* series is a prime venue. Fully televised trials are edited down to one-hour documentaries featuring trial footage, interviews with principals, and commentary by a Court TV host or hostess. They tend to feature, and rerun endlessly, trials involving domestic and sexual violence. The objective appears to be to capitalize on the sensationalism of the topic, even as the hosts comment—explicitly or more subtly—on the problem and its solutions. But this series is very different in its approach to the problem and the possible solutions it offers than the earlier docudramas.

In this chapter, I have two objectives. First, I will compare the way in which representative docudramas of the early 1980s treated the issue of gender violence with the way the newer, emaciated versions of the 1990s have rewritten them to fit a far more conservative turn in American politics. For what is lost in the newer versions of gender violence docudrama—along with so many other socially significant components—is the courtroom drama itself, the place where, in the original versions, narratives of cause and effect, and shifting versions of "justice" and "equality," were treated with some seriousness. Court TV's *Crime Stories* series does include—indeed, is based upon—the courtroom negotiation of these issues. Second, and more importantly, I want to compare those early docudramas with the *Crime Stories* mini-docudramas as a way of drawing attention to the link between forms and genres of representation. I also want to show how traditional genres may in fact live on, in degenerate forms, when the historical moment makes them increasingly irrelevant or unpopular. For it is in the shift from the serious TV movie-docudrama to televised courtroom trials where the drama takes place entirely within the context of the courtroom itself that one sees reflected the parallel shift in dominant ideological and policy approaches to gender violence: its nature, its roots, its social and moral implications, and its appropriate "solutions."

Representation as Social Reproduction

Robert Hariman, in his argument for treating trials as a rhetorical genre, defines a genre as a "form of social knowledge" that reflects "what people 'know,' in the sense of what they rely upon when otherwise in a condition of change, disorientation, or trauma. That is why," he argues, "generic forms that have been relaxed during periods of routine social exchange predominate in moments of social and political transition." For "a genre exists only as long as others agree that it exists"; and one's "knowledge of the genre must be matched by others' willingness to recognize its forms and authority."[3] In other words, genres reflect the beliefs and assumptions about reality and morality that dominate their time. And, while in times of relative social harmony they tend to remain stable and go unquestioned, in changing times they must be amended, sometimes radically, in order for people to recognize and share the new set of dominant assumptions and beliefs.

Trials themselves, however, as Hariman notes, have continued to be generic staples of social knowledge at least since Socrates. This is especially so in times of social and ideological change because, in their very adversarial structure, trials "contain explicitly the problems of comparing and evaluating discourses before an audience of ordinary citizens."[4] As film and later, to a much greater extent, television have taken the trial and created a major genre, "the courtroom drama," for it, the social importance of the trial as dramatized social knowledge has grown in importance, both culturally and ideologically.

As Lisa Cuklanz notes in discussing the media's inordinate interest in rape and rape law, in news as well as drama, the media have made the court trial the primary focus around which public debate of this issue (and, I would add, all other forms of gender violence as well) centers. But she goes farther in analyzing the political role of such media coverage, suggesting that media genres can be used in a variety of ideological ways. "Highly publicized trials are in one sense vehicles of containment and control," she writes, for the media tend always to define and debate social issues within the limits of current hegemonic norms. But "they can also be trumpet calls that bring attention to the issues they involve" in more positive and progressive ways.[5]

Indeed, as many feminist political theorists have argued, as a result of the rise and influence of feminism, feminism has become what Nancy Fraser terms an "oppositional force, intervening, in sometimes quite effective ways, in public sphere debates about gender politics." Fraser speaks of television as a central element of the "public sphere" within which feminists struggle to revise hegemonic discourses as part and parcel of their other agitational and discursive activities—in the classroom, the courtroom, the streets, wherever. "However limited a public may be in its empirical manifestation at any given time," she writes, "its members understand themselves as part of a potentially wider public" whose goal it is to enter the "structured setting where cultural and ideological contest or negotiation among a variety of publics takes place" in the interest of realizing their "emancipatory potential."[6]

This statement has been particularly true in cases involving gender violence, because the role of feminists in putting this issue on the public agenda has been so central. And feminism itself is of course a controversial political movement—and term—about which public opinion is radically divided. Historically, it has risen and fallen in public recognition and sympathy according to the political tenor of the times. Thus, when rape and other forms of gender violence gained media attention, its presentation and reception directly reflected the influence of feminism. For, as political theorist Kathleen Jones has noted in summarizing the assumptions about law and justice that have historically prevailed in American jurisprudence, "The standard analysis of authority in modern Western political theory begins with its definition as a set of rules governing political action, issued by those who are entitled to speak." But these rules traditionally "have excluded females and values associated with the feminine." Thus, the "dominant discourse on authority," in placing "strict limits on the publicly expressible, and limit[ing] critical reflection about the norms and values that structure 'private' life and which affect the melodies of public speech," has traditionally marginalized women's voices and experiences within public arenas such as the courtroom.[7]

But the impact of feminism on public discourse and debate, by the late 1970s, had, as Lisa Cuklanz documents, begun to alter this hegemonic norm. Rape trials, in particular (and, I would add, trials dealing with gender violence generally), did indeed begin to incorporate feminist demands for legal reform in ways that vexed and complicated legal procedures. For the first time, traditional assumptions about the "normality" of gender violence and the victim's responsibility for her own abuse began to be challenged in courtrooms. Women's previously silenced, hidden, or publicly distorted experiences began to be publicly voiced, heard, and discussed. This change, for Cuklanz, was at least a partial victory for feminists. For it is through "discussion of rape trials [that] the climate of public opinion has been adjusted to a slight degree as writers and observers have attempted to adjudicate between a traditional view of rape and a revision based on female experience and voice."[8]

This is an observation that holds for public discussions of gender violence generally. For as Susan Griffin has noted, in the struggles for rape law reform, "public expression itself is an achievement." Thus the power of public speak-outs in which women "spoke bitterness" about their previously hidden and silenced pain. For such occasions, according to Griffin, gave women "the so desperately needed time to speak about a long hidden injury." And through these events, held all over the nation over a period of several years, enough collective strength was generated "to change the more outrageous injustices."[9] Public speak-outs were instrumental in organizing forces to demand legal redress, and the impact on those hearing and seeing such bitterness must have been enormous. The roots of gender violence were presented to an audience of millions over time, through reruns, video rentals, community and classroom viewing, and so on. Movies such as *The Burning Bed* and *Silent Witness* challenged traditional assumptions about gender violence—that it is "natural" or somehow "asked for" by letting the voices and experiences of women speak for themselves in the context of the legal arena. And in a similar way, the *Crime Stories* TV series about domestic abuse and rape has allowed the voices and experiences of victims to be heard and recognized in court proceedings in which, as feminists have demanded, gender violence is inscribed as a criminal offense, punishable by law.

But there is an enormous difference in the *way* women's voices and experiences are heard, described, or dramatized—the way the truths of their experiences are absorbed and evaluated—in the courtroom use of the two genres. The dramatic difference is due to a plethora of diametrically opposed assumptions about why and how such violence occurs and what feminists can and should be doing to stop it. Indeed, in comparing these forms, feminists' demands that women's voices, the "truths" of their experiences, be heard suddenly emerge as more complicated than they may seem. For in a court of law, the word "truth" can be tricky. One takes the stand in a court of law and "swear[s] to tell the truth, the whole truth and nothing but the truth." But as anyone who has studied or participated in the adversarial system of trial law knows, it is not really "the truth" that justice rests upon, but rather the *version* of truth that is most compelling to a judge or jury. The alleged victim may say one thing and the defendant, or his or her representatives, something quite different, even when the essential "facts" are agreed upon by all concerned. Nor is *telling,* in the sense that narrative theorists may use it, sufficient to make the facts and experiences surrounding a crime legally significant or compelling. One must also *tell* them in a certain way. For in the courtroom the *telling* must always conform to the norms of legal discourse. The law, unlike narrative fiction, drama, or autobiography, has very strict rules about how one may say or show one's experiences and feelings or attest to the "truth."

Thus, the extent to which a genre makes use of a courtroom setting in addressing feminist issues affects the way in which women's stories are allowed to be told and—more importantly perhaps—what redress for their suffering they are allowed to receive. In fact, the extent to which a genre uses a courtroom setting implicitly reflects the extent to which its producers have chosen to define the issue at hand in terms of legal and juridical discourses and assumptions. And so, while trials do make perfect settings for "comparing and evaluating discourses" in times of social change, they also carry within them the formal requirement that the social issues being addressed are placed narrowly within the framework of the law, with all its rules about what and how stories can be told, and in what ways they can be resolved.

In fictional series like *The Practice*, for example, all sorts of liberties are taken with the realities of courtroom constraints about what can be said and done. As has been noted, this series allows their lawyers to behave in ways which no actual courtroom would permit. Court TV obviously cannot and does not do that. But there are other ways in which dramatic series—based on fact or not—can expand the limits of how a criminal case can be presented without bending the rules of legal procedure. The TV movies of the 1980s that I will analyze did that to good effect; the actual courtroom scenes are indeed true to legal life. However, what comes *before* the courtroom scenes that are the climax of these movies puts everything that happens within the courtroom in a much broader social context than do the *Crime Stories* mini-movies I will discuss below.

Both *The Burning Bed* and *Silent Witness*, for example, use the courtroom and the framework of law and criminal justice as centrally as *Crime Stories*. But while in *Crime Stories* the courtroom dominates while other material is decidedly subordinate, in the docudramas the reverse is true. Indeed, much of the "truth" told from the female victims' and spokespersons' perspective is heard and seen in a variety of settings outside the courtroom before it ever reaches the trial itself. And that is only the beginning of how the two forms differ in their treatment of the relationship between gender violence, society, and the law.

That Was Then and This Is Now: The Docudrama as Women's Genre

Even as early as 1974, the docudrama format had begun to reflect feminist influences on attitudes toward rape. For it is women, increasingly influenced by feminist thinking, who have always made up the majority of the TV audience and bought most of the advertised products—thus the number of early TV movies that addressed, at least from an implicitly feminist perspective, issues such as rape. Among these films, *The Burning Bed* stands out as a landmark in media representations of gender violence because of its perspective and narrative strategy. Beginning with scenes of the murder itself, and then of Francine Hughes's initial meeting with her court-appointed attorney, it continuously flashes back to the history of the Hughes's marriage and its disintegration. There are regular interruptions of the narrative to allow for a return to the prison conference room in which the attorney attempts to fashion a defense for a crime that is heinous and shocking by "normal," that is to say patriarchal, standards. Indeed, the very fact that a major network would present a film in which a woman sets her husband's bed on fire and walks free from the courtroom in which she is tried and judged is itself so remarkable that it alone would make the film politically and hegemonically noteworthy. For the movie challenges what until then had been unchallengeable ideas about who has a "right" to commit violence, and under what conditions. Men, of course, have long been authorized to kill—most typically in war, as law enforcers, and, until feminism challenged it, in the privacy of the patriarchal home. But women who kill, or commit any act of physical aggression, have always, according to the essentialist norms that govern patriarchal law, been viewed as outrageously "unnatural," no matter what the circumstances.

But in allowing Francine Hughes to tell "her story, in her own words"—as her attorney puts it in his opening arguments—the movie lets us see this "abnormal" act in its social, cultural, institutional, and economic context and thus we can find it more "normal" than the laws and ideological assumptions that prohibit it. Thus it is important to hear the previously silenced victim's voice throughout the narrative. Beginning with her marriage, in the early 1960s, Hughes—first in voiceover introductions to flashback scenes, and later on the witness stand—relates a series of events and encounters with family members, the social welfare bureaucracy, and the police in which it becomes startlingly clear that she has been entangled in a set of sexist (and classist) social structures, both domestic and public, from which she could not escape. She is pressured into marriage—although she dreams of "getting away, getting a job, or something"—because it is expected of women, especially working-class women. Her mother and her in-laws think nothing of her husband Mickey's public assaults on her, telling her that "she's made a hard bed" and must lie in it, and that men are "just made that way" and "don't really mean it." She herself, again typically, believes that she must have done something to deserve such treatment and vows to "be a better wife" and to "try to figure what Mickey wants." When things get unbearable she calls the police, but they do nothing. Neither do the welfare workers who embroil her in a maze of complicated, incomprehensible, illogical, and—most poignantly—wholly ineffective "solutions." Thus the drama—as told in Hughes's words and seen from her own point of view—hammers home in a compelling, even shocking way the structural blockages to women's emancipation from male abuse. When the actual courtroom scenes begin, the viewer has already seen and heard enough to be sensitized to the similarly biased assumptions and processes of the legal system—as represented by the prosecuting attorney—that can only view such a woman as a vicious criminal.

It is also important, in this case, that the battered woman herself appears not as a victim, accusing her abuser and demanding punishment, but rather as a defendant *accused* of a violent crime, a woman who has struck out *as an agent* in an effort to free herself and her children from years of institutionalized victimization. Indeed, her husband Mickey is himself portrayed in terms of social and institutional norms. He is no caricatured monster, perceived as simply evil, as abusers in later TV movies have been depicted. He is rather a somewhat pathetic loser, unable to hold a job or gain any status in society, driven to drink and domestic violence out of a frustrated need to "feel like a man" in a sexist and classist society in which such men are "given permission" to take out their frustrations and failures on women and children.

Silent Witness is equally clear in its focus on the family and institutional norms by which women are held in disciplinary control while men are free to abuse them, as though such behavior were perfectly "normal." The movie, based very loosely on the Big Dan's Tavern gang rape of a female patron, upon which the theatrical film *The Accused* was also based, challenges traditional assumptions concerning rape through a narrative strategy quite different from *The Burning Bed*. The heroine, Anna Dunne, is not the victim but the sister-in-law of one of the rapists, and a witness to the crime. But again, the crime and the trial are placed within the context of gendered family norms as well larger institutional and social beliefs and processes, which act as powerful disciplinary structures. And again, it is the larger narrative of family and social dynamics within which the victimization of one woman and the ultimate rebellion of another are portrayed. Anna, at first reluctant to come forward as a witness against a family member, in the end, heroically, does just that. The movie movingly portrays the female bonding of two women of very different social stations, even as it challenges patriarchal distinctions between "good" and "bad" girls which serve to divide women and keep us in our respective places. The rape victim, Patti, is a woman of dubious reputation and credibility. She is known to drink alone at bars quite regularly and has a history of alcoholism and blackouts which make her a less than reliable witness. But Anna cannot avoid a growing sense of identification with her, especially after visiting her and hearing her—in *her* own words—tell the story of her own sad life. When Patti commits suicide, after a grueling day of brutal attack by the rapists' attorney, Anna is compelled to come forward and testify in her behalf, although it costs her her own reputation and the security and acceptance of her family. For when Anna comes forward, she is indeed ostracized and vilified by her in-laws, who, playing on her loneliness and vulnerability, go so far as to pay an old school friend to seduce her, so that they can claim that she, like Patti, is a "bad" woman and therefore not credible as a witness to the "truth."

Like *The Burning Bed*, then, the movie manages to place the entire legal system—the courtroom and the trial—within the larger context of a social environment in which the roots of gender violence and their naturalization within sexist institutions are exposed and critiqued—through the voices, experiences, and actions of women, first as victims and then as agents. And, like *The Burning Bed*, the male abusers are similarly portrayed within the context of the social norms and institutions which allow—indeed socialize—them to commit such vicious acts without guilt or remorse. They simply cannot *see* the horror of their deeds while their wives and mothers, to maintain their own (dependent but secure and respectable) positions within the family, cannot acknowledge it, even to themselves.

In both these movies, then, there is a serious critique of gender violence and a dramatically effective portrayal of its social roots and of the moral heinousness of a society that condones or ignores it. And in both there is a heroine who resists and an (at least) implicit demand not only for legal but for social reform. Indeed, these films are exemplary narratives of female oppression and ultimate resistance. They provide an impressively complex portrayal of the institutional and ideological linkages within which society functions. They show a subtle but powerful network of forces that ensure the compliance of individuals by raising them from birth to internalize the ideological "truisms" about gender roles and natures that keep patriarchy afloat. Often they even manage, without pushing the envelope of feminist radicalism too far for the comfort of networks and sponsors, to show how those oppressed by sexist institutions can in some exemplary and even inspiring instances manage to fight the system, win, and in the process even force a certain amount of structural change upon those institutions.

In fact, in both narratives, the heroines emerge as freer, more autonomous women, no longer willing to submit to sexist forms of control and abuse. Francine Hughes goes on to obtain a secretarial degree so that she can become financially independent and support her children. And Anna Dunne's marriage is significantly transformed, as her husband ultimately joins her on the witness stand and dramatically breaks with and condemns his family's patriarchal practices and beliefs. The reformist political implications of these movies are thus made dramatically clear.

But there are limits to what the resistant acts of such women, and the reforms they may help to bring about, can ever really do for women, in liberal television narratives or in liberal democratic societies generally. For as political theorist Wendy Brown has noted, mere "resistance to oppressive power structures is at best politically rebellious, and at worst politically amorphous," for it is always "figured by and within rather than externally to the regimes of power it contests." Thus, it must always "stand against, not for; [for] it is [an] often spontaneous and unreflective reaction to domination." Resistance—as opposed to outright revolutionary struggle to destroy illegitimate institutions—is thus "neutral in regard to possible political direction," according to Brown. "It is the practice of freedom," but not its actual end result. In other words, reforms of various kinds may occur—or not—within the complex, always localized, power struggles of everyday life. But what Brown calls true "emancipation"—the power to act *for* oneself and determine one's own social structures and values—is proscribed by simple acts of resistance, heroic as they may be, as it is in even the best of commercial television texts.[10]

Silent Witness and *The Burning Bed* represent the best that liberal, but still politically limited, commercial media can offer progressive forces such as feminism, no matter how influential such forces may become or how much impact their ideas and values may have on media producers. For, like other liberal democratic institutions, the media are inherently and inexorably linked to the forces of power they may, at exemplary moments, resist but never escape. And so, for reasons inherent in the nature of mainstream media, resistance can only lead to a kind of reform—in production norms as well generic conventions—that does not truly upset, much less overthrow, dominant power structures. In both films, for example, there are male characters who support the women and thus represent an amended but not wholly transformed system of gendered power relations.

In *The Burning Bed,* most obviously, while Hughes does indeed speak for herself, it is within the larger context of a legal system whose reformist limits are represented by the male lawyer who, during the trial itself, speaks *for* Hughes, even as he makes it possible for her to speak for herself. And in *Silent Witness* there is a similarly accomodationist ending. It preserves, while amending, hegemonic norms even as it allows for effective resistance and possible reform as Anna's husband joins her as a witness for the prosecution, amplifying and strengthening her own voice and "truth" with his corroborating male voice and version of events. A new definition of marriage emerges in which power relations and ideological assumptions are amended and shifted, but, again, there is no suggestion that women need ask for more than that—from men in general, and the still largely male-run media or legal system in particular.

Nonetheless, with all their limitations, generically and ideologically, these two movies—and many others like them from the early 1980s—represented a significant victory for feminist forces that should not be underestimated. For it was no small thing to push the envelope of hegemonic gender norms, steadfastly in place for centuries, so far as not only to allow women to be heard and recognized in the public arena of the courtroom, but also to put forth a serious critique of American institutions that led to significant reform, if not what Brown would define as freedom. It is only when we look at what has happened to representations of gender violence, as portrayed in the 1990s versions of televised court-room drama, that we can see how advanced these liberal reformist films, and their ideas about gender violence, actually were compared to current representations and assumptions.

From Socially Empowered Women to Victims—and Avengers

As we have seen, in the years since *The Burning Bed* and *Silent Witness* were produced, American politics generally took a radical swing to the right. As this trend has intensified, there has been an interesting, and I would argue problematic, shift in both legal policy toward gender violence and media representation of it. Certainly, new laws and institutional changes—the Domestic Violence Act of 1996 and the rise of new domestic violence courts are typical of this trend—reflect the continuing attention paid to feminist issues and demands. But we may wonder, and perhaps worry, that this issue was singled out at a time when so many others were being neglected and worse. For it raises the interesting question of how the growing public and political concern about gender violence fits with the regressive, *anti*feminist tone of the period in general. Movies like *The Burning Bed* and *Silence Witness* reflect the influence of feminists in making both media and law attentive to this issue. But the wave of "women in danger" TV movies and, far more significantly, the Court TV *Crime Stories* documentaries that have replaced them, while undeniably reflecting a continuing interest in the topic also show a radically different understanding of and approach to the issue. I would argue that feminists should be cautious about embracing this approach too gratefully. For in the postliberal era in which right-wing values have ascended, attitudes toward gender violence and women generally have undergone a shift which, while subtle, is indisputably ominous. This change is most apparent in the increasingly popular "reality" genres like Court TV's *Crime Stories* series and the many imitative, documentary-style, edited-down airings of actual criminal trials that have followed in its wake. In fact, *Law and Order* producer Dick Wolf's new *Crime and Punishment* series, which always features a prosecutor as the (implied) hero, is a perfect example of the swing away from fictional series and fictionalized docudramas to the newer type of pure documentary-style legal genres. In these, the broad social sweep of series like *Law and Order* itself, or docudramas like *The Burning Bed,* give way to the far narrower arena of the courtroom itself.

From Real Life to Lifetime

Before we turn to *Crime Stories*, it is worth pausing to mourn the passing of the early docudrama of resistance and reform, and to cast a rueful eye on the Lifetime "weepies" and "women in danger" movies that have by-and-large replaced it. I want to look briefly at a series of typical Lifetime movies dating from 1993 to 1999. In them one sees, hopefully with some dismay, the reduction of feminist approaches to gender violence to mere televisual cliché, and the displacement of the earlier reformist, but still significantly progressive politics of the early films with a simplistic law-and-order "solution" in which male law enforcement officials save the damsel in distress.

One of the more intriguing aspects of this newly minted version of the genre is its links, in many cases, to the *Unsolved Mysteries* series, which, as has been noted, precedes the *Lifetime Movie* on week nights. Like *America's Most Wanted*, it re-creates horrendous crimes not yet solved and then asks viewers to help solve the case by hunting down the alleged criminal. The 1993 TV movie *Escape from Terror: The Teresa Stamper Story* tells the story of a battered wife whose crazed ex-husband could be apprehended and stopped only when Stamper put her story on *Unsolved Mysteries* and, as luck would have it, reached a (male) viewer who recognized the hunted man and led the police to him.

In many ways, this movie sticks fairly closely to the Francine Hughes story. The abused wife, a naive young working-class woman, tells her story in flashback, recalling how her husband, Paul, for whom she worked as a receptionist in his prosperous mechanical repairs office, "charmed her off [her] feet" with his irresistible charm and glamor. Showering her with flowers and expensive gifts, he soon marries her and almost immediately begins to be possessive, controlling, and abusive. While in *The Burning Bed* we learned much about the gender culture of the times, the ideology that both Fran and Mickey's families had indoctrinated into them, and the complicity of virtually all social and legal institutions in this sexist ideology, in *Escape from Terror* we get nothing of that. The man simply turns from chivalrous to monstrous overnight, and in typical horror movie acceleration of danger and terror, Teresa's every attempt to escape fails as Paul maniacally tracks her down, beats her, and escapes undetected. Teresa meets a new "good" man in this new version, and he sticks by her and her daughter. But it is the police, ultimately aided by ex-G-man Robert Stack's TV show, who finally capture him. The final scene shows the new family celebrating the little girl's birthday in what is, in this 1990s version of the genre, almost de rigueur.

Teresa, in a final statement to the audience, says she is telling her story in the hope that other women will not suffer the terror in which she lived. Of course, Francine had no such hope, since she did not even know her situation was common. But by now we all know all about it, and it is sufficient merely to go through the dramatic motions, almost in pantomime, for the audience to get the point. Only what exactly is the point? Not female empowerment certainly, since it is a group of helpful men who set Teresa free. As we shall see in the *Crime Stories* segments, it is the criminal justice system, in this case explicitly aided by a popular reality television series, that is the apparent and only solution to a problem that now most certainly has a name—a name so well understood that it is no longer necessary even to say it.

Another TV movie, *Dead before Dawn,* this one aired in 1995, is also linked to *Unsolved Mysteries,* and is even more bizarre. This time the couple is not working class but upper class, although they are again white. For as Sarah Projansky rightly notes, in postfeminist versions of gender violence, feminist issues in general are usually coded white, while the similar experiences of women of color are seen as less important or interesting to the demographics that networks like Lifetime target.[11] There is no background story at all to the abusive marriage of the wealthy Edelmans. Apparently the violence has been going on for a long time, often publicly, although the victim's parents seem to be the last to know and are—unlike Francine Hughes's family—appalled and supportive when they learn of it. The heroine files for divorce when she realizes her hopeless plight. Her mad but endlessly successful and charming husband hires a detective to find a contract killer to do away with her, and if necessary her whole family, which harbors her, simply to avoid a costly divorce settlement. Again, the FBI rides to the rescue, and the culprit is cuffed and carried off as the scene shifts to the following year, where our happy heroine and her loved ones, including the handsome FBI agent, celebrate a child's birthday.

In a 1998 update of this scenario, *Dangerous Child,* the batterer is a teenage son who has learned from his father (who is divorced from his mother) to treat his passive, permissive mother disrespectfully, and ultimately violently. As the violence escalates, the woman is endlessly seen at the emergency room. Her and her son's wounds are treated so often that she is finally questioned by the authorities and is threatened with imprisonment for child abuse. In the meantime, her best friend reassures her that all kids go through such "phases," and she fails to report the abuse to anyone. When she is finally forced to see a social worker—before the ultimate brawl in which the son is seriously injured and she is faced with criminal charges—the woman offers her some lame advice about simply leaving the house, and some sensible advice about having the boy removed from the home. The mother shrugs off that possibility. In the end, however, seeing his mother facing imprisonment, the boy breaks down and agrees to therapy, and all's well that ends well as yet another happy birthday is celebrated with yet another new Prince Charming boyfriend. The cycle-of-violence theme is here given lip service, of course. But we know all about that, we Lifetime viewers, so little is made of any social, economic, or cultural causes (except for the ubiquitous damning of black rap music). Nor is there is any explanation for why we should believe that the new "good man" will be any different from the old.

Perhaps the most interesting of these recent movies is *I Saw What You Did* (1999). This time the victim is a high-powered, successful defense attorney who defends rapists by doing what most TV defense attorneys do: crassly and cruelly attacking the victim and bringing her to tears in a successful effort to have her guilty client freed to rape again. When she herself is a victim of acquaintance rape and murders her attacker after the rape is over, she knows too well that the law will not forgive her, since she did not act in immediate self-defense but after the fact. She buries the dead body, gradually falls apart emotionally, keeps her police detective boyfriend—this time the "good man" is both a boyfriend and a rescuing cop—at arm's length, and is hounded by a blackmailer who saw her actions and continuously stalks, harasses, and extorts her.

Finally she goes to a rape crisis center pretending she is acting on behalf of "a client," where she is treated with disdain as "the enemy" and sent packing. But predictably, her boyfriend figures out what happened and captures her blackmailer. In the final scene—this one in a courtroom—she tearfully tells her story, repents her arrogant, sinful life as a defense attorney, and is given a sentence of community service in—what else—a rape crisis center.

What is most disturbing about this movie is its attack on successful, powerful women—not to mention the entire defense bar. The woman is not only saved by her policeman lover, she is brought to her knees for practicing her profession so well and made to renounce her past successes in favor of a happy-ending honeymoon and a commitment to victim advocacy. This movie uses the long-understood basics of rape and gender violence—without bothering to analyze their social, cultural, or political causes—to attack, indeed threaten, those few (mostly white) women who have actually made it in a man's world. It brings them to their knees, reducing their fragile sense of empowerment to terrorized victimhood with no hope whatsoever, except through the criminal justice system, of liberating themselves from the sexist status of victim. This, of course, was the entire point of early feminism—and earlier TV movies—when addressing this issue. Feminist readers may read a caveat into what I am saying here. A common issue discussed in clinical law school programs, where many young women have understandable reasonable doubts about the possibility of having one day to defend rapists and batterers, is: isn't it appropriate for rapists to go to jail? These young women, and feminist men, often ask how they will be able to live with themselves if they do their job properly and possibly free someone deserving of punishment—someone, perhaps, like O. J. Simpson, who many believe did in fact "beat the system" through the clever chicanery of highly skilled, much maligned lawyers. This is the same issue raised earlier in discussing *The Practice*, and the one that is the trickiest but the most important to answer. It is worth repeating that the very basis of the American legal system stands or falls on our understanding of the importance of every defendant, no matter how unsympathetic or grotesque his character or alleged actions, receiving the best possible defense.

But this issue speaks to a broader question for feminists. For even if one rejects the legal and constitutional argument that even the allegedly most guilty are given the best defense, there is still the question of whether the criminal justice system itself is the best or even an adequate solution for the greater problem of gender violence itself. Gender violence is just one of many crimes for which sexism as a system must take responsibility. This is the issue that movies like *I Saw What You Did* obscures and elides. For like much of the recent TV programming we are analyzing, it confuses the issue through the use of melodrama and horror movie conventions that code all women as powerless victims and point to the male-controlled criminal justice system, and ultimately to its ability to incarcerate convicted offenders, as the only hope women have of escaping the threat of male violence. Like the other TV movies of the 1990s, it forecloses our vision of any other alternative to this threat by simply denying, by masking out, all mention of the institutional structures through which gender violence thrives, and is in fact authorized, in sexist societies.

But is it really in our best interest as women to put our faith in this system and turn to its male heroes for protection? We have already seen how poorly the prison system—the only solution offered by the criminal justice system—works to rehabilitate criminals of any kind; how it manages, especially around issues of violence, to be more a school for career offenders than a corrective invitation that opens new doors that might lead to better lives. The implication in all of this is an essentialist view of both men and women as inherently and unalterably victims and victimizers. And its lesson is far from a liberating one. As we shall see when we turn to the real-life courtroom dramas presented in edited form on *Crime Stories*, the solution offered by the criminal justice system does little to empower women, much less end sexism. In fact, it tends to reinforce feelings of helplessness and the need for male rescue and protection.

More than that, as these movies demonstrate, the solution is tainted by an inherently race and class bias that makes the original ideal of feminism—that all women everywhere would ultimately be equally free and powerful—nearly impossible. For if even a successful, independent white attorney can be brought so low by male violence that she gives up her power in favor of the dubious protection of the male-run justice system, what hope is there for women who are less privileged? What hope indeed? As mentioned in chapter 2, the actual statistics on who is being hounded, tried, and ultimately incarcerated by the criminal justice system indicate quite clearly that it is hardly white men, especially privileged white men, who are now overcrowding our prisons. Although fictional series like the Lifetime movies, or even *Oz*, distort these statistics, when we look at real trials we cannot help but see that even Court TV cannot find enough trials to fill its daytime live trial coverage or convert to prime-time mini-docudramas. Here and in the chapters that follow, as we examine these trials and their conclusions, we will see more clearly how the world of reality television, which is an ever-increasing source of audiences and revenues for all manner of networks, does in fact come closer to presenting the class and race realities that now permeate so problematically what we call criminal justice.

Is this a positive or negative development? Given the way that these reality-based programs are produced, it cannot be considered positive, since the portrayal of working-class and minority "criminals" who make up most of those who regularly come into conflict with the criminal justice system is primarily negative. What one sees on fictional series, even such nasty fictional series as *Oz*, does not reflect the reality of the class and race makeup of those who enter criminal courtrooms and prisons. Rather, these series—for contradictory reasons—tend to exaggerate the number of white people who make up this population. On the one hand, of course, television still favors white male heroes and primary characters in general—for race-biased reasons that actors of color have long protested. But on the other hand, there is a clear concern for fictional programming with a certain kind of political correctness. Producers of fictional series tend to steer clear of charges of racism as much as possible. They have been through their troubles with feminist, black, and gay rights movement protests, many of them highly publicized, and so they make a conscious effort to avoid antagonizing the now well-organized groups and their "media-watch" branches.

What we see on Court TV, however, is, for better or worse, the real thing. And if it is a more accurate picture of who actually encounters the harsh hand of criminal justice the most, it is not a flattering picture of that population. Nonetheless, for those who are truly concerned about these matters—and I am writing this book in the hopes that many more of us will be—it provides much better documentation of what is in fact a highly class- and race-biased system.

Crime Stories: The Camera Doesn't Lie, or Does It?

The 1990s TV movies just examined differ radically in style, characterization, and narrative strategy and resolution from their predecessors. They become almost cartoonish in their black-and-white portrayals of villains, heroic rescuers, and victims-turned-avengers. Their failure to attempt to place their titillating stories in a social, much less political context, and their use of the courtroom as an arena of melodramatic highjinks or sheer violent acts, reduce them to little more than horror movies writ small.

When we turn to *Crime Stories*, however, we have a very different if equally problematic approach to issues of gender violence. While they are closer to movies like *The Burning Bed* and *Silent Witness* in the seriousness with which they portray courtroom procedures, they are—perhaps for that reason—more troubling in their ultimate ideological conclusions about how such issues of systemic sexism should best be resolved. No one, after all, takes seriously the "vengeance is mine" scenarios of recent TV movies. The villains are too cartoonish; the heroics of the women are too unbelievable; the final-frame "save" by the rescuing hero is too fairy-tale-like to give us more than a gratifying momentary fantasy of revenge, which is, after all, the main appeal of such movies. *Crime Stories* and the gavel-to-gavel coverages of the actual trials from which they are derived differ from the 1980s movies discussed earlier far more radically. They are meant to be taken much more seriously, since they are, after all, "reality" genres in which, as in series like *Cops*, the camera apparently does not lie (even though it certainly, if slyly, edits and editorializes).

Like the 1980s TV movies about gender violence, *Crime Stories* centers on courtroom processes and decisions. But while the early docudramas do so in ways which place the courtroom and the criminal justice system in the broader context of personal narratives and social institutions, Court TV, by its very nature, locates its drama far more narrowly within the arena of the legal process itself. Only the briefest and most limited view or discussion of the broader context within which the alleged criminal act occurred is given. There are, for example, brief talking-head interviews with attorneys, jurors, and other interested parties, but they focus almost exclusively on opinions about the process itself, and—due to the nature of Court TV—tend to present "both sides" with no particular slant in either direction. In fact, if there is a bias to the series and to Court TV as a whole, it is—as the justices who allowed the trials to be televised originally hoped—toward the validity and credibility of the system itself. Women are certainly allowed to speak in these trials, but their voices and experiences are heard only within the context of legal discourse and process. And such discourse and process are primarily constructed to reflect the interests of (male) power and authority, for which the concerns of women figure only if and when they serve those interests. The idea is to show that the system works, after all, and not, certainly, that it is in need of reform.

One sees this most clearly in the narrative points of view of the two forms. In the classic TV movies, it was the woman and her representatives whose point of view was central. But on Court TV, although the jury cannot be shown on screen, it is this group of twelve citizens, the defendant's "peers," who—along with the judge—are the representatives of the "collective conscience," empowered with the awesome authority to judge and punish. Henry Louis Gates captures the significance of this situation when he describes the jury as "a symbol of popular and local sovereignty" empowered with the authority to "confer legitimacy upon the most invasive thing a State can do: strip a person of life, liberty or property."[12] On Court TV in general, it is this sense of the awesome and always legitimate authority of the state and its representatives that most solidly grounds the representations of crime and punishment. The system itself cannot be questioned or critiqued, as in docudramas about social issues.

This displacement of the contesting narratives of "truth" presented by opposing attorneys with the sovereign authority of judge and jury creates a dramatic arena in which the questions to be asked and answered give a very different spin to the implications of a woman's power to have a voice and have her experiences heard and credited. This is nowhere more clearly demonstrated than in the *Crime Stories* series. Briefly, the structure of the series is as follows. The commentator introduces the story and lays out the issues and questions that must be answered and resolved by hour's end. The basic structure of a criminal trial is then followed: opening arguments; prosecutor's case and the cross-examination of her or his witnesses; defense case and cross; closing arguments; verdict; and, in some cases, the penalty phase in which the sentence is determined. Interspersed in this documentary footage are, perhaps, a few shots of the crime site or other relevant background sites or objects, interviews with participants, and the ongoing comments of the narrator, who throughout the hour, points the viewer toward the ultimate moment of closure: the verdict.

It is important to note that trials take place not only after the entire background stories and situations which led to the crime have occurred, but also after the various back-room negotiations and motions among attorneys, defendants, and judges have taken place. Thus we get an extremely truncated version of "the truth," no matter who is "swearing" to tell it. There is none of the social, cultural, or economic context we get in serious TV movies, in which both victim and accused are presented at a level of complexity and depth that allows the conditions which led to the act to be understood. For even the rapists and wife batterers of our docudramas were seen as products of a sexist social environment which at once empowered and authorized their acts, even as it often deprived them of other more important forms of social power because of class or race.

But *Crime Stories* and Court TV generally, like the current legal system itself, exist at a time in history when the reforms demanded by early feminists have already been largely acknowledged. A victim's right to speak, her right to have her abuse taken seriously no matter what her social class or lifestyle, and her right to have her injuries recognized and punished as crimes are—at least in principle if not always in practice—now inscribed in law. Thus, the portrayal of trials involving gender violence, in which "justice" is seen to be achieved, raises complicated issues for feminists, since law and order, stiff prison terms and conditions, and victims' rights to retribution and revenge have become rallying cries for right-wing forces. For while, in all these trials, the attorneys certainly and explicitly use feminist arguments to make their cases, the demands they, and their clients, make on the larger society are far from what feminist political theorists like Wendy Brown would define as emancipatory.

Feminist Justice as Seen on TV

To compare the TV movies of the early 1980s with the televised trials of the 1990s, let us look briefly at a typical *Crime Stories* segment dealing with domestic violence.[13] In *Ohio v. Redding*, a case in which a woman and her teenage son went on trial for murdering the man they claim was an abusive husband and father for many years. The segment is entitled "Death of a Father: A Battered Woman Defense" and begins with the commentator giving harrowing statistics about the incidence of domestic abuse in America. Thus, the "issue" of domestic violence is made clear from the start. But there is something odd about the *way* in which it is incorporated into the narrative of judgment and punishment. For it is always employed, by defense or prosecution attorneys, in the context of a system of justice in which evidence, witness testimony, and legal precedent are dominant, and social or political issues subservient. Indeed, there is, I would argue, something uncomfortably opportunistic about the way in which the new acknowledgment of rape and domestic violence as criminal offenses is employed by most attorneys. For what is at issue is invariably "Who did what to whom and why?" And attorneys only bring in feminist phrases and assumptions when and if it suits their purposes: to persuade a jury to convict or acquit.

It is also important to note that in the vast majority of *Crime Stories* involving rape and domestic violence I examined, women accused of murdering abusive partners were almost always African American and/or working class, and they were, almost invariably, convicted. And similarly, in rape cases in which the victim is of color, sexually "suspect" in some way, or in any way of a lower social station than the man accused, the defendant generally goes free. The most notorious and early of these cases involved an alleged rapist belonging to a particularly prominent upper-class family and an accusing victim who was white and middle class: the case of *Florida v. Smith*, in which William Kennedy Smith, a cousin of the illustrious Kennedy clan, was the defendant. In this case, the woman bringing charges was a respectable professional woman whom Kennedy met at a bar frequented by the "beautiful people" of Palm Beach. According to the plaintiff, Kennedy invited her to a party at the family compound and then proceeded, during a stroll on the beach, to viciously rape her, tearing at her pricey Ann Taylor dress and Victoria's Secret underthings—items which became titillating exhibits that were endlessly passed around to the jury and shown on TV screens. As is typical in rape trials, the plaintiff's character was attacked. She was, it was "revealed," a friend of the bartender at the bar where they met and where, as he testified, she dropped in on occasion, usually dressed casually in jeans and a sweater. Nothing much more could be found to defame her. And still, when the Kennedys, including Senator Ted Kennedy—armed with a high-rent law team and jury consultant—appeared as prosecution witnesses, there was a clear sense of awe in the courtroom and even among media commentators.[14] Among other things, the family's proud history of public service and personal tragedy was invoked. The plaintiff, a virtual "nobody" compared to the man she was accusing, was humiliated and the prosecution defeated. Such is the importance of gender and class difference, even when a white professional woman brings charges, in the most typical criminal cases involving gender violence. Similarly, in the case of *Ohio v. Mesa*, the Cleveland Indians' star pitcher, Jose Mesa, was quickly acquitted of rape charges brought by one of the many women fans he had dated. In these cases, television functions in a way that certainly reinforces race, class, and gender biases inherent in American society and, unlike the 1980s movies discussed, it does nothing to correct for those biases, for the cases themselves did not allow for such corrections.

In less glamorous cases—no matter what the class or race status of the principal—it is always a good bet that the person of higher status will win out against the socially less privileged. And when race or class are not at issue, it is generally the woman who will come out with the short end of the legal stick. In the very typical case of *Florida v. Trice*, for example, a lower-working-class woman claiming self-defense in her trial for the murder of her abusive husband was quickly convicted in a trial in which both partners were portrayed, by prosecutors and witnesses, as prone to drink, abusive language, and mutually violent altercations. That the defendant herself could show medical records of her long history of abuse did not influence the jury, who—apparently swayed by the unsavory portrayal of Ms. Trice—convicted her. Indeed, this rule of thumb is broken only when the behavior of the defendants has already been documented as too egregious to ignore, as in the cases of long-term serial killers such as Ted Bundy or Harold Rolling (*Florida v. Rolling*) or in the case of the kidnap, torture, rape, and murder of Michelle McGrath by a drug abuser named Thomas Gudinas (*Florida v. Gudinas*). Thus, again, the televising of such trials serves uncritically to portray a system in which "justice," as the courts define it, is achieved at the expense of the least powerful and articulate among us. And the more one watches such trials, the more one sees such versions of "justice."

Another interesting trend in cases involving gender abuse and violence involves the legal and media treatment of women who break with "gender norms" in committing crimes that are more typical of men. The most notorious of these is the case of *Florida v. Wuornos*. Wuornos, "the first female serial killer," a woman with an undeniable history of amazingly brutal abuse, abandonment, and violence at the hands of men, was working as a prostitute on freeway intersections, picking up men for quick sex and money. On a few occasions, not surprisingly considering the nature of her work, her johns turned violent and aggressive and allegedly raped her quite brutally. Her response was to fight back in what she claimed was self-defense. In more than one case, the man was killed. The case certainly was sordid, but no more so, surely, than the far more frequent cases of male serial rapist/murderers in whose cases self-defense was not even an issue. Still, Wuornos was vilified by the media and the jury, and sentenced to death. Even at her execution, in October 2002, the media had a field day with this by now clearly deranged woman who, as a final statement, vowed to return in a spaceship. In interviews with the wives of her victims, the press tended to quote the most vengeful of interviewees rather than any of Wuornos's friends.[15] When asked if she thought justice had been done and she had achieved "closure," one such woman, for example, said, "Yes, I feel satisfied now that she is dead, even if she is a whacko." Television footage included similar interviews.

Less gruesome cases involving women who break gender taboos by seducing students similarly tend to enrage and offend jurors. As in the case of the accused in *Oregon v. Mary Beth LeTourneau*, now imprisoned for her affair with a sixth-grade student, and in *Massachusetts v. Cross*, imprisoned for her affair with one of her high school students, penalties are severe enough, arguably, to reflect the bias of jurors against women who take the lead in sexual relations with younger males. In these cases, women are treated as particularly monstrous by the media, in comparison with the far greater number of male teachers—and, as we now know, clergy—whose similar behavior is often simply accepted by those who know about their affairs. Even when prosecuted, they are treated with far less vitriol than when the genders are reversed. Indeed, such are the privileges patriarchy so often confers on males.

The Exception That Proves the Rule

It is in this context of gender, race, and class bias that the case of *Georgia v. Redding* must be understood. For this case is a rarity in the system by virtue of its very unusual and fortuitous—for the victims if not the defendant—reversal of the classic race, class, and gender biases inherent in the criminal justice system. For this reason, its symbolic status as a true "feminist victory" needs to be looked at in a more complex way than many feminists—and certainly Court TV and its generic formula—allow. For it raises problematic issues of race and class bias in the criminal justice system—and in society in general—which seriously question the political value to women of such a strategy. The problem it poses is twofold: first, if the system only favors women of a higher social status than the men they accuse, is it truly "feminist"—in the sense that feminism generally stands for equal justice for *all* women, not merely a privileged few; and second—and this problem will be dealt with in greater detail below— is the criminal justice system, as an arm of the patriarchal state, an arena in which *any* outcome can be seen to further the struggle for female freedom, equality, and justice?

Georgia v. Redding is indeed an extraordinary and moving example of a certain kind of feminist victory. Like movies made in the 1980s, it offers a clear and unusual sense of feminist-inflected victory to viewers. But the definition of "feminist victory" becomes problematic in this highly watchable and moving trial. The case involved the rapes of two women, living only blocks apart, within a period of two months. They join forces to bring their attacker to justice, a process that takes seven years of passionate, continuous agitation and litigation. In this case, the victims did indeed receive "justice" and wept tears of joy at the successful conviction of their alleged attacker.

Again, the segment begins with horrifying statistics about rape in America. As in *Ohio v. Redding*, a series of talking-head interviews show the abused women describing the horrors and shedding copious tears of anguish at the painful memories. But in this case, the women are far more articulate and compelling for reasons that reveal some of the contradictions of feminist involvement with the criminal justice system as an ally and protector. Kathy Winkler, the more articulate of the two and the one whose words are given more airtime, is a white feminist professor of anthropology. During her ordeal, which lasted three and a half hours, she tried to reason and plead with her attacker, to no avail. Hettie Bennett, the other victim, is a working-class single mother who also tells a horrifying tale of being raped within earshot of her sleeping daughter for an unendurably long time. The defendant, a black man, sits silently throughout the trial and has only his mother to beg for his life after he is convicted. "He ain't no saint," she tells the court sadly, "but he is not capable of the things he was accused of."

As in the previous trial, the better part of the hour is taken up with legal details, mostly involving DNA testing and the inability of the two women to positively identify Redding as the perpetrator. As it turns out, the hours of scientific testimony on DNA—which, as viewers of the O. J. Simpson case will remember, can easily put a jury to sleep or leave them totally confused—is inconclusive. But the passionate testimony of the women—especially Winkler, who cries, "How can they believe science over a woman's word?" in one of her talking-head interviews—finally wins out, and the "reasonable doubt" that is Redding's only hope is overridden by the jurors' belief in the women's stories. "I feel like I've died and gone to heaven," says Bennett when the guilty verdict comes in and the women embrace and cry.

Mae West, Feminism, and the Not-So-Liberal State

In the proceedings described above, then, we have a case in which virtually every demand feminists have made upon the legal system for reform of rape law has been met. Women are heard, their pain and anguish are displayed as "legal events," and their demands for justice are granted. Indeed, the trial is particularly moving because—as in *Silent Witness*—we have a deep bonding between women of very different stations in life around the issue of rape. Their alleged attacker is put away for life; indeed he is given five consecutive life sentences with no chance of parole and will never again see the light of day outside the prison gates. But what, in the end, have women won through this admittedly moving spectacle of judgment and punishment? Have they achieved any significant reform of the sexist institutions that are so clearly addressed in the TV movies discussed? Have they in any way contributed to the kind of emancipation and control over the conditions of their lives that Wendy Brown defines as true freedom? Have they, indeed, freed themselves in any sense from the disciplinary control of the masculinist state?

I would argue that what they have won is a moral victory of a particularly Durkheimian kind. They have managed forcefully to dramatize and reinforce—in the public arena of the courtroom, and then the television screen—the idea that gender violence is a moral outrage against the collective conscience of the community, and thus a "crime" to be publicly condemned and punished. But on another level, they have allowed themselves to be defined, by the state, as victims in need of protection and rescue. Moreover, as Alison Young has rightly noted, they have joined a community in which belonging and membership are based on a sense of "shared victimization" and "shared awareness of risk and danger."[16] That in fact is the very basis of their feminist bonding. But perhaps most troubling are the political implications of the turn to the courtroom for redress of feminist grievances. For, as Brown suggests, there is something "profoundly undemocratic . . . in transferring from the relatively accessible sphere of popular contestation to the highly restricted sphere of juridical authority the project of representing politicized identity and adjudicating its . . . demands."[17]

Thus, I would argue, in taking up the feminist demand for redress of gender violence, the state has gained more *from* women than we have gained from it. For unless you are of the mind that vengeance and punishment are a "good enough" ending to women's harrowing stories of rape and battery, and that moral victory is a "good enough" remedy for sexist oppression, there is simply too much that is still ignored, denied and distorted in this kind of "happy ending," for women and men alike. For if we treat sexual offenders and batterers as merely and essentially "evil," and women as in need of nothing more than protection or revenge by the state, where have our demands gone for ending sexism, much less for the freedom to determine the terms by which our lives, in general, are lived?

In *The Burning Bed* and *Silent Witness*, whatever their flaws and limits, the idea was that men too were social products of a sexist society, which, once restructured, might well produce very different individuals. Indeed, at one point, the idea that Mickey Hughes might need therapy is even suggested. "Mickey needs help," Francine pleads to her in-laws, and his mother even agrees that "he ain't been right" for a while. But when the father, in predictably patriarchal fashion, vows that "no son of mine is going to no mental hospital" and actually leaves home for several weeks, in outrage at his wife's view that their son needs help, such a "solution" is never again mentioned. Nonetheless, it is raised within the text as a possible avenue of relief in a way that rarely occurs in *Crime Stories*, since issues of treatment and rehabilitation are beyond the scope of what is usually at issue in a trial. Indeed, in both movies the men are presented as opaque, mute, socially decontextualized presences whose only identification is in terms of their "alleged" acts of violence. Thus the essentialist notion of male violence as an inherent, defining characteristic is, if not explicit, dramatically *im*plicit. We women are left to deal with our legitimate fears in no way except through the processes of judgment and extreme, preferably permanent, punishment. Get them off the streets, is the cry of the day. And so we do, in such large numbers in the black community that family and community dysfunction—not to mention the burden on taxpayers—has grown to alarming levels.

The politics of victimization is thus, I would argue, in many ways the antithesis of the politics of feminist emancipation. For, as Lauren Berlant has argued, such a "politics of sentimentality" depends on "revelations of trauma, incitements to rescue, the reprivatization of victims as the ground of hope," and the assumption that "the nation's duty [is] to eradicate . . . painful feelings,"[18] rather than end sexism itself. Indeed, far from suggesting that women should be free to "play house with the world," as Simone de Beauvoir once put it, and remold it in their own interests, such a politics tacitly accepts the legitimacy and authority of the state and relies upon it for protection and redress of suffering. But, as Brown argues, "Whether one is dealing with the state, the Mafia, pimps, police, or husbands, the heavy price of institutionalized protection is always a measure of dependence and agreement to abide by the protector's rules." For "institutionalized police protection necessarily entails surrendering individual and collective power to legislate and adjudicate for ourselves in exchange for external guarantees of physical security." But there is a cruel irony in such a bargain. For "to be protected by the very power one fears, perpetuates dependence and powerlessness."[19]

Of course, this is an old feminist debate, or schism, perhaps the first serious sign that the apparent utopian harmony of second-wave feminist sisterhood might, over time, become an arena of struggle over political and ideological differences. In this case, as Brown notes in an analysis of Catharine MacKinnon's feminist theories, the issue might be posed in terms of freedom versus security. For MacKinnon and her followers—as Brown reads them—believe that in a sexist society "women need protection more than freedom."[20]

These are honest disagreements and important debates among feminists. However, I am suggesting that the debate has taken on a very different meaning at the turn of the century than it did when it first arose in the 1970s. For we are living in a time—far different from the 1970s—in which the political cry of the day, from Democrats and Republicans alike, is for stiffer penalties for lesser crimes, more prisons and prisoners generally (the fastest-growing segment of whom are women), more executions for more and more legal infringements previously considered lesser crimes, incarceration of younger and younger offenders in adult prisons, and so on. The state, in this context, cannot be seen—as theorists such as MacKinnon tend to do—as a friend and protector, much less emancipator, of women. On the contrary, any alliance with the powers that be must be seriously interrogated. For in a state dedicated to incarcerating more and more people, particularly those who fall into the categories of the powerless—the poor, the sexually "different," the non-white, and certainly the female—the role of victim is a necessary evil. It serves the needs of a government intent on punishment and incapacitation, which today are becoming the primary rationales for imprisonment, according to criminologist Franklin Zimring.[21]

Therefore, it is increasingly dangerous for all progressive people, especially feminists, to fall into the trap of playing the victim role, no matter how victimized we may in fact have been by a male abuser. In the context of current political and ideological trends, we need to think about the larger implications, for all Americans, of giving up the early struggle of left-leaning feminists for true emancipation in favor of a retreat into the "protective" arms of a state whose policies are increasingly driven by essentialist notions of evil, the valorization of victimhood and victimization, and the desire to see—literally *see*—punishment administered as a form of vengeance against the alien "Other." It is as elementary as Feminism 101 that women are and will always be the "Other" in a sexist state. And for that reason, we can never allow ourselves to feel too safe under its "protective" wings.

6

Television and
Family Dysfunction
From the Talk Show to the Courtroom

Of all the issues we have so far examined, there is none which has a more chilling potential to affect all of us than the topic of this chapter: the criminalization of family relations. For once laws are set in place—as they increasingly are—which provide for criminal indictment and punishment of family members merely because of accusations made by neighbors, children, spouses or partners, we are indeed on very shaky ground. Children can and are being taken from parents; and parents can and are being imprisoned for behaviors and situations which, until very recently, were seen as the purview of such extralegal professionals as the clergy, the social worker, and most recently the therapist.

That such cases are increasingly being televised on Court TV and made into particularly moving and melodramatic *Crime Stories* is not surprising. After all, as in so many of the issues we have examined—violence, victimization, out-of-control youth—family dysfunction is a particularly appropriate and effective topic for the most popular of television genres and styles: melodrama. As we have seen, even law series such as *Law and Order* and *The Practice* have often relied on family dysfunction as the basis for the criminal cases featured. But of all these issues and genres, none is more indicative of the trend toward pushing the envelope of criminal law to a more and more chillingly inclusive realm of behaviors. It is revealing in the particular way in which television genres and conventions have aided in this trend by increasingly focusing on families, in their every day interactions, as sites of criminal activity.

Readers are likely to have heard of this topic far less, so far, than gender issues or youth violence. Nonetheless, it is a trend to be watched carefully, for it is a particularly ominous sign of the times, and one which, for all the reasons given in previous chapters, is likely to strike a sympathetic chord in the hearts and minds of television viewers and citizens concerned not only about crime, but about "the breakdown of the family."

Television and the Preservation of "Family Values"

Family narratives and dramas, including television commercials, in which typical family problems are solved by providing "proper" models of healthy family life, have been an important mainstay of television programming since its establishment in the 1950s. Whether through endless discussions between Ward and June Cleaver about "a problem with the Beaver," or through the equally endless commercials in which the proper detergent or breakfast cereal is seen to heal overly dramatized moments of marital and generational discord, television has always been in the business of keeping families together in decades of increasingly stressful and difficult social tensions and turmoil. Commercial products have been one of the most obvious (if absurd) "solutions" offered for obvious reasons. But the other, more serious, format for shoring disintegrating families has been entertainment programming—from sitcoms to, most recently, daytime talk shows.

To view this trend historically is to understand its logic and to see most clearly that above all else, television, in the face of rising divorce and delinquency rates, has assumed the role of primary socializer. It is replacing the increasingly weakened role of the patriarchal head of household with a corporate-based, media "voice of authority." In fact, television arrived on the scene during the post–World War II era in which major upheavals in lifestyles, workplaces, and living arrangements, due to postindustrialism, were causing increasing stress and strain on traditional family norms. The invention of television—a medium actually available since the 1930s but not adopted until the postwar, postindustrial 1950s—appeared as a godsend to those trying valiantly to keep order in their lives. The traditional ways of doing things had—by then—been sorely disrupted by the radical economic and social changes wrought by industrialization and the new corporate world order.[1]

Television, then, was always more than an entertainment form in America. The original draw to buy television sets may well have been early sitcoms like *The Honeymooners*, *The Life of Riley*, and *The Gold-*

bergs, which featured working-class, often immigrant, families and cultures. But it is no accident that these early shows were quickly replaced by others—*Father Knows Best, Leave It to Beaver, The Donna Reed Show*—which presented the dominant model of an upscale, traditional, white, suburban nuclear family whose lives revolved, implicitly or explicitly, around ideals of success and consumer living. For these were far more ideologically consistent with the needs of sponsors and government regulators in their pushing of middle-class norms of consumption and family order. Thus television, from the start, was set up as an institution through which Americans, while living through social and cultural upheaval and change, might be informed about, and socialized into, the brave new world of postindustrial democracy. The white male patriarchal figures who figured most prominently on TV screens—the newscasters, the sitcom heads of household, the well-known celebrities (Ronald Reagan was one such, in his role as host of *GE Theater*) who served as corporate spokesmen—public mentors and role models. The brought and interpreted news of the new world order, and acted out, for the public's edification, the new roles that men and women, boys and girls, were meant to play in it.

Nonetheless, the very fact that early television programmers felt the need to stress the still-central role of fathers and patriarchy was a sign of the already straining internal contradictions and weaknesses of the traditional model of family life in the new era. The role of early television was, after all, to shore up the old images of family unity and male domination and authority against the growing pressures—built into the new economic order—that were tearing it apart. Among the most obvious of television's contradictions, from the start—and its greatest difference from theatrical films, which generally assumed a male viewer and male worldview—is its emphasis on family viewers and the implicit assumption that the audience is a member of a family. In a medium built for home consumption and intent on hailing us all as nuclear family members, it was assumed implicitly that "father" was the head of the household. Television was built upon this idea as much as on the need to preserve the family, but the switch to a consumerist economy made *mother*, not *father*, the key target of the TV announcer's messages. But perhaps equally important to the networks and the FCC was the increasingly difficult role of women in the family as socializers of children, in which the "generation gap" and the rise of teen rebellion and juvenile delinquency became increasingly problematic.

This promise was hard to keep, however, especially in the realm of gender and family relations and assumptions. For the politicized personal and sexual issues and controversies raised by feminists in the 1960s and 1970s have gone to the heart of the most basic ways in which we live and think about our lives. The public-sphere role of television—as gatekeeper, agenda setter, and negotiator of these matters—is crucial in such troubling times if we are to maintain any semblance of a politically and socially unified and coherent national identity. The maintenance of traditional family norms and values is at the heart of these issues. Thus, it is far from surprising that family themes have continued to play a central role on television. Nor is it surprising that, as the social fabric becomes more and more fragile, not only sitcoms but crime series themselves have focused attention on the family's role in maintaining or tearing more fiercely at the fabric of our social unity and harmony. Where the cops and lawyers of early television had no personal lives, since the 1980s the cop and law series have, like the rest of television, focused more and more attention on the symbiotic relationship between the personal and the public, in the lives of criminals as well as crime fighters.

Indeed, the more the realities of American domestic life have belied the harmony and joy of marriage and family life, and as gender and generational relations have grown more and more strained and even hostile, the more difficult and complicated the role of TV producers has become. How does one keep up with obvious shifts in American lifestyles while still maintaining essential family and social values? It has not been an easy puzzle to solve, and television's producers have been forced to work vigorously and cleverly to update their product and incorporate, and then recuperate, family and gender changes into their programming. They have had to incorporate the changes in social life due to both social and political forces, and to still maintain and reinforce dominant hegemonic messages about American life and its norms and values.

The difficulties facing programmers can easily be seen in the often tortured and contradictory texts that were increasingly produced for post-1960s American television. Sitcoms especially reveal the faultlines in American social and cultural life and TV's efforts to manage and control them. In the 1970s, TV produced updated sitcoms. For example, *The Brady Bunch* featured a "blended" family made up of the six children of two previously married parents. The Norman Lear–produced sitcoms such as *All in the Family*, *One Day at a Time*, and *Good Times* featured, respectively, a family racked with political and generational conflict, a family run by a single mother, and an African American inner-city family. They put forth images of nontraditional families struggling to survive under the many pressures of social change.

Even more prominent were sitcoms like *The Mary Tyler Moore Show* and *Julia*, which featured single working women as protagonists and showed the clear stamp of feminist influence on TV programming. This trend, started in the 1970s, has continued to be of profound importance. Among the most popular and long-lived 1990s series, for example, were *Roseanne*, about a working-class family with a powerful female heroine, and *Murphy Brown*, about a powerful TV news program anchor who is also a single mother by choice. The last two decades have also seen such shows as *Who's the Boss?* which featured a male housekeeper employed by a female executive, and the *The Cosby Show*, which featured an African American family headed by a physician father and a corporate-lawyer mother. All these programs were very far from standard 1950s white, middle-class family norms and they gained huge success. But no matter how unconventional the family and gender roles portrayed were, these shows always ended on the same point of hegemonic consensus: no matter how things change, we can accommodate ourselves to new situations and demands without really changing the basic structure of things—the basic rules about power and money and decision making.

Talk Shows and the Crisis of the Family

Ultimately, however, it has been a losing battle. Families and relationships on cop shows are hardly models of domestic or sexual bliss. Indeed, anyone who has been paying attention knows that the era of the classic family sitcom came to an end in the 1990s. With the demise of *The Cosby Show*, the best example of this classic format, and *Father Knows Best*, the middle-class format that was always dominant, the idea that the family still looked like the Cleavers or Andersons—intact nuclear families in which family problems were predictable and could be easily contained and resolved within the simplistic conventions of the thirty-minute sitcom—was no longer credible.

In fact, with the coming of Aaron Spelling's mold-breaking *Beverly Hills 90210*, in which teenagers were seen to be very much on their own as parents receded into the irrelevant distance, sitcoms and dramatic series geared to young audiences generally began to avoid all mention of family issues. Instead, they favored idealized images of teenagers and young adults doing just fine on their own, with no connection to family, much less family values, at all. As a listing of the hit series of the last decades of the century demonstrate—from *Seinfeld*, *Friends*, and *Ellen* to *Felicity*, *Dawson's Creek*, and the campy *Buffy the Vampire Slayer*—the sitcom had by then become a genre in which families no longer even existed except as an occasional nuisance, when Mom and Dad decide to visit. In all these shows, the lead characters were either teens relating primarily to their peers, or young people living together in an extended period of prolonged adolescent irresponsibility—free of family, job, or child-rearing woes.

Interestingly enough, and perhaps not surprisingly, the events of September 11, 2001, seem to have ushered in a resurgence of new family sitcoms that are far closer to the classic model than the series just mentioned. In fact, while the new season that fall saw only three family sitcoms make the list of the top thirty series among the coveted 18–49-year-old demographic, the fall 2002 season saw nine such series make the list. But even these series, as reassuringly wholesome and comforting as they are, do not necessarily portray traditional nuclear families. Even when they do, they do not portray them as free of such issues as sex, drugs, and even violence. A series like *Everwood*, for example, which is perhaps the most striking example of a series attempting to revive wholesome family values, still deals with serious parenting issues such as drugs and sex. Indeed, the very title of another such wholesome series, *8 Simple Rules for Dating My Teenage Daughter*, has a clear undercurrent of sexual anxiety and uncertainty. And series like *Life with Bonnie* and *The Gilmore Girls* deal with far from conventional family life. In portraying the trials of single motherhood combined with career anxieties and tensions that arise when a single mother has a sex life or a child faces the serious problems that today's kids and teenagers do face, they recognize that raising a family—even a very functional, happy family—is fraught with pitfalls and conflicts not seen in earlier eras when family series were most popular.

This desire for cultural comfort food may or may not last. Even if it does, the breakdown of family life and its many areas of strife, confusion, and conflict is—and has long been—a real fact of American life. All the happy faces on the TV screens of the nation cannot simply make them disappear with the wave of a virtual wand. It is still with us on the many law series we have already looked at, in which, as we have seen in the ever

more popular *Law and Order* franchise and *The Practice*, family problems are very much at the heart of the darker, more serious legal programs. And, as we shall see, they increasingly are also in the real courtrooms of America.

But back in the 1970s, when television first began to treat these issues
as major fodder for their corporate mills, family dysfunction was treated
very differently from what we are now seeing on courtroom dramas and
in live televised courtrooms. In fact, the daytime talk show genre, which
was so amazingly popular until quite recently, dealt almost exclusively
with family and relationship issues of the most disturbing kinds. Starting
with the *Phil Donahue Show* but reaching its peak of popularity and influence in the 1980s, with the rise of *Oprah*, *Geraldo*, and *Sally Jessy
Raphael*—and their many, increasingly sleazy clones, from *Montel* to
Jenny Jones to *Ricki Lake*—it was the daytime talk show that replaced
the sitcom as the major public sphere through which family crises of all
kinds were dealt with and "resolved."

It is important to note the distinct differences between the traditional
family drama or sitcom and the relatively new talk show genre. For one
thing, talk shows, like *Crime Stories*, feature real people with real, very
often serious problems. In fact, with shows like *Oprah* (which still exists
but has pretty much given up on family trauma in favor of celebrity ha-
giography, spiritual uplift, and guest makeovers), *Geraldo*, and *Sally
Jessy*, the whole issue of "family problems," as traditionally defined by
commercial televison, took a radical turn. No more the Beaver's squab-
bles with friends or the Cosby kids' desire for more expensive consumer
items than they already had. Now we were seeing families in which incest, domestic violence, homosexuality, addictions, juvenile delinquency—from theft to prostitution—and any number of unusual family
arrangements, from bisexual threesomes to polygamous households,
were featured. And while these more sensational sexual themes were the
segments most commonly cited by critics who saw these shows as ex-
ploitative and overly sensational, the very fact that real people involved
in nontraditional family arrangements were seen on television telling
their stories in their own words was unsettling for reasons beyond mere
sensationalism. For what these shows did—beyond making lots of money
for sponsors because for their sensationalism—was to blow the lid off the
traditional TV version of American family life as at best idyllic and at
worst troubled in easily manageable ways. Now we saw trouble, real
trouble, in American homes. And if it was usually working-class families

who chose to go on these shows and air their dirty linen, one need only to listen in office, coffee shop, and supermarket conversations about "the latest *Oprah*" to realize that many of these shows—particularly the ones featuring problems with children and spouses—struck a nerve with more upscale viewers. In fact, while most people are reluctant to admit to watching these shows, it takes very little prodding to get them to inadvertently admit to a far greater familiarity with them than they would like to admit. Of course, they are hard to avoid in hospital and car repair waiting rooms and other such public places. But the interest they compel cannot be attributed to mere curiosity or "captivity." For, like the docudramas we examined, these shows, if in a far less classy way, indeed touch a nerve with many of us whose family troubles are rarely openly discussed but are nonetheless all too common.

Most noticeable when watching the earlier versions of the daytime talk show—what distinctively distinguishes them from the *Father Knows Best* simplicity of the traditional sitcom—is its reliance on therapeutic discourse to describe, analyze, and offer "cures" for the family problems presented by guests. Also noticeable is the important role played by the audience members as major players in the "working out" of the issues raised. Like an unruly, Alice-in-Wonderland mad tea party, the audiences for these shows serve as a kind of unofficial "jury" deliberating and debating among themselves the culpability and just resolutions of the guests on stage. Theirs, however, is never the final word. For the host or hostess and the necessarily present "expert"—a therapist or self-help book author—always have the last word. And their "word" is invariably couched in the terminology of therapeutic discourse. Families are now "dysfunctional," and "toxic." Relationships are "codependent" or "addictive." In fact, the language of the 12 Step/Anonymous programs set up originally to help alcoholics "recover," but now used by no fewer than five hundred different "fellowships" to describe and treat everything from eating disorders, gambling problems, "shopaholism," and cosmetic surgery, has become a lingua franca of American culture. We all find ourselves using it to describe our own and our friends lives. This is because the language itself is truly useful in describing—if not curing—so many family and interpersonal issues common to postindustrial, millennial society.[2]

In their earliest incarnations, these shows combined a canny mix of pseudo-therapy and pseudo-jury trial. For their rationale, they relied on a set of assumptions about human behavior and its flaws that characterized the liberal democratic assumptions of criminal justice policy and law series like *Law and Order* that characterized 1980s courtrooms and tele-vision programming. By the mid-1990s, however, this train of thought, even on the more serious talk shows like *Oprah*, had begun to reveal sub-tle shifts in focus away from therapeutic expertise to issues of criminal punishment. Like the examples of *Crime Stories* segments examined in the previous chapter, this shift first appeared as a more or less balanced ideological struggle between two contesting versions of how to under-stand and treat troubled families and children. But as time went on, the stress on punishment began to prevail. By the late 1990s, as actual crim-inal trials became so popular, the shows themselves had increasingly lost their audiences. They either died, became bizarre fighting matches like *The Jerry Springer Show*, or shifted very far from family problems of all kinds to focus, as Oprah has done, on puff pieces, makeovers, and "high-brow" plugs for serious novels. But the family problem genre did not dis-appear. As with youth crime and gender violence, it was taken over by the *Crime Stories* series, in which therapeutic discourse virtually disappeared and harsh and vengeful criminal punishments were handed down to un-happy parents and parents-to-be for the kinds of flaws and errors previ-ously treated as therapeutically "curable."

I am certainly not arguing that therapeutic discourses on addiction and "damaged inner children" are adequate to solve anyone's problems, and certainly not the really serious ones most often presented on these shows. For what talk shows and therapeutic discourse never address are the larger forces—sexism, class bias, racism—that put such conditions in place. All they can offer as "help" are the clichés of self-help, a set of ax-ioms that invariably assume that one's problems can be solved merely by one's own changed attitudes and behaviors. There is never a suggestion that the larger social structure needs to be altered so that this kind of fam-ily trauma and abuse might no longer seem either permissible or be one's only option for gaining, power, respect, status, love.

Nonetheless, I *would* argue that despite these serious limitations, the language of therapy—with its optimistic sense that even the most dam-aged among us is capable of change; that even the most fractured of human relations can be healed; that even the most grievous of disputes and hostilities can be resolved and reconciled—has some advantage over the alternative that has replaced it: criminalization, punishment, and the "closure" that supposedly comes with vengeance. It may never solve the ultimate problems at the root of family, generational, and social discord. Indeed, if it could, it is highly unlikely that corporate sponsors would put it on the air. After all, once the problems of American life are solved, who will buy the Excedrin? The point is that, as with the criminal justice system itself, there has been a dramatic sea change in the last decade of the twentieth century in which admittedly faulty, limited, and often disingenuous liberal approaches to social problems of all kinds have given way to a far worse alternative. We now have the pessimistic and punitive approach to all such problems in which rehabilitation, the possibility of human redemption, and the commitment to provide social resources to make such possibilities real have been almost entirely renounced.

To see how this has happened, it is instructive to look at a few examples from early *Oprah* and *Sally* segments and compare them to typical segments from the late 1990s. From there, the move away from talk altogether, and toward shows like *Crime Stories* in which family trauma is defined in terms of criminality rather than psychology, becomes so logical as to have been inevitable.

The following examples are taken from a random sample of five shows, selected for their addiction-related titles, gleaned from the files of *Donahue, Sally Jessy Raphael, Geraldo,* and *Oprah*. The titles are typical: "Addicted to Addiction," "I'm Sorry for What My Addiction Did to You," "Women Who Love Sex Addicts," "Shop till You Drop but Feel Compelled to Buy More: Shopaholics," "I Gambled My Life Away," and "An Abusive Father Begs Forgiveness." In each case, the problems addressed in one way or another deal with family breakdown issues in which abuse of drugs, sexually self-destructive behaviors, and financial irresponsibility appear as symptoms of extreme crises in the orderly functioning of family life, as defined by "the American Dream" depicted on 1950s sitcoms. Men gamble away the family income; daughters become prostitutes; sons become drug addicts; and mothers spend all their time compulsively shopping as a way of gaining the pleasure and self-esteem their daily lives do not provide.

Each of these shows also featured an often well known therapist and author. "Addicted to Addiction" was capped off by a visit from Ann Wilson Schaef, the author of several of the most influential recovery self-help books, whose agenda was quite obvious—to sell her latest book and her many commercial services. The guests on the show suffered from a variety of compulsions—shopping, relationship addiction, compulsive escape from intimacy, workaholism, and self-abuse. Dr. Schaef neatly managed to offer several insights and suggestions for each of the guests, which did indeed make sense. The workaholic was probably avoiding intimacy with his family and substituting money—the high income his "addiction" pro-vided—for love. The woman addicted to love was obviously deprived of her sense of feminine attractiveness by an emotionally distant father. The self-abusing child was seeking the attention her self-absorbed, immature parents denied her. And so on. In each case, of course, a self-help group or family therapy was offered as the "cure" for these dysfunctional families.

In cases where the dysfunctional behavior was in fact criminal, these early shows were still committed to self-help and therapy, and no mention of criminal justice ever occurs. On one *Oprah* segment, a daughter apologized to her mother for the suffering her sexual promiscuity and ultimate descent into prostitution and drugs caused her. And while, from a feminist perspective, it might well have seemed that the wrong member of the family was apologizing, since the mother herself was revealed to be a fanatically religious and repressive parent who had denied her daughter all the normal childhood and adolescent pleasures of most young girls, the segment ended on a note of reconciliation: the young woman saying she would join drug and prostitute "recovery" groups and her mother "forgiving" her. No mention was made of the sexual repression of young girls in American society or, even more disturbing, of the fact that most prostitutes are not rebelling from repressive homes. Most turn to this line of work for the same reason any of us chooses any job: because at the time it seems the best way to make a living and support our children.

On another *Oprah* segment, a father who had sexually abused his daughter confronted his victim, apologized, and begged her forgiveness. As both wept, the girl told the father of her pain and suffering and, in the end, again with advice about 12 Step programs and therapy, the two were reconciled. This was actually a rather moving hour. It provided something rarely seen on television these days: the picture of a child sex abuser who was indeed capable of remorse and rehabilitation. These last two examples, of a daughter who becomes a prostitute and a father who abuses his daughter, fall into the realm of criminal activity. Had either of these two been arrested for their past actions they would most certainly have been incarcerated and, in the case of the man, forced to lead the rest of his life as a registered sex offender. So it seems actually quite amazing that the subject of crime and punishment never came up on these early talk shows. But these are also stories of family dysfunction and trauma of a kind far beyond anything seen on television before, except for the exceptional early 1980s docudramas like *The Burning Bed*. Some of the best of these—including *Little Ladies of the Night* and *Off the Minnesota Strip*—treated the issues of teen prostitutes and incestuous fathers and ended on a similar note of reconciliation through family or group therapy.[3]

But by the mid-1990s these talk shows began to change their perspective, at first subtly and then more blatantly. Suddenly, as the nation became more concerned about crime and less sympathetic to therapeutic "psychobabble" and "abuse excuses," talk shows too picked up the increasingly popular theme of the criminalization of family problems. At first, as with Court TV's turn from *Trial Stories* to *Crime Stories*, the shows presented a balanced dialogue in which both sides were presented and debated. But gradually, and not surprisingly, by the late 1990s more and more of these segments—and their audiences—seemed increasingly vengeful and bloodthirsty as cries for criminal charges and penalties, including the death penalty, became popular topics. While the talk shows continued to focus on families and their issues—the mainstay of daytime TV on both talk shows and soap operas—the insidious intrusion of criminalization as a way of discussing and "resolving" the problems became more common and more strident. And Oprah, like Court TV's Terry Moran, began gradually to use words like "evil" to describe guests and actions, where before she would have used the discourses of therapy and redemption.

From Therapy to Criminalization

Looking at a few typical *Oprah* shows from 1996 to 1998, when she began her move away from sensation and controversy to celebrity profiles, fashion makeovers, literary pursuits, and spiritualism, we can see the gradual shift—similar to that on Court TV's treatment of youth crime—from sympathy and rehabilitation to vengeance and punishment. In September 1996, for example, Oprah ran a segment on "Pregnant Women Who Use Drugs and Alcohol." This, coincidentally, was the show on which she introduced her new feature, "Oprah's Book Club," which was destined within a year or two to replace the role of "sleaze" on the show entirely, but became defunct in 2002. While the "grab attention" opener promised the audience they were about to meet "the most dangerous drug addicts in the world—pregnant mothers"—the better part of the segment was actually filled with uplifting tales of women who had recognized what they had done to their children, gotten clean, and were now living productive family lives. "Jackie," for example, told of going to her child's school, telling them her child had been drug-exposed, and asking for help. When asked by Oprah "What saved you?" she credited her counselors at her drug rehabilitation program, the first people in her life who "ever asked me how do I feel or cared about me." Then came an "expert," Laurie Tanner, author or *The Mother's Guide to Recovery*, with her predictable list of rules and guidelines for addicted mothers and her insistence that addiction was indeed a disease for which treatment was the only rational road to recovery.

But in the final segment of the show, a new idea was introduced: that addicted pregnant women should be charged with attempted murder or at least child endangerment and imprisoned. Barbara Harris, a "homemaker" from California, had successfully led a campaign to have legislation to that effect passed in her state legislature. She was challenged by a physician who, again, insisted that addiction was a disease. At this point several more "panelists" entered the fray and, while the disease and treatment model still prevailed, it was clear that the tide was turning and that—as one panelist insisted—the issue was shifting from an emphasis on the women themselves to "the children." Echoing the rhetoric of the Right-to-Life movement, Ms. Harris insisted, "Everybody wants to make this a woman's issue. But it's not about the women. It's about the children." And so the battle was engaged.

The following month, another, far more bizarre episode ran in which the idea of imprisonment of parents for "crimes" against their children was suggested again. This time, however, the crime, for which the couple did temporarily lose custody of their two children—was keeping a "trashy" house. The neighbors had complained; the police had come; and they had determined that the house was not fit for children and removed them from their parents' care. As it turned out, the couple were using drugs and the woman described herself as suffering from "low self-esteem." But the reason for removing the children was the state of the household. This time, again, the story ended happily. The couple got counseling, the house got cleaned up, and the parents regained custody. Nonetheless, the increasing presence of police authority on a show that had for so many years offered only therapy and self-help as "cures" was ominous.

By May 1997, Oprah had turned increasingly to law enforcement officials as panelists and "experts" in segments involving family and relationship problems. On a segment on "Teen Dating Violence," for example, Oprah began with the story of sixteen-year-old Jamie Fuller, who "was convicted of first-degree murder and sentenced to life without parole" for killing his fourteen-year-old girlfriend. She described the story as "horrifying but . . . not uncommon" and went on to tell even more gruesome tales of teen violence, including the story of "sixteen-year-old Rebecca" who "was so savagely beaten that she was hospitalized for three weeks." Against her mother's urging, Rebecca refused to press charges, however, and a few weeks later she was dead.

Of course, domestic violence has been a staple on talk shows since the airing of *The Burning Bed* made it a household issue, and it is a tribute to hosts like Oprah, Geraldo, and Sally Jessy that they have been instrumental in keeping it alive. But there is a huge difference between the way it was presented in earlier days and this new emphasis on crime, punishment, and incarceration. There was never a mention of incarceration in *The Burning Bed;* the only suggested remedy for Mickey Hughes, rejected by his father, was therapy. But by the mid-1990s, the most common experts addressing these issues were no longer therapists or self-help gurus but, increasingly, law enforcement agents like Westchester County District Attorney Jeannine Pirro. Pirro dominated the discussion with her insistence that there was only one issue in such cases: the fact that gender violence is a crime, punishable by law. "It's illegal," she insisted, "don't call it anything but illegal." To this the audience gave a roaring ovation. And of course murder *is* illegal—and horrendous. But what is at issue here is the overwhelming turn to the criminal justice system, to the incarceration of batterers (most of whom are not the vicious murderers described on this show), and away from counseling, therapy, and, most importantly, from the empowerment of women—economically, educationally, and psychologically—so that they can leave the situation. The issue here, as in the segment on addicted pregnant women, was no longer women. It was crime and punishment, and women and children, once again, were seen as mere "victims" for whom the criminal justice system was the only institution that could help them.

By late 1997, Oprah's topics were increasingly gruesome and terrifying. On a December segment called "Would You Watch an Execution," Senator Brooks Douglass of Oklahoma appeared to publicize his successful campaign to allow victims' families to witness the executions of those convicted of murdering their loved ones. Of course, to prepare for such a sensational discussion, the first half of the program was filled with first-person reports of witnessing murders or barely escaping while others were victimized. The details were gruesome and the tellers tearful and often near hysteria. Oprah was appropriately horrified and consoling.

Then came the testimony of the daughter, who had witnessed her parents' murder. The daughter had been horrified to learn earlier that the "person being executed could select five people to be there with him. . . . And yet, once again, the victims and the victims' family had to wait outside the prison walls. And—and they are the ones that have the most to benefit."

"What," asked Oprah, "was the benefit?" The answer was chilling. The daughter's most intense feeling was that it was unfair that the killer was allowed to die so easily. She had hoped to see him suffer as her parents had. For the senator, who did watch, it was a "moment of closure." As he watched, he found satisfaction in saying, "For fifteen years I've wanted to see you dead and now I am satisfied." As for Oprah, she was as sympathetic to all this emotion and rhetoric as she has always been to all her guests, no matter how ideologically and emotionally different this group of guests was from those of earlier years.

By May 1998 Oprah's law-and-order stance was pretty much a standard focus of an unusually large number of her shows. "Child Alert: Pedophiles," for example, featured a number of victims, their parents, law enforcement officials, and prison psychiatrists, all of whom agreed that these criminals were incurable, incorrigible, and should be locked away for life. Short of that, they widely approved of the now common laws about identifying sex offenders who have served their time and reentered society and informing any community they move to that they are in the vicinity. No one appeared to represent "the other side"—that the offender may in fact be in control of his impulses; that he may even have been wrongly convicted; and that the lifetime of harassment and inability to live and work once one has paid one's debt to society may be construed as "cruel and unusual." There simply was no "other side" to something so horrendous as child abuse. For the victim was now, unquestionably, the only person involved in a crime whose feelings and "rights" were valid.

Oprah ended with a strong political statement, unusual for her in earlier days. The stories we had just heard, she insisted, "prove that evil does exist on this planet. . . . In a few short months America will have national elections. . . . And you know what? Protection of our children . . . which should be the bedrock on which our nation is built won't even be a plank in [either party's] platform. . . . This time I'm praying, America, that we will not settle for the usual tough-on-crime rhetoric we've been hearing; that we'll demand that the protection of our children in this country from predators will be a major plank in the platform of any party you are going to vote for." And as we all know, Oprah generally gets what she wants. "Evil predators" have indeed—like Communists in the 1950s—been increasingly found lurking in the most private, sacred places of our communities. Posing as "real human beings," they increasingly seem to be committing deeds for which no psychological or social explanation is deemed relevant. Indeed, we are increasingly voting, whether Republicans or Democrats, for tougher and tougher laws that will not only keep us forever safe from these demons, but also give us the satisfaction of knowing—increasingly even *seeing*—that they are dead.

Oprah Gets Her Way: Real Parents on Trial

While it is true, as I have been arguing, that the shift from therapeutic to criminal "solutions" to family dysfunction became dramatic in the mid- to late-1980s on *Oprah*, it is important to note again that such ideological shifts do not occur in as clear-cut a linear fashion as I may have inadvertently suggested. As we have seen in the Menendez case, and in the 1996 segments of *Oprah* dealing with parent-child issues, psychological and sociological explanations and solutions do not simply disappear as criminal procedures take over. On the contrary, although the self-help "experts" on *Oprah* tended to be in private practice or authors of books, the rise of the therapeutic approach to family troubles was, from the start, echoed in government policy on such issues. However, these policies were, at first, under the purview of governmental social service and educational institutions rather than criminal justice courts and prisons.

Nonetheless, the coming of therapeutic discourses and practices was, from the start, intended as a means by which authority over children would be gradually taken over by governmental institutions. Indeed, in 1977, Jacques Donzelot, a political scientist at the University of Paris, wrote a book called *The Policing of Families*. In it he devoted a central section to the issue of "Government through the Family," in which he de-

scribed the salutary effects of a new trend in family governance: the turn
to government administrators as arbiters of family problems:

> Assistance (to the abandoned) and repression (of family rebels) were
> combined in one and the same preventive activity . . . thanks to the med-
> ical norm and the laws that ensued, with a widened margin of interven-
> tion within families . . . the neutralization of patriarchal authority would
> permit a procedure of tutelage to be established, joining sanitary and ed-
> ucative procedures with methods of moral and economic surveillance.
> This procedure involved the *reduction* of family autonomy . . . facili-
> tated by a whole series of bridges and connections between Public Assis-
> tance, juvenile law, medicine and psychiatry. . . . [Thus] one reversed the
> relationship of collusion between state and family, making the family a
> sphere of direct intervention.[4]

This formulation of the strategy for disciplining and controlling dysfunctional families and rebellious youth, at a time—as Donzelot states explicitly—when the role of the father in the home had declined is in fact a
model for what later came to be called the welfare state. Donzelot makes
clear that the role of social worker and psychologist will replace the role
of parents in determining how to "rehabilitate" or solve problems of family turmoil and juvenile delinquency. The children targeted were, he explained, "too numerous to be gotten rid of through prison and too 'wild'
to be dealt with by charitable organizations"; thus "education under
court order" was the only solution. But, he notes, this solution, in order
to work, had to transform psychiatry from a private-sector practice to
"an extrajudicial jurisdiction."[5]

Under the new regime, the state would become the official parent and
take full responsibility for what was then still referred to as the "education" of the juvenile delinquent. The implication of course is that the family itself is no longer capable of raising decent, law-abiding citizens. The
loss of paternal guidance is stressed, and the assumption that, absent such
strong parental control, the delinquent child will have little chance of
thriving in a healthy way is clear.

However, as we have seen in other chapters, the model of control
through professional sociological, psychological, and educational inter-
vention—which as Donzolot asserts, was intended originally to keep
children *out of* prisons—has not proved sufficient. Prisons have indeed
become the warehouses for unruly youth. Therapeutic strategies for

rehabilitation have, as we have seen, given way to policies based on vengeful, bloodthirsty quests for punishment and the hopelessly cynical and resigned theory that only absolute, lifelong incapacitation can stop criminal behavior. These prisons, and the ideologies that control them, are thus far less focused on discipline and rehabilitation than sheer punishment for those considered incorrigible, less than human, and worthy of being treated no better than animals.

But, as the later *Oprah* shows dramatically illustrate, the state's impulse to intervene and control family life did not end with the "education" or even punishment of youth. Increasingly, as the criminal and juvenile justice systems have been seen to fail, the trend has been for government and its handmaiden, the media, to turn in ever greater desperation to the parents themselves, who have now, in an increasing number of states and cities, been held criminally liable for the behavior of their children.

As the trend toward seeing children—and of course fetuses—as *victims* has gained passion and volume, an increasing number of laws are being passed in which the murder or even the abuse or neglect of a child is being given special attention by the criminal justice system, as in the murder of police officers. This trend, as we have seen, has been a godsend for television, with its love of melodrama and of stories in which the innocent and helpless are victimized.

These *Crime Stories*, in which parents are put on trial, are dramatically and visually engaging, to say the least. But the emotions they target are not those of tolerance and compassion, as in the early talk shows, but rather of rage and vengeance. They do this in a context that shifts from a discourse of therapy and compassion to a strict legal discourse in which the conflict between "law" and "sympathy" is spelled out in ways that make for intriguing and emotionally engaging drama. We should look at a few of the more typical *Crime Stories* segments in which legal sanctions against parents and other "child killers" are employed to impose criminal sanctions on behaviors that—even in the original *Oprah* shows—would never have been discussed in such harsh terms.

A particularly appropriate example is the use of dramatic visual images of children and babies—even fetuses—to win sympathy for the criminalization and harsh punishment of behaviors that in earlier days would have been treated less severely. "Ohio vs. Alfieri: Road Rage," as it was titled on *Crime Stories*, is such a case. Here, two young women, Renee Andrews, six months pregnant, and Tracy Alfieri, the mother of two, both in a hurry to get to work, seemed to be engaged in a competitive kind of "warfare" on the highway. It was never clear which of the two was primarily responsible for the ensuing accident, since witnesses on each side contradicted each other. Nonetheless, Andrews's car went off the road and crashed and, since she wore no seat belt, she was thrown from the car and lost her baby. Alfieri, who testified she had done nothing wrong, drove on to work.

Throughout the segment, pictures of the dead fetus, dressed in a snuggly suit with a teddy bear at his side, were shown again and again. The baby was christened "Reese Tyler" and was referred to by that name throughout the trial by the prosecution. His casket and grave were also pictured frequently, and family members were shown in the most heightened emotional states. According to Andrews's sobbing aunt, "Reese was sent to us as an angel; he died so that his mother could live." Andrews's enraged mother took a different tack, yelling at Tracy's mother, after the sentencing, "Your daughter should have gotten the death penalty!" Tracy Alfieri appeared "cold and remorseless" to jurors although she was not "the blatantly horrible person" they had hoped she would be. She too was apparently a loving mother and wife, if a less emotionally open person than Andrews, who sobbed throughout the trial.

Alfieri was convicted of "aggravated vehicular homicide," for which the prosecution, and the Andrews family, requested the harshest sentence of six and a half years. The judge, taking in account Tracy's own children, sentenced her to eighteen months. But the history of the Ohio law that made it possible to consider the death of a fetus "homicide" is itself interesting. As in most of the cases considered in this chapter, the law was relatively new, put on the books as a result of citizen lobbying, after a similar case, in which a mother and her fetus were killed in a car crash, resulted in a conviction of murder only in the case of the mother. A coalition of Pro-Life and Victims' Rights groups found this verdict so outrageous that they successfully demanded that in such cases the fetus too should be considered a "murder victim." And so it now is, not only in Ohio but in "a growing number of other states," according to the Court TV commentator.

Unlike the famous "Nanny Case" in which both women—the "evil" babysitter and the "selfish" working mother—were demonized by the media, this case actually presented a more traditionally sexist set of stereotypes: the "good" mother and the "bad" career woman. Women who become pregnant and choose to give birth are valorized in American culture as "good" women, until and unless they do something to stigmatize them as "bad mothers." But any woman—especially one with a career, in a hurry to get to work—who even accidentally harms a fetus is almost automatically demonized. Such are the melodramatic stereotypes, in place for centuries of Western culture, upon which television still relies for heart-rending, ratings-winning, dramatic narratives. As national policy moves increasingly toward an all-encompassing view of family life, and especially sees the protection of children and fetuses in terms of criminal law and harsh punishment, not only Court TV, but television news and talk channels in general have found fertile ground for attracting enormous audiences, eager to see and hear the gory details and know that the villains are severely punished. Think of the JonBenet Ramsey case, in which a beautiful little beauty queen was brutally murdered in her own home on Christmas Day in 1996. This case has never been solved, but the image of the innocent, lovely young girl, blonde and blue-eyed, still appears on TV screens at every opportunity. "New information on the Ramsey case" has become a common media phrase, which, as viewers must now realize, generally leads to a trivial and meaningless fact with no news value whatever. But, oh, that face! Who can resist looking at it and yet again watch the sad refrains of tragedy and sorrow that accompany any story of harm to an innocent child, especially a beautiful, white child. Melodrama and sentimentality fuel these pointless but audience-attracting "news" stories. But as Lauren Berlant and others have argued, sentimentality is generally a mask covering something much uglier than a compassion for victims. It is more often the benign cover for the increasing lust for vengeance of a most brutal kind that runs rampant in America today.[6]

That these tales are told, in visual detail, on Court TV points to the power of television to use images that compel deep emotion to make the case for harsh criminal justice laws. As I have mentioned, we are a highly visual culture, trained to "look" more than hear, smell, taste, touch—or perhaps even think. And as Erika Doss notes insightfully in discussing Elvis Presley's rise to stardom in the televisual 1950s, "Elvis, perhaps more than any other performer in the 1950s, recognized [the power of the visual] . . . and consciously blended sound . . . and sight (the style of his clothing, the movement of his body) into sensual and seductive spectacles." Later she notes that we talk of going to "see" (rather than hear) Madonna or Prince, "which," she observes, "tells us something about how profoundly visual our culture has become."[7]

This emphasis on the visual in television's portrayal of legal issues has important and problematic race and class implications. For here, as we saw also in the previous chapter, issues of race and class play a major role in determining which "family crimes" or tragedies will be given airtime on the news and, to a far lesser extent, on Court TV's *Crime Series*, which, by necessity, must be more realistic about crime. But on the news itself, it is white, middle-class, and generally suburban populations whose sad tales of victimization get the most airtime, even though the cases are statistically rare. The abduction and possible mutilation of lovely, fair-skinned, blue-eyed little girls like JonBenet Ramsey, Polly Klaas, and Elizabeth Smart are endlessly played for all they are worth on news channels.

But a black child needs to do something truly amazing, like escaping her kidnappers through sheer guts and ingenuity, as did seven-year-old Erica Pratt in Philadelphia in 2002, before we can consider it "news." Similarly, it is considered shockingly newsworthy when "nice" middle-class white kids do away with an unwanted baby by throwing it in a dumpster, or leaving it in a bathroom and then returning to the senior prom to dance the night away. Similar cases involving people of color are rarely covered at all, except on the nightly local news segments devoted to humiliating footage of hooded, hands-over-faces blacks doing the famous "perp walk" as they are taken, hand cuffed, to the waiting police cars. In other cases in which race determines newsworthiness, for better or worse, white families who have miraculous multiple births are featured all over news magazines and channels, and are heaped with gifts and attention. It is difficult to remember a single instance in which a black family was so honored, although there surely have had to be at least a few over the years in which fertility technologies have become so widely used.

Many of the cases in which family behavior is criminalized illustrate a strong strain of misogyny as well, for as Jacques Donzelot notes, it is not only the breakdown of parental authority, but the increasing "absence of the father, the patriarchal figure of authority" in modern society that has disturbed government officials, from the eighteenth century to the present. Similarly, we see cases in which teenage mothers kill their newborn infants out of shame and desperation, or, as in the case of Susan Smith, impulsively murder their children for reasons as irrational as they are tragic. The misogynist sense of rage against such women, and the relatively moderate concern about the men involved and their responsibilities for the women's plights, is so common as to seem unremarkable.

As Alison Young rightly notes, the image of the single mother is among the least sympathetic when it comes to matters of child neglect or delinquency.[8] In the case of *Tennessee v. Ducker*, for example, a young mother with a history of severe mental illness and poverty left her two small boys in a locked car in a motel parking lot while she went inside to visit a boyfriend. A manic depressive with a severe sleep disorder that kept her sleepless for days on end, after which she would pass out for hours—as her family members and treating psychiatrists testified—she fell asleep with all her clothes on and, as the sun rose and the day became hot, the boys suffocated. She was charged with first-degree murder. While the prosecution presented her, understandably, as a promiscuous party girl who cared nothing for her children's lives, the defense witnesses, including the boyfriend, described her as seriously ill and, in the days and nights of sleeplessness, often terrified of being alone. She had also attempted suicide several times and was only twenty years old at the time of the tragedy. Thus, according to them, she would often turn up at the boyfriend's home to sleep. She was fully clothed and no sex had occurred, according to both Ducker and her friend.

During the trial, she behaved in a number of bizarre ways, often slumping to sleep at the defense table or sobbing uncontrollably. While it is possible, as the prosecution argued, to see all this as an act, it was difficult to imagine (at least for this viewer) that a person so emotionally and intellectually dysfunctional—her vocabulary and reasoning were almost juvenile, as was her inability to control her emotions—could have intentionally left her children to die. But that, it seemed, was no longer the issue in Tennessee. For, as in the Alfieri case, the state had recently passed a new, citizen-driven law making intentionality no longer necessary for a charge of first-degree murder. This law not only defined child abuse as first-degree murder but also made it punishable by death. It came as the result of a case in which the boyfriend of a young mother abused and killed her child, but since he had not "intended" murder, he was convicted of a lesser charge.[9]

Throughout the *Crime Stories* segment, pictures of the two little boys at play, and then of their small caskets, appeared regularly. The father—who had impregnated Ducker, married her, and then moved out of town—suddenly appeared as the aggrieved father, filled with the most vicious hatred for Ducker and making self-righteous demands for her death. He was even shown sobbing at the boys' graves, as though they had been a major part of his life. Because she had chosen to testify,

Ducker was forced to undergo the most grueling cross-examination in which every aspect of her lifestyle was presented as morally decadent, and every claim of mental illness was scoffed at. While her mother and father supported her in every way possible, bearing witness to her many mental problems and admitting, when asked, that they failed to find treatment for her because, according to her mother, "I didn't know anything about psychiatrists," the jury was largely unconvinced of such mitigating circumstances.

Three jurors had in fact voted for acquittal. But, as one woman put it, "I felt like I was in a den packed with wolves," so intense was the majority demand for a first-degree murder verdict. In the end, the jurors reached a "compromise," agreeing to convict Ducker of child abuse but not first-degree murder, for which the sentence would be fifteen to twenty-five years at the judge's discretion. The three sympathetic jurors "hoped the judge would give help."

At the sentencing, after prison doctors had put her on medication for manic depression, Ducker appeared in control, lucid, and far more adult in her behavior. It was a dramatic change. Nonetheless, the judge found Ducker to be "without remorse" (although throughout the trial she sobbed endlessly, took full responsibility, and was on twenty-four-hour suicide watch) and sentenced her to eighteen years. Cheers went up in the courtroom as another "bad" single mother was given due punishment. And so, we were meant to think, the problem of child abuse had somehow been "solved" through harsh punishment. The poverty-related issues of mental illness, ignorance, and lack of resources to find help *before* such tragedies occur were never even mentioned.

On Court TV, after all, the main issue is, "Does the system work?" The system places legal limits on the discourse permitted in a trial and features the rapid growth of citizen-influenced laws that are more and more punishing of more and more acts and accidents and less and less concerned with the *causes* of these acts and how they might be remedied *before* the fact. A conviction of anyone for anything makes a winner of the courts, politicians who are "tough on crime," citizens whose misplaced anger needs to focus on some scapegoat, and, of course, the media. As for the pathetic defendants who are punished, well, once the gavel pounds, we see and hear no more of them.

Would the courts have been as hard on the father of the Ducker boys, had he been the negligent parent? There is very little reason to think so. For, as in the case of Susan Smith, the horror of maternal neglect and the already assumed "unnaturalness" and "criminality"—to use Young's term—of the single mother make single mothers easy targets for prosecutors. Especially if, as in both these cases, extramarital sex is a factor. No matter that Smith was actually abused by her own stepfather, or that Ducker's boyfriend testified that it was loneliness and terror, not a "good time," that had brought her to his home. Single mothers are almost always presumed guilty of something. Because a large percentage of black families are in fact matriarchal, the misogyny is inherently mixed in with an unspoken if virulent touch of racism. Black women who find themselves in such situations don't as often make the news or Court TV, like the more "shocking" cases of the Susan Smiths and Andrea Yateses— good white Christian women from good middle-class homes. So there is always the implicit assumption underlying the lack of coverage of blacks that such behavior, when it occurs in black homes, is less "shocking" because it is more predictable, even expected, in the black community.

Nonetheless, race does quite often enter into Court TV's range of vision. As in the cases examined above involving gender violence, race is all too often presented in ways that make explicit the subtextual racism inherent in the criminal justice system, and race is reflected—by omission or commission—in TV coverage of racial incidents. Indeed, the most troubling example of a *Crime Stories* segment involving a single mother on trial for abuse also points out the irrationality of a system that sees punishment as an answer to family discord and refuses to consider the larger social, economic, and cultural factors that leave so many single mothers—especially those who are poor and black—desperate and powerless as their children become unruly and vulnerable to unhealthy community influences. In a segment called "Tough Love: The Case of *Florida v. Temple*," a black single mother with two teenage sons was accused of abuse when her son called the police and reported that she had thrown him down, handcuffed him for hours, and seriously bruised and hurt him.

The woman in question was, by all rational standards, a model mother and citizen. She had put herself through night school so she could qualify for a position as a corrections officer and thereby afford to move her children out of the rough neighborhood that was already influencing the accusing son, Jason, in negative ways. The home she bought, in a middle-class neighborhood, and the work she was doing indicated that she had lived her life entirely in a way that put her concern for children's well-being above everything. In fact, as the trial proceeded, we learned that she had received a scholarship to Princeton and had turned it down in order to raise her children. She was also an active church and PTA member with no possible blemish on her record.

Nonetheless, when, in an argument with her already troubled son, she had resorted to using her handcuffs to restrain him when he lashed out at her for punishing him for breaking a rule, she was instantly and harshly prosecuted for child abuse and false imprisonment. The trial itself revealed the prejudice against single mothers and the bias toward fathers, even largely absentee fathers, in family disputes. While Temple's younger son staunchly supported his mother and her version of the facts, the older boy, now living with his father (who had initially given up custody), was reported to be doing well in school and shown playing the piano in his father's house.

Of course the complexities of this family drama were not revealed in all their contradictory and confusing density. But what was absolutely clear was that this case was not really about a "crime" so much as a case in which class, race, and gender figured prominently and yet were ignored. Possible cultural differences between black and white families in disciplining children physically—especially when the black parent is a single mother—were never mentioned. The question of the son's motives in accusing his mother was not raised. The issue of how much "brutality" the boy actually suffered was also confusing since photos revealed very little bruising and the younger son corroborated his mother's story: that in a moment of desperation she had resorted to subduing her out-of-control child with handcuffs as a way of showing, she testified, that "this was how he would be treated in jail," where, the implication was, he was heading.

The prosecutors and social workers, however, were adamant about serving the side of the angels by convicting and punishing the abusive parent. Child abuse is a hot issue, due at least in part to the rise of the Victims' Rights movement, which we will examine below. Also at play is the segment of the women's movement which, as in the case of sexual violence, sees victimization as the primary political condition of those considered politically weaker and turns to the state for punishment and retribution. But what happens in the cases where these well-meaning souls are successful? In the case of Ms. Temple, she was convicted of a felony, and while her sentence was three years' probation, she has lost everything she has worked for—her home, her right to practice her profession, and, not least, a son who could not possibly be helped by knowing that his mother and brother are living, once again, in shame and poverty due to his impulsively angry action.

While most cases involving white single mothers accused of abuse focus on the plight of the "innocent" victim, when race or class enter the picture—as in this tragic case—things often tend to get more complicated. For one thing, black women, even those with impeccable records as parents and providers, tend to be judged more harshly than their white middle-class counterparts. As we saw in the Temple case, young black males are more likely to be seen as delinquents than white boys. In fact, the only reason this possibility was *not* highlighted in the Temple case was because the prosecution successfully convinced the jury that once the boy's father—previously a largely absent parent—took custody, the boy immediately straightened out. Thus, of course, his behavior must have been the fault of his inadequate mother. And because of the limited legal constraints of the *Crime Stories* genre, no background information was given about the father's previous behavior or—more to the point—how well, in the long run, the boy actually did in his father's care.

But in cases where children and youths are found guilty of crimes, or even just out of control in school or at home, the law is increasingly stepping in to hold parents criminally responsible for the behavior of their offspring, often when the youths involved are as old as eighteen. Alison Young, in a telling article entitled "The Single Mother and the Criminal Child," traces how criminologists have generally analyzed and treated juvenile delinquency since the 1950s. Her essay centers on the "invention of images of responsibility for crime" and how changes in those dominant images reflect parallel changes in actual criminological theory and legal practice. In the 1950s and 1960s, criminologists used the image of "the broken family" as the site of criminogenesis and particularly singled out for blame the absent father and inadequate single mother. During this period, influential theorists such as J. Bowlby and D. West argued against the "radical" theories of social causation of delinquency and insisted upon the personal, domestic sphere as wholly responsible for the actions of their offspring. For as Young puts it, in the views of these early theorists, women who "choose" to be single mothers lost their feminine identities and became images of "abnormality" and unfitness.[10]

These views, according to Young, have recently reemerged with great impact in criminological theory and policy. Personal "responsibility," she argues, "has become a key trope in current governmental policy on the family." And in this trope it is most often the mother who is "figured as the scapegoat to be sacrificed" in the interests of social harmony. Young gives several examples of single mothers imprisoned for leaving children at home to go to work because they could not afford child care, the very same "crime" which, on a 1997 segment of *Oprah*, brought the audience to its feet in a mass attack upon the poor woman being interviewed. "You deserve to be put in jail!" yelled one of the self-righteous audience members, while others hurled scurrilous epithets at the woman that suggested she was less than human.[11]

Certainly, this attack on single motherhood, from Dan Quayle's ill-advised attack on *Murphy Brown* to President Clinton's cruel cutbacks in welfare support for such women, has become a cutting-edge issue in social and media discourse and representation. When we turn to criminal trials in which parents are held responsible for their children's "bad acts" or are accused of negligence or abuse, it is most often single mothers, such as those discussed above, who find themselves at the defendant's table.

But I would not push this argument as far as Young does. In viewing the *Crime Stories* segments in which parents are on trial for crimes of omission or commission, it is clear that other forms of family dysfunction figure prominently as media images of "how not to raise a family." While some of these cases are indeed sexist in their representations of strong, often unloving mothers and weak, ineffectual fathers, others promote images of what appear to be intact, functional, white middle-class families who are still incompetent to raise children, and are responsible for either a child's delinquency or some grotesque accident in the home that the court prosecutor argues should have been prevented.

In fact, as *Crime Stories* demonstrates, the criminalization of even white middle-class family dysfunction is increasingly common. The criminalization of parents for their children's deeds or for negligence or abuse—issues previously handled in family services agencies rather than criminal courts—has become increasingly popular. This is true not only in the United States but in Canada, Australia, and Great Britain as well, where the rhetoric of "personal responsibility" is replacing the increasingly unpopular turn to the state's social services to manage such matters. In fact, in the last few years, we have seen headlines like "Truants' Parents Face Crackdown across Country,"[12] "What Causes Brutality? The People Nurturing It,"[13] and "Parents Blaming Parents."[14] Often in

these articles the "crime" is trivial or the parents had clearly done everything in their power to get help for troubled children and had been denied
such help by the state.

Judges often do deny parents' pleas for such help, and police and social service agencies often have inadequate services to offer. It is all too
common, in fact, when parents testify at a child's sentencing hearing, to
hear them tearfully explain in heartbreaking detail how hard they tried to
get help for the convicted child and how fruitless their longtime efforts
had been. As in the case of Francine Hughes, the government and its
agencies too often fail to recognize or aid troubled families, and then,
when the ultimate—predictable—violent act occurs, they are only too
quick to prosecute the troubled or abused victim. In fact, it is ironic that
the term "victim" is so easily appended to anyone the state and media
find sympathetic figures, while it is denied to those whose true victimization has been so intense and long-lived that it brings them to the point of
violence as a last resort. By this stage they are viewed as demons rather
than the actual victims of social neglect they have been for so many years.

To see the range of such cases, let us survey some of the most typical
that involve white, middle-class, law-abiding, often loving parents caught
up in a legal system that increasingly makes parents the scapegoats for
much larger social problems. If these cases were investigated, they would
lead to an obvious conclusion: that there are serious social and economic
problems in this country whose solution would require huge restructur-
ings of institutions and reallocations of state and federal budgets. But no,
it is far simpler—and from a media point of view, far more dramatically
compelling—to focus melodramatically on the tragic stories of families in
trouble and, unlike the early talk shows and made-for-TV movies, remove
even the slightest mention of larger social forces or possible remedies that
do not involve incarceration. Everyone likes to see families with troubles
worse their own, almost as much as they seem to like to see people pinned
with the tag of "villain" and expunged from the social unit. The media
and law have evolved in ways that encourage us to sleep soundly in our
beds, knowing that all is right with the world—that the "system" is working to protect us "good guys" from those "bad guys."

To start with a tragic example, the case of *Florida v. Newton & Newton*, dubbed "Kids and Guns: Who's Responsible?" concerned a devoutly
religious couple whose three-and-a-half-year-old child found a gun hidden under the parents' mattress and accidentally shot her two-year-old
brother. As is typical of these programs, everything was presented almost

entirely in terms of legal doctrine rather than social or cultural factors. And legal doctrine, since 1989, has stated, in at least ten states, including Florida, that having a loaded firearm where a child can reach it is a felony. Obviously, there was some evidence of poor judgment here. But there was also, as is increasingly common, a fear of violence in the neighborhood in which this working-class family lived. And despite a long list of character witnesses, including the couple's minister, attesting to the fact that the Newtons were "the best parents [they] had ever known," the jury was instructed, explicitly, that "sympathy [was] not a legal concept" and that they were to "set [it] aside" in their deliberations. After two hours of deliberation, the jury came back with guilty verdicts for both parents on counts of "culpable negligence," a crime requiring a five-year sentence. Jurors interviewed after the trial overwhelmingly attested to feelings of great compassion for the couple. Nonetheless, they were, they felt, obliged by law to convict. And of course the ever-present images of the dead two-year-old worked in melodramatic terms to balance at least some of the sympathy for the parents. Dead children, as we have seen throughout this study, are the most prominent and effective images in the fight to shift attention and sympathy away from defendants and toward the suffering victims and their loved ones.

Nonetheless, this was a somewhat unusual example because the parents were so clearly decent, caring people, caught in a system in which—"for the greater good of society and the protection of its children," to quote the prosecutor who, along with the judge and most of the local citizens, was himself a gun owner—the individual circumstances were deemed irrelevant. If all such cases involved defendants like the Newtons it would surely be at least a bit more difficult for laws criminalizing parents to gain the emotional and political support they now enjoy. Not surprisingly, however, most of the parents put on trial for negligence, abuse, or responsibility for their children's actions are far less sympathetic, largely because they tend to conform to negative social stereotypes, which the media has of course helped to construct and reinforce in a major way.

Two final examples from popular segments of *Crime Stories* that are often rerun seem more ridiculous than tragic, although the parents involved would certainly not see it that way. Both involve white middle-class intact nuclear families whose major fault, as presented in the trials and in the edited versions of them, seems to be either a "weak" father or an "unnaturally" strong mother. The gender bias here is subtle only because it is so deeply ingrained in popular culture. A father who loses control of a child is seen as a weakling, which in a patriarchal society can, apparently, lead to criminal charges. A mother who takes control of the disciplinary functions of a family in which such a "weak" father fails is, on the other hand, quickly made the villain of the piece. For a too-strong mother is even more unsympathetic in the eyes of the courts and TV audiences than a weak father with an equally weak wife.

In the case of *Michigan v. Skousen*, a professional middle-class mother of two was accused, by her eighteen-year-old daughter, of aggravated domestic violence. Her mother had slapped her face during an argument about the girl's staying out all night with her boyfriend without even calling home. During the course of the trial, Skousen's three other children supported her while the father, described by friends and relatives as "a big marshmallow" when it came to disciplining the children, supported his daughter.

As the drama progressed, one felt as if one were watching a Hollywood melodrama of the 1940s—*Mildred Pierce*, perhaps—in which the strong controlling mother is revealed to be an unnatural, almost inhuman shrew while the mild-mannered father, largely absent or ineffective until the major crisis emerges, suddenly emerges as the good guy. Indeed, the same could almost be said of the *Florida v. Temple* segment if it weren't for the race and class differences. For in both cases we see strong competent women, struggling to raise children under extremely difficult cultural (and, in the case of Temple, financial) circumstances, with little or no help from the male parent. And yet, in all three cases it is the mother who is judged to be harsh and unnatural and subjected to unusually cruel punishment for stepping out of her traditional subservient role. Skousen was indeed convicted and, while offered probation on condition of getting psychological help, refused the guilty verdict and preferred to appeal, at the risk of facing prison.

Harshly disciplining an insolent, unruly child (if face slapping is deemed to be harsh), it seems, can get you into prison. But so, most confusingly, can failing to discipline severely enough. In the case of *St. Clair Shores v. Provenzino*, for example, we have another middle-class white family on trial, this time for failing to keep a delinquent son from committing the crime of breaking and entering. The son, at the time of the trial, was already in juvenile detention and testified on behalf of his parents, who insisted they bore no responsibility for his actions. Nonetheless, the Provenzinos too were convicted under the parental responsibility laws which are now on the books in thirty-six states. While the mother in this case was not a particularly strong figure, it was, again, the image of an overly weak father that was most distinctive and compelling about this family dynamic. For while Ms. Skousen was convicted of slapping her daughter, Mr. Provenzino had himself, on several occasions, been the victim of severe battering by his out-of-control son. And yet it was the father's testimony that most strongly convinced the interviewed jurors to convict the couple, because he "had done nothing" to stop his son's behavior and in fact appeared as a contemptible figure. For an "unmanly" father, it seems, is far less sympathetic than a father who is virtually absent from his children's lives, as in the Temple case.

In both of these cases—indeed in all of the cases looked at—it is clear, despite the murkiness of many legal "facts," that the families involved were all in need of help. For every one of the parents convicted was either suffering from extremely negative social forces, mental illness, or family dysfunction so severe that all parties were suffering and bewildered, angry and desperate. Is the courtroom the proper place for such problems to be handled? Is prison the proper institution for solving them? Is the discourse of crime and punishment in any way adequate to address what is leading all these people to acts of physical violence, no matter how mild or severe? The answer would seem to be obvious to anyone watching these trials. But when one accepts as given the authority of the state and the criminal justice system to adjudicate such matters—as is increasingly the dominant ideological thrust of our age—one is not easily led to raise such questions. The law is the law, after all, and with the gender, race, and class biases, and the stereotypes that subtly infiltrate the "objective" laws by which all citizens are assumed equal, it is difficult for audiences and juries not to be influenced by the prejudices of the system and the cruelty and irrationality of its precepts.

If we look back at the talk shows of the 1980s, with their therapeutic discourses of disease, addiction, and recovery, we cannot but feel that even with all their ideological and political flaws and elisions, they offered a far more caring and even in some cases helpful approach to the underlying causes of family dysfunction and violence. Oprah or Geraldo, in the 1980s, would have handled these case with far more compassion and insight than today's criminal justice system, as shown by these bizarre trials. Yet, it is an irony of media trends that Geraldo himself— ever vigilant of media trends—gave up his daytime talk show when he saw the writing on the wall and reinvented himself as *Rivera Live* on nighttime cable. Here he presided briefly over a talk show in which legal experts debated current legal issues and cases, and in which he himself—once the defense attorney for radical young Latino activists—appeared as a passionate spokesperson for law and order, victims' rights, and even the death penalty.

As the mother of two children, both of whom put me through the usual traumas—rebelliousness, limit testing, experimenting with dangerous associates and activities, and so on—in their teen years, I must confess to feeling the most chilling emotions watching this particular set of *Crime Stories*. "There but for the grace of God go I," I kept thinking as I recalled some of the more frustrating episodes in what I believe to be the typical life of a mother of teenagers. For while I did not physically punish my children, at any age, I could certainly remember moments in which the urge to do so was strong. And while both of my children are now responsible, socially productive adults, there were surely moments when I had my doubts about whether they would make it through high school, much less college, without some terrible incident altering their lives, and mine. And I have often thought, when talking to parents who deny having such feelings or experiences, that, with some exceptions, of course, they may have been blinding themselves to what was going on in their own minds and in their children's lives. After all, we are living in times when social services for children and parents are in scarce supply; neighborhoods, even "good" ones, offer children seductive opportunities to get into serious trouble; and popular culture, consumer society, and society in general, as we have seen, have increasingly valorized youth and undermined parental authority (right-wing exhortations about "family values" to the contrary notwithstanding). Parents, especially single mothers, have a hard time in any event because adequate child care and after-school programs are increasingly rare, and children—through economic necessity—are left on their own. The stress of mere survival, for far too many of us, not to mention the cycles of violence and abuse that too many parents bring to family life, understandably bring many to the brink of violence and, in the most unfortunate cases, far over the brink. All sorts of new "rage" syndromes are indicative of the difficulties of living in this society. We experience "road rage" and we "go postal." Even "real estate rage" is increasingly growing in urban centers where only the rich can afford decent housing, and we increasingly witness outbreaks of violence at sports and music events. All indicate a state of mind, in so many of us, that is filled with justified anger at our difficulties, predominantly economic ones. In 2000, a pickup hockey game between children resulted in one father killing another over a minor incident. For many, sports are no longer games for children, but (unrealistic) paths to fortune that the parents themselves have failed to achieve.

And so a mother slaps a disrespectful, out-of-control daughter; a father fails to keep a son out of trouble; a desperate mother handcuffs a violent son; a mentally ill young mother, deprived of social or psychiatric help and living a life of poverty and hopelessness, stupidly leaves her two children in a locked car while she attends a party; a religious, upstanding set of parents, so fearful of neighborhood crime that they keep a gun under a mattress, tragically lose one of their small children when another child finds and fires it.

These stories will go on until we look beyond the courtrooms and the rhetoric of criminal justice to the larger social and economic problems of our society.

7

Television and the
Demonization of Youth

If the only measure of any generation were the worst acts that any of its members might commit, each generation in the United States would be viewed as an unqualified disaster. In fact, to see only the negative in any generation of a nation's youth is almost implausibly silly   —Franklin Zimring

So the elevator comes and there's these two white kids inside. "Whoa, man," I said, "ain't no way I'm going in there. Those guys might shoot me."   —African American comedian Chris Rock

The criminalization of families, especially when child abuse is at issue, has indeed become a major concern of the criminal justice system, and the juiciest of fodder for the sensation-seeking TV mills. However, it is ironically contradictory that, even as parents are being prosecuted and convicted for mistreating "innocent" children, an even more stridently punishing area of criminal justice has also arisen, which in many ways contradicts the former. For while parents are being convicted, fined, and even jailed for abusing children, the children themselves are similarly being treated with more and more harshly punitive measures for their own alleged crimes. In fact, had the mother in the Skousen case been the first to turn to juvenile justice, she might well have had a very good case for treating her disobedient, disrespectful, "out of control" daughter as an offender in need of judicial handling of some kind, possibly in an institutional setting.

Indeed, the demonization of youth in America dates back much farther than the more recent turn to criminalizing parents. In the introduction to his book *America at Century's End*, Alan Wolfe counts among the many dramatic changes in the last decades one that is particularly disturbing. "America has long thought of itself as a child-oriented society," he writes, "but hair-raising stories of sexual abuse, poor schools, latchkey kids, and an inadequate childcare system suggest otherwise. Even as we celebrate the innocence of childhood, we deprive children of the opportunity just to be children."[1] How to explain this apparent contradiction? A recent study called *Young People and Youth Justice* suggests a rather radical answer. In spite of democratic rhetoric to the contrary, we are in fact a nation that increasingly harbors quite negative attitudes toward youth in general. "American society does not like young people,"[2] say the authors quite bluntly. This is a sentiment that many Americans, as I have learned the hard way, find shocking and insulting. After all, they will tell you, we are the nation that cries, and demands justice for perpetrators of child abuse, child pornographers, and those mysterious figures responsible for the untold numbers of "missing children" whose lovable little faces appear on public service announcements, community bulletin boards, and milk cartons. We are the nation whose very history reflects an increasing (if problematic) fascination with and adulation of all things youthful, from clothing styles, to celebrity figures, to musical forms, to the newest slang phrases. We have been taught to live our lives for our children, so that they will have more and more and more of everything that we ourselves have strived for; move higher and higher into the ranks of the privileged than we ourselves have managed to climb. We are the nation of Baby Gap; of preschools with years-long waiting lists and inscrutable entrance requirements; of pricey "educational toys" meant to push our children, from the earliest ages, toward these lofty goals.

Why then, one might wonder, have we also become, as Wolfe documents, the nation that invests less and less in public education and health care; that incarcerates more and more children at younger and younger ages; that stares hypnotized at the TV screens that tell us, night after night, of new acts of atrocity committed by young people—black, white, and brown; rich, poor, and average—and applaud the public figures that demand stiffer punishments for these children? We hear them speak knowingly of a new generation of "superpredators" who have somehow slipped through the cracks of our nurturing, social structures, apparently because they are genetic mutants, "bad seeds" inexplicably emerging from our warm fertile soil.

So which is it? Do we love or hate our children? Do we shower them with care and affection or with neglect and abuse? Do we look up to and emulate them (in a bizarre reversal of the traditions of most advanced civilizations), or secretly hate and fear them, viewing them as some alien race of monsters who have somehow—as in the 1950s classic sci-fi movie *Invasion of the Body Snatchers*—taken the form and mannerisms of our own flesh and blood but who, in fact, are evil demons hell bent on mayhem and destruction, especially of those closest to them?

I have no doubt at all about the answer to these questions. We are indeed a nation living in fear and dread of a generation of children and youth who have become—absent a more likely (if equally irrational) ideological enemy such as Communism—the scapegoats for all that is wrong in this society. These kids are viewed generally—but especially by the privileged who have resources and access to media and political power—as the main cause of an abiding, perhaps unconscious, sense of anxiety and even guilt about the state of the nation, even as the eager consumers gobble up its goods and services and collect its stock market dividends. The depiction of youth by the media is much the same as that of "criminals" as presented by the tabloids: the social and economic contexts are wholly absent. After all, putting a story into context would involve implicitly pointing a finger at the parents and legislators who have created the private and public environments in which these kids have grown up. Youth, especially inner-city black youth, appear sui generis as some alien race for whom we take no responsibility and for whom we can only imagine incarceration as a solution to the problems they are seen to cause.

In what follows I will demonstrate my argument in three ways: first, statistically, by refuting the most common media-circulated "demonization myths" about youth, which belie our avowed love of them; second, historically, by looking at the rise of youth culture within the context of industrialization and the coming of consumer culture; and finally and most importantly, by tracing the permutations in the representation of youth in popular culture, from the earliest days of advertising, through the rise and proliferation of youth-oriented movies since the 1950s and the current views of youth and its relationship to the larger society in recent television programming. For the last, I will include news as well as the made-for-TV movies and "Crime Stories" docudramas we have already looked at in relation to gender violence. As I have done throughout this study, I do this to demonstrate the parallels in media representations of issues of crime and justice and the changing legal and political trends these media trends reflect and reinforce. Without them it would be difficult to convince voters and jurors, who can only make judgments through personal experiences, to buy the arguments in support of current, increasingly punitive trends in juvenile law and policy. In particular, in the wake of recent high-profile murder cases involving white, well-to-do suburban youth, I am interested in looking at the way in which race and class figure in the discussions and analyses of the so-called epidemic of youth crime as the traditional scapegoat—black, inner-city youth—has been joined by a new, in some ways more frightening, icon of demon youth: the "good (white) kid" mysteriously, and apparently instantaneously, gone bad.

Youth and Crime: The Myths and the Realities

In Chicago, two black boys in the single-digit age group drop a five-year-old neighbor from the window of a high-rise project and kill him. In Columbine, two upper middle class youths go on a shooting rampage in their high school, killing and injuring dozens of their peers. In Beverly Hills, two youths of enormous wealth and privilege plot and execute a plan to kill both of their parents in cold blood as they sit in their den watching television and eating ice cream. In Lake Worth, Florida, a thirteen-year-old is sent home from school for throwing water balloons in class and returns, a few hours later, to shoot and kill his teacher. In Las Vegas, a high school honor student lures a small black girl into a restroom and sexually abuses, tortures, and kills her.

I needn't go further; everyone has heard about and seen, ad infinitum, these and many other such tales in the last few years. And we will undoubtedly hear and see footage of countless more such incidents before this chapter goes into print. The sensationalism of the acts and, more significantly, the proliferation of cable news channels which have endless hours to fill with eye-catching, emotional news stories in their endless race to garner ratings and stave off the competition, make it an economic necessity to air such events. They will be run and rerun, discussed and debated, commemorated and analyzed as long as audiences are willing to consume, digest, and revisit them. And while it is all too easy (and hypocritical) to blame the audiences—ourselves, that is—for our crassness and voyeurism, it is important to combat that argument. For these stories—especially as they are presented—are indeed worthy of our interest, concern, and discussion.

The problem is not audience interest; it is the media's framing of the stories themselves in ways that falsify and sensationalize such incidents in ways that mystify and distort their true significance. Is there, in fact, as these "major media events" suggest, an "epidemic" of youth crime? Is there a rising population, such as America has never before seen, of children and teenagers who are amoral, remorseless, incorrigible "superpredators" for whom the only answer is lifelong, institutional incapacitation? For those who have studied the statistics from a historical perspective, the answer is a resounding "no." Indeed, statistics reveal that even as the media and its favorite spokespersons continue to raise the bar in their rhetoric of hysteria over youth and youth crime, rates of crime—especially violent crime—have been dramatically falling, along with crime rates generally, in the years in which television's "moral panic" scenarios have been increasing in amounts of airtime as well as level of fear-inducing hysteria.[3]

Kevin Harner and Mark Drakeford list a series of techniques by which the media have constructed the largely mythical moral panic about the state of American youth today. First and most obvious, they cite the expanded coverage of juvenile crime in the last decade. The idea is that if we see and hear something over and over again, we come to believe—quite erroneously—that there is a correlation between media coverage and actual incidents of youth crime. And of course, as a corollary to that observation, is the equally obvious fact that it is the most heinous and shocking of youth crimes that get the most coverage, at least where white youth are concerned. (For black and Latino youth, virtually any act of violence or criminal activity is worthy of note, especially on the local news.)[4] We then get a heightened emphasis on the suffering of victims and their friends and families, which serves to lend even more coverage of an even more emotionally loaded quality to reports of juvenile crime. In a similar vein, Harder and Drakeford cite the media's tendency to play on and reinforce public criticisms of the courts as being "soft on crime" or "having their hands tied" by "defendant-favoring" laws. And finally they note the tendency to depict juveniles generally from a point of view that *assumes* a certain level of "badness" as a given and then defines kids in terms of the categories of "bad" and "not so bad."[5]

Other criminologists cite still further reasons for the distortion of media constructions of youth and youth crime. For one thing, as media mergers proliferate, there are fewer and fewer sources of alternative voices and viewpoints. Thus, what communication theorists term a "spi-

ral of silence" occurs, in which minority views are more and more silenced until, at last, the dominant view becomes accepted as unassailable
truth. And that unassailable truth, in the case of youth crime, becomes a
particularly dangerous one: the most sensational, heinous—*and atypical*—of crimes come to be seen as exactly what they are not: the most typical and common. What makes this a particularly easy, if ultimately illogical, jump is the lack of social or economic context in the reporting of
these crimes.[6] One of the most egregious cases of this kind of narrow, distorted framing of youth crime coverage is the case of Jeremy Strohmeyer,
the youth convicted of luring a little girl into a restroom and sexually torturing and killing her. Nowhere in the coverage of that sensational case
was it mentioned that Strohmeyer, adopted by an upper-middle-class family, was the biological child of two parents with serious histories of mental illness and chemical abuse, and that he was born with fetal alcohol
syndrome. To the extent that any kind of analysis *is* offered to explain
such ultimately unexplainable acts—at least in terms of current social science theory—it tends to be highly unsatisfactory. "Who knows?" would,
at this point, be the most honest answer. But television abhors a lack of
closure, a failure to tie up loose ends. It wants to send us off to bed feeling enlightened and therefore more secure that someone will "handle"
these things properly. And so the old bromides are dragged out: the media
made them do it; parental neglect was the culprit; the breakdown of social and religious values are at fault—and so on. In fact, statistically
speaking, crimes like those at Columbine and Lake Worth are so rare as
to be statistically meaningless. The actual best answer in the most shocking cases may well be one given by that fount of wisdom, Chris Rock:
"Some people are just cra-a-a-a-zy!"

It would however be unfair and inaccurate to leave it at that—as re-
freshing as Rock's unpopular and rarely stated sentiment might be. For of
course we do have real problems with young people today. In fact, I
would argue that one of the media's most egregious distortions is its un-
faltering focus on aberrant, statistically meaningless acts of unexplainable atrocity. Instead, they should look much more closely at a far less
sensational, but ultimately more serious problem: the growing number of
kids of all races and classes who are indeed unhappy, troubled, self-destructive, and lost, but whose problems are either not obvious, are ignored, or—when they become too obvious to ignore—are handled, as is
juvenile crime in general, through institutions that serve primarily to remove them from society for as long as the law or their parents' economic

resources allow. Mike Males, who has perhaps been the most astute and diligent of researchers and analysts on this aspect of society's hatred and mishandling of its youth, offers a variety of insightful analyses of how adult institutions, and adults generally, have managed to twist or distort the truth about society's role in mistreating and abusing our youth. Reinforced and endorsed by the media, society cleverly blames the victims, in this case American youth, for the crimes of adult society, for which so many young people are suffering in so many ways instead.

Most obvious among Males's observations is that youth have become the scapegoats for issues for which adults are unwilling to face or take responsibility. After all, he notes, even John Diulio, the coiner of the "superpredator" youth theory, admits that most juvenile crime is committed by kids who have been abused. Yet he, and the media that love him, never seem to consider that there might be an "epidemic" worthy of "moral panic" over adult crime. He notes, too, that much of the new fear of youth is due to adult anxiety over the shifting racial mix in the general population. As we become a more and more multicultural nation, one in which whites are increasingly making up smaller and smaller percentages of the population, fear of black and brown youth is thus quite possibly a way of projecting onto all of youth a real fear of racial changes in the population at large: a fear, that is, of black and brown peoples. Equally illogical, but understandable, is the scapegoating of youth for much larger social ills that arose in the second half of the twentieth century as a result of the rise of consumer society and youth culture itself (a topic which we will look at closely later). For as adults have been encouraged and seduced, largely by media, to emulate rather than be role models for youth, it is the kids, rather than the economic and social values of which they are products, that take the punishment. In the case of poor and minority kids, it is of course incarceration that "solves" the problem. And for the wealthier, it is treatment centers for the "troubled child" that serve to remove them from society. In fact, such treatment centers, as Males and others note,[7] have become billion-dollar enterprises, taking in larger and larger numbers of troubled kids through referrals from schools, therapists, and parents for as long as insurance policies or bank accounts hold out. All this in lieu of addressing the real causes of so much pain, anguish, violence, and self-destruction in today's youth.

And so America's war against its own kids escalates, as the legal system, aided and abetted by media sensationalism, goes farther and farther in its efforts to impose stiffer and stiffer penalties on younger and younger children. As reported in a 1998 article surveying national legislative initiatives in the realm of juvenile justice, "At both federal and state levels, lawmakers are targeting juvenile offenders with ever more punitive legislation." The article cites in particular a bill in Congress called S 10—the Violent and Repeat Juvenile Offender Act, which would lower the age at which juveniles could be tried as adults, as "symptomatic" of national trends. By 1994, the researchers say, half the states had already lowered the ages for trying juveniles as adults and, if found guilty, have been sent to adult prisons.[8] Perhaps the harshest of these laws is Michigan's, which sets no limit whatever on the age at which a juvenile offender may tried as an adult. The law, according to Jeffrey Fieger, the attorney for Nathaniel Abraham, an eleven-year-old with the mental capacity of a six-year-old who was being tried for first-degree murder in that state, would allow even a three-year-old to be tried for murder. "Then where do we go?" asked Feiger. "Is there a diminished capacity defense there? . . . And [if so] diminished from what?"[9]

Whatever the particulars of each state's laws in this area, there is no doubt that nationally the trend to treat juvenile offenders more and more harshly is dramatic. More and more youths, for example, are being placed in adult facilities with adult offenders. According to Maryland officials, virtually every adult facility in that state now houses youth. And a study done in Florida indicates that such youth are far more likely to turn to adult lives of crime and reincarceration than those in juvenile detention. Not that juvenile detention centers do much better for kids. In New York, youth from the ages of ten to sixteen are housed together in barges originally intended for serious adult offenders, so rapid is the rise in juvenile prisoners. And many of these youths suffer from mental disorders that go untreated.[10]

As Franklin Zimring observes, we are a nation caught in a dilemma. On the one hand, there is the ideal we purport to uphold: that a society has a responsibility to protect and nurture its youth. But on the other hand, there is the increasingly vengeful desire to see crime punished and the increasing rise of antipathy and fear of the very youth we are supposed to love and care for. The solution, according to Zimring—and it is a chillingly cynical one—is simply to elide the problem by arbitrarily deciding to lower the bar on who is considered an adult. Thus we can punish "criminals" in single-digit age groups with no compunction, since we now can simply call them "adults."[11] The documentation for this kind of thing is abundant.[12] Perhaps the most disturbing of all the statistics, however, is the rising rate of actual executions of youths in the United States. In fact, we are among only six nations—the others being Yemen, Pakistan, Iran, Saudi Arabia, and Nigeria—who have executed juveniles since 1990. And of the nineteen such juveniles executed worldwide, ten—more than half—were American children.[13]

To understand the meaning of all these facts and figures, we need to look back to the beginnings of the juvenile justice system, understand the rationale for its inception, and trace its history and ideological shifts in the context of shifts and changes in American society and its dominant ideologies generally. Only then can we begin to understand the roots and rising tide of America's war on youth, and—finally—the role of the media, especially television, in fueling its fires.

In the early nineteenth century, the idea of a special category called "juvenile justice" had not yet been developed. Children under seven years of age were, even then, considered too young to have the capacity to plan a crime; and those between seven and fourteen, while subject to adult penalties, could bring forth evidence to prove that they were influenced by an adult or mentally deficient and so not subject to adult charges.[14] But youths of fourteen and older were subject to adult trials and penalties and were in fact tried and convicted in great numbers. In 1880, more than two thousand youths were incarcerated in adult prisons.[15]

The campaign to change the laws applying to youth began in the 1820s, when the idea of setting up "houses of refuge" for troubled youth of various kinds—"half prison and half school," as one observer described one of the earliest of these homes. These institutions harbored orphans, the destitute, as well as criminals. In the 1840s the first Reform School for Boys was established in Massachusetts; and in 1889 the first juvenile court was established in San Francisco. In both cases the trend to lump together "the bad and the bad-off" continued.[16]

As the trend to establish such institutions spread across the country, controversy arose among criminologists and other social critics about the efficacy and even the political implications of these trends. While those who instigated the changes—centering around the leadership of Jane Addams, the founder of Hull House—were well intentioned, some on the left argued that the results of their efforts were far from progressive. For one thing, as their fiercest critic, Anthony Platt, argued, making "juveniles" a separate category of criminal worked, as Foucault would later argue, to "invent" the concept of "delinquency" and to relegate certain elements of the youth population—primarily the poor and destitute—to an inferior social status, thus institutionalizing the oppression of lower-class youth.[17]

Lawrence Friedman, in his acclaimed history of the American criminal justice system, disputes this analysis to some extent. He argues that there were indeed sound reasons for considering the youths of the lower classes more likely to turn to crime than others, that, in fact, it was quite often the parents of these children who, finding them incorrigible and unmanageable, took them to these courts themselves. The stresses of family life in working-class communities, and the "bad influences" of the neighborhoods in which these children lived, he argues, were indeed likely to produce more delinquents than middle-class families and communities.[18] This argument, however, seems problematic. For, then as now, incarceration and incapacitation are hardly likely to solve the problems of youth crime, no matter what their causes. And as for the causes, in those days as in our own, it is surely the conditions of the communities into which most "delinquent" youth are born that need to be addressed if the problems of youth are to be taken seriously.

In any event, once these juvenile justice institutions were in place, they became integral elements of the criminal justice system as a whole, and so tended to reflect the changing ideological trends in American society generally. Not surprisingly, it was the Warren Court which, in 1967, cast a careful eye on the legalities under which youth were remanded to juvenile detention centers. In *In re Gault* it ruled that such institutions, under the guise of being "nurturing," caring "homes" for the unfortunate, were in fact prisons to which the young were remanded without due process and for unlimited amounts of time. Since that ruling, all juvenile justice proceedings have been forced to conduct their business more in keeping with the way adult courts do, with all the rights of adult defendants given to accused juveniles.[19]

But in an ironic twist of fate, as the country turned sharply to the right and the backlash against Warren Court decisions generally grew stronger, this ruling tended more and more to work against juvenile defendants, opening the way for the increasingly harsh punishments now being handed down against younger and younger children. Starting in 1978, when a juvenile was convicted of murdering two subway passengers in New York City, a cry went up for harsher sentences and for lowering the bar on how young a child could be to be tried as an adult. The result was legislation allowing thirteen-year-olds to be tried as adults for murder and fourteen- and fifteen-year-olds for other serious crimes.[20] As we have seen, in the quarter century since then—and especially since 1990—the severity of such laws, and the number of states adopting them, has risen to astonishing proportions and numbers.

Youth Culture:
America's Love/Hate Relationship with Our Children

In this overly quick review of juvenile justice trends in the United States, much of the economic and cultural background material necessary for an understanding of the historical shifts in juvenile justice policy is missing.

In particular, the ironic double bind implicit in the Warren Court's 1967 ruling needs to be put in cultural perspective. In the 1960s, liberal ideas, and youth culture generally, were looked upon more favorably than at any time before, and certainly since. But except for that short-lived blip in the arc of twentieth-century history, the period from the early nineteenth century to the present has been marked by economic and cultural changes in American society that have placed the very concept of "youth" in a most central and contradictory position, made even more complicated by issues of race, class, and gender.

Indeed, the coming of industrialization, and its symbiotically linked twin, our mass-mediated and thus increasingly "popular" culture, created a situation in which not just "youth" in general, but working-class youth in particular began a "lifestyle" that was deeply disturbing to both the older generations and the middle and upper classes. For with the coming of universal schooling and cheap, widely available, culture, working-class youth in America as well as in England and other European countries as well suddenly had increasingly high literacy rates, enabling them to be employed at early ages and in relatively lucrative jobs. With this shift came a parallel rise in leisure time and the economic ability to consume the new, increasingly cheap print materials, much of it now geared to the new adolescent consuming class.[21] In fact, the parallel rise of literate, employable youth and of popular culture was already, by the mid-nineteenth century, linked in the popular mind—and in criminal justice policy—with the parallel rise in juvenile delinquency. The first statistics on this new term, paralleling the historic point at which American criminal justice policy also began its focus on juvenile delinquency as a new problem, were gathered in 1834. At that time, it was reported that one quarter of all crime was committed by youths between ages fifteen and twenty, an age group making up only one-tenth of the general population.[22] This figure, as most historians agree, is highly unreliable. Nonetheless, it points to the rising hysteria about youth and youth culture at a time when industrialization itself was creating havoc with traditional institutions such as the family, the church, and the community.[23]

The rise of youth culture, in general then, is intimately connected to the rise of industrialism, and later to consumerism and mass media. But nowhere was this more significant than in the United States where, by the end of Word War II, consumerism had become the absolute mainstay of the economy. Before the age of mass production, the most common form of life for Americans was the family business or farm. This economic formation was based on the dynamics and values of the patriarchal family in which the father was the central figure of authority, since it was his work—visible and invaluable—which kept the family alive and thriving. According to Stuart Ewen, the average family at the turn of the last century spent an average of ten dollars per year on consumer goods such as nails, coffee, and fabric for sewing clothes. Everything else they needed for survival was produced at home.[24] Obviously, in such an arrangement, every member of the family—women and children included—was an integral and necessary cog in the wheel of home production. Children stayed home from school during harvest season, and women worked alongside their husbands in a division of labor that made for a harmonious team of self-sufficient home production.

But by the 1920s, with the coming of the machine and the simultaneous (and symbiotic) rise of mass production of commercial goods and images, this patriarchal system of family unity and self-sufficiency gave way, gradually but dramatically, to a radically different way of life. Now men, women, and children no longer worked side by side but rather diverged along separate paths to separate arenas of activity and geography. Men became wage earners, no longer heads of households whose physical labor could be seen to keep life going. They became paid employees whose paychecks—mere pieces of paper with no tangible meaning to the children it now supported—depended upon a new kind of subservience: a need to follow the orders of superiors and please those upon whom they were now dependent for their livelihood.

Women of the upper classes stayed home to tend to household responsibilities, which now involved a good deal more shopping than producing. They also became a good deal more dependent on commercial magazine articles and advertisements about how to manage the new "modern" way of life, so different from the "finger knowledge" passed on from generation to generation of women that had stood them in good stead for so many generations. While poorer women went to work in factories, children were sent off to schools in which the skills demanded for workers in the industrial economy—skills their parents could hardly teach them—were learned.

According to Ewen, "by the 1920s family life had become contested ground," already eroded by a rising divorce rate, pressures from the women's movement, and a rise in juvenile delinquency. The latter, as we have seen, produced the rise of institutions for troubled youth, and the gradually increasing severity of the treatment of those young people unlucky enough to find themselves in them. In other words, what we now call "the breakdown of the family" arose early on as a result of the forces of industrialization and its effects on traditional family dynamics and values.[25]

But there was another side of the story, especially where youth were concerned. For if, on the one hand, the problem of "juvenile delinquency" became a social problem of great concern, on the other hand, youth itself became an essential component in the new industrial order, serving more and more centrally and importantly as both workers and consumers. For by the end of the 1920s, a full two-thirds of the nation's income came from the sale of retail goods. In a sense, then, the traditional patriarchal family was turned on its head, as fathers lost authority, mothers' roles came to be seen more and more—by the newly minted advertising and media industries—as nurturers of youth. And youth itself became the most valuable element of the economic structure, the most important members of the new industrial work force. Strength, vitality, and energy—the qualities which young people held in abundance while their fathers increasingly lost them—were the qualities considered most desirable by employers. And mothers were thus urged more and more emphatically to center their attention on the nurturing of youth.

The Lynds famous study *Middletown* contains any number of quotes from those they interviewed in a typical American city of the 1920s. "Whenever you get old," said a forty-one-year-old laborer, "they are done with you. The only thing a man can do is to keep as young as he can and stay as young as he can." One woman spoke frankly about how youth was her family's most precious commodity. Speaking of her husband, she prophesied, "He is forty and in about ten years now will be on the shelf. . . ." She added that, "We are not saving a penny but we are saving our boys."[26]

The coming of this economic rise of youth brought with it a parallel rise in consumer production and advertising for products geared to a youth market. Mothers were at once urged to buy the best foods—Quaker Oats, Jell-O, and other mass-produced, processed foods—to insure that their children grew strong and healthy. At the same time, they had to work hard to keep themselves looking young, now that youth was the marker of value, with the many cosmetic products appearing more and more rapidly in advertisements and on shop shelves. Moreover, as youth became wage earners, the targeting of younger and younger consumers became the hue and cry of all corporate manufacturers and advertisers.[27]

There is certainly no difficulty in reading the signs in this trend as they have impacted upon our own world. Nor is it difficult to understand—given this brief economic and cultural background review—why Americans, in general, have such mixed feelings about youth. On the one hand, whether it is the realm of music, clothing styles, images of sexual desirability, television programming, film production, and consumer goods generally, it is youth that sets the standard; youth to whom all corporate forces look for approval and consumer dollars; youth to whom adults themselves increasingly look to learn and imitate the latest styles and trends in all these areas. Popular TV shows increasingly portray parents as hopelessly out of it and teenagers and even very young children either ignoring or being disrespectful to their parents, as the parents—dressed as youthfully as possible—look on happily and the laugh track hits its highest decibel level. The sexualization of children, not only in pornography but in mainstream advertising, is a well-known, oft-lamented phenomenon, as is the rise in the number women and men undergoing cosmetic surgery in an effort to look as close to half their age as they can manage.

Such a situation cannot help but produce a kind of social schizophrenia in adult attitudes toward youth—their own and everyone else's. Envy, rage, self-contempt, frustration with discipline problems pitted against the desire to keep up with the Joneses by giving their children every possible advantage and product available—all this can only lead to the kind of love/hate relationship that we are seeing in the manifestation of youth as the current scapegoat for all social problems. All this even as we shell out more and more money—at home, at the movies, at concert halls and in every conceivable mall boutique—to gaze adoringly at and try to emulate the latest teen screen idol or supermodel.

Movies, Television, and the Demonization of Teens

Which brings us to the main issue: the rise of youth culture and especially of popular culture in which young people are centrally featured, and its role in the current demonization of youth in the American criminal justice system. It is important to understand from a historical perspective how the rise of youth as an economically privileged group, as workers as well as consumers, manifested itself in popular culture representation, particularly movies and television. We need to understand how television today, and most importantly the coverage of youth crimes and trials, has come to play so important a role in the rise in support for, and institutionalization of, the harsh, youth-hating laws and policies documented above. For the image of "the teenager" as a cultural icon is as new to American culture as it is to American society as a whole.

It is often said that James Dean, particularly in his 1956 role in *Rebel without a Cause*, was "the first American teenager," the cultural figure that first presented and embodied a concept previously unknown in American culture. There is much truth to that notion. For until the 1950s, although the social conditions that created youth culture were—as we have seen—in a process of change for as long as a century before that decade, it was the movies of the 1950s, especially Dean's mere three movies, that brought to wide-scale public attention what had been a building trend for so many decades previously.[28]

As Thomas Doherty has documented in his study of *Teenagers and Teenpics: The Juvenilization of American Movies in the 1950s*, until the 1950s Hollywood teenagers were not a major presence in film. They were likely to be found in the Mickey Rooney *Andy Hardy* series, in which youth were still depicted as essentially *children*, as integrated members of a still patriarchal, nuclear family. But many factors, according to Doherty, contributed to the construction of the new "teenager" figure in the movies (if not the television series) of the 1950s, besides the ones already noted.[29] To be sure, Doherty notes the particular significance of the invention of the teenager as a commercial strategy to attract the newly financially independent youth audience. "The trouble with teenagers," he notes at one point, "began when some smart salesman made a group of them in order to sell bobby sox."[30]

But there was also the problem of television. In the 1950s, it loomed very large indeed to Hollywood studio executives as a direct threat to their box office sales. After all, television had chosen as its favorite genre the kind of family-oriented sitcoms in which teenagers were featured, as in the Andy Hardy films and similar Hollywood hits featuring wholesome "kids" with wholesome values engaged in wholesome projects. It now saw itself as socializer to a nation in the throes, as we have seen, of social disruption. Hollywood, feeling coopted, decided it needed to go in another, more sensational direction in order to regain its audience. In general, the major direction was toward spectacular musical extravaganzas rather than the social-issue films now being produced on television—at least during the "golden age" of the 1950s. But the second important new direction, as Doherty documents, was to create films in which generational clashes and controversies replaced the harmony of 1930s and 1940 movies—and perhaps most significantly, 1950s TV, where teenagers were still as clean cut, obedient, and innocent as Andy Hardy. Thus came the rise of a new genre: the youth film in which teenagers were portrayed as troubled at best and criminally dangerous—even monstrous—at worst.

Of course, this was the age when songs like "How Much Is That Doggy in the Window" gave way to the earth-shattering rise of rock and roll. And as the new music was perceived as a sign of the degeneration of youth and youth culture, movies featuring this music—*Rock around the Clock, Blackboard Jungle, City across the River* (based on the controversial novel *The Amboy Dukes*), *Crime in the Streets*, and of course *Rebel*— all presented juvenile delinquency as a major problem and portrayed the new youth culture as violent, disrespectful of authority, and generally out of control (and so implicitly in need of social control of a stricter nature than in the past). Needless to say, these films were particularly emphatic in their portrayal of working-class youth as the most out of control. (Dean, in *Rebel*, for example, was ultimately returned to the decent middle-class world he came from, through the guidance of a sympathetic law enforcement officer.) But the 1950s portrayals of dangerous youth went even farther in its tendency toward demonization. This, after all, was the decade that saw such bizarre but highly successful B movies as *I Was a Teen Age Werewolf, Teen Age Zombies,* and *Teenagers from Outer Space*.[31]

Social Victims or Bad Seeds? The Changing Portrayal of Teens

Henry Giroux places this increasing demonization of youth in a broader social context, suggesting that it has been in Hollywood's (and I would add, society's) interest to oversimplify the complex, shifting, and contradictory category of "youth" within the dominant public sphere and to withhold from this sphere the "diverse vices of the young" themselves, as "moral and political agents." Thus, in popular culture, youth becomes "an empty category inhabited by the desires, fantasies and interests of the adult world." Put bluntly, he asserts, "American society . . . exudes both a deep-rooted hostility and chilling indifference toward youth" which serves to reinforce "the dismal conditions under which young people are increasingly living." And like Mike Males, Giroux places the media representation of youth in direct conjunction with the "attacks on youth with respect to policy measures." Quoting conservative social commentator James Q. Wilson, he sums up the now dominant view of youth which the increasing media demonization has helped to promote. "Youth," according to Wilson, "represent a menacing cloud beyond which lurks 30,000 more muggers, killers, and thieves than we have now."[32]

As accurate as Doherty's and Giroux's charting of the rising demonization of youth, especially working-class youth, in Hollywood drama of the 1950s is, I would argue that it needs to be seen in a perhaps more subtle, nuanced, and contradictory way. For while it is certainly true that youth has been, and is increasingly, demonized as the criminal justice policies affecting them have become more and more harsh and punitive, it is also true that there has been—and I would argue still is—a more dialectic process going on the mass media. As we have seen in other aspects of media and law interface, two quite different approaches to the problem of youth crime and delinquency have vied for hegemony: the psychologically and medically based view of crime as a "disease," and the more recent and increasingly powerful vision of youth crime as a sign of the coming of a new breed of young people who, like the demonized "criminals" in tabloid TV series, are simply perceived as an alien, uncivilizable new "race" of "superpredators" for whom there is no hope of salvation.

In fact, even as early as the 1950s and 1960s, Hollywood presented two conflicting versions of problem youth. As the 1970s and 1980s media developed, television too reflected these contradictory visions, although increasingly with less and less sympathy for the former and a more insistent emphasis on the latter. Even in the Dean movies, for example, there is a clear sense of social determinism, in which consumer society, the breakdown of the family, and—unfortunately—the rise of female dominance in the once patriarchal family were clearly marked as factors in the confusion and self-destructive (rather than antisocial) behavior of characters played by Dean and his co-stars, Natalie Wood and Sal Mineo. All come from dysfunctional families in which material values have replaced family values, and young people are unable to communicate with parents, who are portrayed as neglectful, self-absorbed, and themselves struggling to find ways to survive in the new, frightening postwar society. And even films like *Blackboard Jungle* and *City across the River*, while they certainly meant to alarm, even terrify, adults, nonetheless presented the problems of youth in a social, often class-conscious way which created an undercurrent of contradiction and complexity.

In fact, there is a whole school of films, from the 1950s to the 1980s, in which youth culture is portrayed as alienated and divorced from adult society and values, but in which primacy is placed not on the kids themselves, but on the larger society that has spawned them. Even a film like *Badlands*, a 1970s fictionalized version of the Charlie Starkweather crime spree—one of the first to shock the nation—portrays the ruthless and brutal criminals as products of society. And in the 1980s, similarly, films like *Reckless* and *At Close Range*, which also portray young people as brutal criminals, place the criminals and crimes in a social context in which social institutions, including the family, are seen as causal factors. Perhaps the most moving of these films is the 1987 *River's Edge*, based on the true story of a group of California teenagers who witness a good friend brutally murder his girlfriend and wait several days before informing the police. The film makes clear, however, that these kids have been raised in an adult society in which a moral vacuum has replaced notions of right and wrong, and there are simply no adult role models with any credibility whatsoever. Indeed, *River's Edge* is most astute in presenting all the adults—from the high school teacher, to the parents, to the mentally unbalanced drug dealer to whom they turn most often—as over-aged adolescents themselves, refusing to grow and assume adult responsibility. In fact, they implicitly encourage the teenagers in their care in their failure to grow up because—as Ewen points out—they are part of a world which is so envied and emulated by adults, that immaturity and irresponsibility become the only values they convey to their young charges.[33]

The other dominant strain of youth films of this period—the comedies and youth-centered dramas of John Hughes presenting teenagers not as criminals but as relatively decent, kids—similarly present a world in which no adult authority (indeed almost no adults at all) play a role.

Parents are all but absent, or, when present, totally self-absorbed in their own pleasures. Teachers are simply portrayed as simpleminded nerds and fools. *Fast Times at Ridgemont High* and *Risky Business*—both of which portray kids on their own finding their ways with the help of peers, not adults—are the best of these films. The John Hughes canon includes such films as *The Breakfast Club*, about a group of high school kids from different cliques forced to spend a long time together in detention, who, in the process, learn tolerance and mutual respect from each other; and *Pretty in Pink,* about a working-class girl who cares for her largely indigent father, sews her own unique clothes, and ultimately triumphs over class snobbery. Both are particularly interesting examples of a genre that hardly demonizes kids, but rather presents them as rising above the negative social forces and values that dominate the times in rather impressive, not to so noble, ways. In fact, all the Hughes films deal with class conflicts in which the working-class kids become heroes while the snobbish rich kids ultimately are rejected as shallow, mean spirited, and morally defective. In all of these films—both the films about delinquency and those about average kids working out healthy social and moral value systems within peer groups—there is a sympathy. In the case of Hughes, there is also a sincere respect for the children of a society and a generation in which adult authority is absent, or utterly destructive and toxic.

Television and the Shift from Social to Biological Determinism

What I am suggesting here is that the popular culture of the last half of the twentieth century, while preoccupied, even obsessed, with youth and youth culture, was not always or entirely hostile to youth. Indeed, while the beginnings of the now dominant mode of portraying teenagers as aliens, vampires, werewolves, and other such metaphorically nonhuman creatures of inherently bestial and antisocial natures begins in the 1950s, it has until quite recently been balanced—or at least battled—by a clear, if increasingly weakened perspective. In this view, kids—even the most violent of kids—have been portrayed within the context of an increasingly decadent and indifferent society, which, at least to some extent, if even implicitly, is seen as a factor in the fates of the kids featured.

This is not to say that films like *River's Edge* do not belong to a genre in which young people seem, probably to most viewers, inscrutable and even terrifying, and thus contribute to the growing sense of hatred and fear of youth in the general public. But while the dark grimness of these films and some of the actions of the characters are certainly meant to shock and terrify adult audiences, the films present a larger message to those open to hearing it: that decency still exists within much of the youth population, and that it is the absence of social and moral role models and messages from adult society that, on one hand, leads so many kids to acts of antisocial criminality, and on the other, forces the good kids to work so hard to find their way to the right road. There is, then, an ideological battle, best seen in the growing tide of youth-centered film and television drama, over how to interpret—and thus implicitly deal with—alienated and delinquent youth. It is a battle that has been evident since the 1950s, when "juvenile delinquency," and youth as a social category apart from adult society, became widely discussed issues of grave concern.

But while, even within the criminal justice system of the 1990s, remnants of this "debate" are evident, even in the 1990s and currently they are increasingly unpopular, both within criminal justice circles and popular culture. The major media discourse around the so-called abuse excuse that dominated so much of 1990s public discourse, for example, was a significant sign of the changing times. It provoked the virulent backlash against explanations—and defenses—based on the notion that a young person's admittedly criminal act might best be understood and judged in terms of her or his social and family background and experience. "Personal responsibility" for one's actions increasingly became the popular response to such "mushy-headed liberal" invocations. Even such prominent liberal attorneys as Alan Dershowitz and Susan Estrich argued these were socially dangerous appeals to sentiment by which virtually all criminal defendants might be found "not guilty" by virtue of the social conditions in which they grew up—in the case of poor and minority defendants—and familial neglect or abuse, in the case of the wealthier.[34]

It is in the context of this shifting debate, and the increasing unpopularity of the more liberal stance, that we must return to the study of trends in popular culture. For if, even in the 1980s, movies were presenting subtly contradictory and complex readings of ever more gruesome youth crimes, television—that bastion of uplifting social messages—was already becoming far more pessimistic about the state of youth in America and what might be done about it. Particularly in the made-for-TV movies that have, as we have seen, served until recently as the primary genre for treating social issues, the message was a subtle one. For it depended far more on almost subliminal messages about how America was losing its children than the openly didactic messages of earlier TV movies. Here, I would argue, is where we see the subtle shift from a psychological, social perspective to a far more biological and moral perspective in which criminal acts become products of, in some way, "defective," "alien" children.

In the 1970s, the progressive era of TV docudrama, family dramas involving increasingly typical problems experienced by (mostly) middle-class families with teenage offspring invariably presented these problems from a socially progressive and optimistic viewpoint. Movies from the 1970s and early 1980s such as *Sarah T: Portrait of a Teen Age Alcoholic*, and *Off the Minnesota Strip* and *Little Ladies of the Night*, both about teenage runaways who become prostitutes, follow a classic pattern. A troubled family, oblivious to what is going on with its teenage children because of their own dysfunctional relationships and habits, is forced to confront the fact that it has been instrumental in causing the near fatal destinies of their troubled children. A social worker or therapist is called; the family recognizes and changes its ways; and the children are returned to normal, productive, middle-class lives. This, of course, is the pattern of classic 1950s films like *Rebel without a Cause*. The major difference is that the big-screen versions tended more often to include tragic consequences, such as the death of Sal Mineo's character in *Rebel*, while the TV movies, though sometimes including such realistic incidents, were—as we would expect from television—less likely to stress the casualties of the generation gap and more likely to end on an upbeat note. Viewing audiences are thus left with uplifting messages about how to notice, and handle, the increasingly serious problems of (again almost exclusively) middle-class white youth.[35]

But in the late 1980s this trend gave way to a far more troubling one. Movies like *A Stranger in the Family*, about a near perfect young teenage boy who, after an automobile accident affecting his brain, turns into a kind of zombie, lacking the ability to relate in any emotional way to his family or anyone else. At one point, he seeks out a group of runaways, another group of lost souls cut off from normal emotional relations with adult society. He feels more connection to them than he does to his family, who seem to want from him an emotional bonding he is no longer capable of feeling. *I Know My First Name Is Steven* is a based-on-fact story of a small boy kidnaped by a sexual molester with whom he lives as a slave for seven years before finding his way back home. Here, too, we have a decent kid who, through no fault of the family, becomes an emotionless, alien stranger who finally moves out of the family home and never regains his previous personality. Female versions of this theme include *Bring Back Our Daughter*, about a young woman, again a victim of a car accident, who becomes a sexual predator, living only for more and more dangerous and extreme sexual experiences and contacts. (This one, I should add, is in no way "based on fact.")

What we see in these typical late 1980s and 1990s movies is a significant shift in television's portrayal of troubled kids and—more significantly—in its message to parents about how to respond to such problems. No more the hopeful turn to therapy or 12 Step programs. Now the message has become far darker—for parents and for society generally, not to mention for youth itself. Your kids are out of your control, they tell us. They have somehow become alien monsters, lacking in human feeling or affect and hopelessly incapable of salvation. We must, they tell us, tragic as this sounds, simply give up on them and let them go. And while crime and prison aren't necessarily mentioned, the implication—one need only think about it for a moment—is clear: these kids may be capable of anything, and since we can't save them, the logical conclusion, as Zimring suggests is the dominant strategy for criminal justice today, is incapacitation, institutionalization, for as long as necessary. And since these kids have been permanently transformed into zombielike aliens, that means permanently.

Popular Culture and the Rise of the "Superpredator"

These movies are quite in keeping with a general trend in popular culture—and the legal system—to portray teens as monsters and aliens, a trend that is particularly visible in the actual trials presented on Court TV, in which kids, who are often psychologically and emotionally damaged in ways clearly related to the social conditions in which they live, are tried and portrayed as pure demons. We will examine some case studies, selected by Court TV (and other media) for particular attention and then endlessly rerun in the interest of their ability to garner high ratings through their extreme sensationalism. But first we need to take a brief but extremely important detour in another direction. As may already have become obvious, and troubling, from our discussion of the demonization of youth in media, we have not yet addressed in this chapter the issue of race. Indeed, an apparent paradox demanding explanation is that while, on the one hand, it is widely noted and indeed obvious to even the most casual television viewer that it is black inner-city youth who are most dramatically singled out by politicians and news media. They are the most common targets and scapegoats in discussions not only of crime but also of the related issue of the assumed role of popular culture—notably rap and hip-hop music—in causing and then perpetuating violent youth crime. Every night on the local news—whether you live in New York City or Kansas City—you are painfully familiar with the almost nightly footage of the "perp walks" of young black males, and increasingly females as well. Jackets are pulled over their heads to hide their faces, they are taken off to jail for some alleged act of drug dealing, vandalism, or violence, or for the abandonment, neglect, or abuse of their young children. The singling-out of racial minorities, along with sexual "deviants" and dark-skinned immigrants, as typical of the criminal element on popular tabloid TV shows is a topic we have already discussed at some length earlier.

Why then, we might well ask, has this chapter about media and youth crime seemed to focus so exclusively on the crimes of white youth, perhaps even especially middle-class white youth? It's an important question that leads to some important, but so far neglected, aspects of the role of media in reflecting and reinforcing the current highly punitive and vengeful criminal justice policies that have made harsh sentences, shaming tactics, all-time-high incarceration rates, executions, and so on so popular with the public. The answer is not as mysterious as it may seem. For while it is certainly true that blacks generally, and poor black youths in particular, are the paradigmatic media symbol for the "problem" of "crime" in America, it is the very ubiquitousness of this image and its meaning, its "taken for grantedness" that makes it less "newsworthy" to the media in particular instances. Indeed, even in the cases I've mentioned in which black youth *were* the perpetrators, they have all been particularly newsworthy not because of the *race* of the youth involved but his *age*. Of all the black youth paraded across our TV screens each night, it is only the young ones—thirteen-year-old Nathaniel Abraham and Nathan Brazil, for example—whose names may be familiar. But the names of Dylan Klebold and Eric Harris, who massacred their fellow students in Columbine, are recognized by almost everyone in America because of the particular shock wave sent out by the real "news" of an affluent, white middle-class youth committing atrocities usually—and now so casually—associated with black youth.

As Herman Gray has noted, it has long been the image of "poor urban blacks" that has, in the dominant media, "marked the boundaries of appropriate middle class behavior and acceptable routes to success." In other words, as Gray argues, we have accepted as "natural" the image of poor blacks as *the* criminal element in America, as well as many other qualities and behaviors associated with "badness," failure, and inferiority of all kinds, from intelligence to ambition. Gray further suggests that this image, and the implications that go with it, has been even further promoted and "naturalized" by the great popularity, in the 1980s, of series like *The Cosby Show*, in which fictional black middle-class success is so cruelly juxtaposed with nightly news reports of underclass black failure and violence. For in Gray's view, the success of Cosby's construction of black professional "normality," of the Huxtables' apparently easy access to everything the American Dream symbolizes, effectively erases the issue of racism from mainstream culture, making it seem as though the problem has been solved. Thus, goes Gray's argument, the nightly parade of black criminals and losers is dramatically plucked from the social, racial, and economic context in which it is produced. They are implicitly seen as emblems of an "essential" inferiority that has nothing to do with institutionalized racism—look at the Cosbys; look at Bill Cosby himself—but with an inherent defect in poor blacks themselves. It is something so taken for granted as to be beyond the need for comment or analysis.[36] Indeed, as we have seen, black youth crime only makes the "big-time" news when it points to something truly new and newsworthy: the lowering of the bar on the age of black criminals. Then, for a while at least, we are again shocked and terrified by the specter of an ever younger population of poor blacks suddenly joining the ranks of the criminally vicious. And then, for a while, we discuss solutions to such "new" problems, and invariably, as Zimring points out, we come to the obvious conclusion that such children can no longer be considered children but must, somehow, be seen and treated as adults. And so the naturalization of poor blacks as criminals and social defectives—even those as young as nine or ten—simply intensifies in its connotation of "normality" and ceases, or will soon cease, to be "news."

Ah, but white-middle-class youth crime! That is indeed newsworthy, indeed a serious assault on the idealized American Dream which television in general promotes and naturalizes. And it is therefore only reasonable that—whether in horror films, TV movies or sensational trials—it is the acts of "good" white kids, those from whom we expect the best, that demand special attention. There is a true paradox in this media strategy, however, in that it tends to distort, in the most bizarre ways, the true problem behind youth crime. For whether it is an eleven-year-old black child or an honor student from an affluent white middle-American suburb receiving endlessly re-viewed, analyzed, and sensationalized media attention, the effect is to make the American population believe that such incidents—which are in fact statistically so rare as to be meaningless[37]—are as common in real life as they are on television. And so we up the ante on criminal punishment legislation and spend more and more of our hard-earned tax dollars on such things as school security systems and high-tech maximum security prisons to ferret out these nonexistent young criminals and warehouse them for the rest of their lives in cages we cannot afford and very few need to be in.

How then do the media rile us up to the point where we are willing to invest so much in such useless and cruel paraphernalia, rather than what we really need: better communities, schools, and health care for the huge numbers of kids, especially poor black kids, who are indeed destined for lives of crime (although primarily nonviolent crime) and serial incarcerations, but who—through what Gray rightly sees as the media's naturalization of their situations—are seen as hopeless and not worth our money or attention? We have already seen a variety of ways in which the ideas that fuel these attitudes and policies are subtly suggested through news and, especially, entertainment media. But it is the real trials of the real cases—singled out by the media *because* of their very rareness—in which middle-class, often affluent, white children commit truly shocking crimes followed by an endless flurry of media analysis and debate that most clearly demonstrate the media's increasing complicity in the youth demonization that has so senselessly and dramatically been intensifying the treatment of children by the criminal justice system.

Crime Stories:
From the Menendez Brothers to the Teenage Vampire

To conclude, I will examine the *Crime Stories* presentation of several much-publicized cases involving sensational crimes committed by white teenagers. These exemplify an important theme running through this book: the ideological struggle over the two dominant versions, or "explanations," of such crimes, and the slow demise in popularity of the psychological and social approach in favor of the now dominant view of young criminals as somehow biologically tainted, cursed, alien beings beyond our help or responsibility.

Perhaps the most high-profile, hotly debated of all these cases was that of the Menendez brothers, two wealthy Beverly Hills youth who, in 1989, brutally murdered their parents as they sat watching television and eating ice cream. During the course of the preparation for, and then televised coverage of, the first of two lengthy trials of these young men, virtually no one in the media or the general public seemed able to see these killers as anything but evil demons, "bad seeds" whose greed and callousness led them to coldbloodedly commit an act of parricide which, to most of us, seemed beyond the pale of "human" behavior. If I can judge by my own personal conversations about the case with many, many friends, associates, and strangers over the course of several years, most people still cannot.

Nonetheless, one of the things that kept the trial—and its meaning—so firmly in the public and media eye for so long was the unexpected nature of the trial itself. To the surprise of most observers, and most especially the prosecutors assigned to the case, it became a site of intense ideological struggle over the causes of the murders and their ultimate social significance. For if the prosecution—and most of the public—assumed a slam-dunk conviction and death sentence for the two, the defense counsel, Leslie Abramson for the younger brother Erik and Jill Lansing for Lyle, managed to turn these expectations on their heads by successfully introducing a scenario and explanation that depended upon the logic of the "battered woman defense" used in the Francine Hughes case. Using the financial resources available to the brothers (but far from available to most murder defendants), they managed to produce a wealth of witnesses and evidence sufficient to convince enough of the jurors of both juries (there were two juries, although only one trial) that the brothers were driven by a perhaps irrational, but to them quite real fear. They were in danger of being killed by their father, the juries were told, as a result of a lifetime of extreme emotional, physical, and sexual abuse at his tyrannical hands. As a result, the juries were hung, and in a second trial, in which much of the "abuse" evidence was not allowed, the brothers were convicted but spared the death penalty. They were sentenced to life imprisonment without parole.

In the *Crime Stories* segment produced in 1994 called "The Menendez Brothers on Trial: The Real Story," one sees and hears quite vividly the way in which these competing ideological interpretations of the case went toe to toe, making the trial, beyond its sensational nature, an intriguing intellectual and political battle over which *theory* of criminal behavior would win out. To the prosecutors' and others involved in the case against the brothers, Erik and Lyle were described as "sociopathic murderers" who "swaggered smugly" into the courtroom or tried to hide their evil natures by affecting a clearly "phony school boy appearance." To their lawyers and family supporters, on the other hand, they were "decent," even "likable" boys who, despite their almost unbelievably horrendous treatment at the hands of their father, retained a "core of decency" that would make them capable of becoming productive, contributing citizens with the help of psychiatric treatment.

Most commentators and callers to television and radio talk shows weren't buying it, however, although a small percentage of those who called—mostly college students or child abuse survivors—sympathized with the defense. Indeed, in retrospect, we can see the clear significance of the case and its theoretical underpinnings not only in the public and media response to the case, but in the proceedings of the second, definitive trial. Not only did the so-called abuse excuse fail to convince, but it became an increasingly unpopular defense in general, as the cases that followed in the late 1990s, and their treatment on Court TV's *Crime Stories*, make clear. Notions of illness and treatment have increasingly given way, in both the courts and the media, to theories of innate evil and the increasing monstrousness of youth.

One thing that has not changed, however, is the melodramatic conventions and ideologies through which such cases are discussed and presented. The Menendez trial was most definitively a family melodrama, which, in keeping the cultural turns of the times, had dramatic and terrifying elements of the horror film genre. As in traditional melodrama, the defense held that the defendants were innocent victims at the hands of a tyrannical patriarch intent upon control of his sons and influenced primarily by the desire for money and status. In his mind, his "disciplinary" strategies would instill these in his sons, making them as ruthlessly successful in business as he himself—a Cuban immigrant—had become. Douglas Sirk, the director of many classic Hollywood family melodramas of the 1950s, couldn't have found a better story to film. The Hitchcock of the 1950s and early 1960s would have loved it, too, if only the abusive parent had been the mother. But to the prosecution, and most of the media and public, the melodrama was far more in keeping with 1980s and 1990s horror films in which the murderous children were far from victims but inhuman, alien offspring, given every privilege, luxury, and advantage and yet, inexplicably, drawn to the brutal, cold-blooded murder of the parents to whom they were so indebted.

In 1996, the case of Barry Lukaitis, a fourteen-year-old boy, was among the first of the white teenage killing spree cases to attract intense national attention and alarm. Apparently influenced by a Stephen King novel called *Rage*, about a boy who shoots up his classroom; a song by Pearl Jam, about a similar incident; and the Oliver Stone film *Natural Born Killers*, about a teenage couple on a murderous rampage, he dressed in a black trench coat, took a shotgun and went to his school classroom and shot and killed several people. The *Crime Stories* segment about the case, called "Washington vs. Lukaitis: Killer in Class," again reveals the gradual shift from social to biological or religious interpretations of such crimes, as well as their increasing popularity as television fare. Again we have a battle—although a highly unbalanced one now—between a defense trying to argue for the social and family forces that caused Lukaitis to become "mentally ill" and a prosecution bent on portraying the killer as the embodiment of sheer, inhuman "evil." That the latter view is already winning out on television as well as in the courtroom is evident by the very different style in which this drama—produced only two years after the Menendez segment—is presented. While the Menendez tape is presented in traditional documentary style, emphasizing the ideas and issues rather than the horror (no horrifying images appear in this segment), the Lukaitis tape is quite dramatically and disturbingly presented in the style of tabloid shows like *Cops* and begins with a warning to parents of "graphic material." Grainy images of shadowy, run-down urban landscapes and distorted, ominous images of Lukaitis himself (as reenacted for the segment by an actor), with trench coat on and machine gun in hand, begin the segment. We are told that it was 10 degrees out that day and in the background we hear eerie music to suit the cold, shadowy darkness of the scene and the story we are about to be told.

Even the defense's attempt to explain the boy's actions in terms of family trauma is creepy. No Beverly Hills mansions, and no ice-cream-eating, TV-watching parents for this child. His mother—who actually bought him the strange outfit in which he killed—explains how traumatized Barry was by her own bizarre behavior. At one point, for example, she describes telling him, when he was only in seventh grade, how she planned to go to her estranged husband's home, tie him and his girlfriend to a chair, and shoot herself in front of them. But it is Barry's own bizarre behavior in court that most strongly impresses viewers, and no doubt jurors, with the inhuman, emotionless nature of this truly strange child. Day after day he sits motionless and expressionless in court, like the "zombie" the prosecutors call him. And witnesses to the crime describe him, even in school, as behaving "like a sleepwalker" or "in a trance."

That this child is and was deeply disturbed emotionally if not mentally seems too obvious to belabor. But the horror of his actions, in the context of his and his parents' bizarre appearance and behavior before and during the trial, especially given the horror movie conventions chosen by Court TV to present the tale, all lend themselves far more easily to the "evil demon" theory than any "abuse excuse" or social or psychiatric analysis. Indeed, the entire presentation of this case is so different from that of the Menendez brothers as to seem to exist in two different universes, as indeed they do. For with the Menendez case we are still in the realm of reason, debate, the possibility of redemption and normality. But with Barry Lukaitis, we enter a region of sheer nightmare and horror, where only the likes of Michael Meyers and Freddy Krueger walk; no sunny days are spent on tennis courts; and classrooms in which kids wear Shetland sweaters and Gap jeans simply do not exist. Neither do hung juries. Barry Lukaitis's jury took relatively little time to find him guilty of two counts of first-degree murder, among other lesser charges. They sentenced him, as an adult, to a juvenile detention center until the age of eighteen, after which he will be transferred to an adult facility, where he will spend the rest of his life with no chance of parole.

Among the many trials televised on Court TV and condensed into *Crime Stories* segments from 1997 to 1999, a full fifty-nine involved teen and juvenile offenders, tried for murder and sentenced to life without parole or—in some cases—death. These *Crime Stories* invariably tend to be presented in the style of the Lukaitis segment, using the conventions of horror films and the visual style of low-budget tabloid crime shows. The reasons for this dramatic shift from the far more dignified, documentary-style treatment of the Menendez case, and all the other trials televised and condensed to docudrama format in the first years of the network's existence, are many and intertwined. Economics cannot be overlooked, however. In the early years, when the network—and televised trials as media events generally—were a novelty, it was enough simply to televise the trials straight, so to speak. But as time went on, the novelty wore off, and only the most sensational trials drew audiences. Court TV gradually shifted its emphasis away from daily coverage and nightly commentary about whatever trials seemed most interesting at the moment. Even then, of course, the driving force was to choose trials that on some level involved the kind of sensationalism or social controversy that would draw audiences.

Nightly news and coverage gave way to reruns of crime series like *Homicide* and *Cops*, as well as original, tabloidesque series like *Inside Cell Block F: The Toughest Prison in America*, as a way of garnering ratings and staying in business. Indeed, the original title of the *Crime Stories* series was *Trial Stories*, but in the late 1990s, as the style and generic conventions of the series changed, so too did its title—now emphasizing the element of crime rather than law. In keeping with the title change, along came stylistic and generic changes. Thus, again, we see how economics, aesthetics, and criminal justice policy converge to create a form of television programming which, inherently—and not necessarily for conscious political reasons—reinforced the growing trend in legal policy toward viewing crime and criminals in terms of alien, monstrous, predators looming in the dark shadows of the American landscape, filled with irrational, inhuman compulsions to violence, especially against those closest to them.

Of all the *Crime Stories* segments about youths convicted of murder, I'll end with two disturbingly typical cases. In these, punishment of the harshest order was handed down to young white men. Their crimes, while certainly horrific and shocking if hardly typical of the run-of-the-mill cases that pass through juvenile courts every day in America, were particularly suited to the conventions of the melodramatic horror genre and the attention-getting sensationalism of the twenty-four-hour news and talk channels. The cases were sensationalized as "Facing the Death Penalty: The Trial of Private Burmeister" and "The Vampire Murderer." The Burmeister case concerned a young man in the military who became a member of a Nazi skinhead organization, which was apparently operating quite openly within the barracks of the military installation. He was convicted of murdering two black people—a middle-aged, working-class couple—as a rite of passage that would qualify him to obtain the spider web tattoo on his arm that marked him as proudly "having killed a nigger."

The segment was narrated by Terry Moran, one of the brightest and most eloquent of the Court TV anchors. But his presentation was noticeably different in this case than in the Menendez segment. "Evil lives in

America," he began, as a series of ominous images of Nazi flags, caches of weapons of mass destruction, and other violent and racist parapher-nalia were displayed, tabloid-style, on the screen. Since video cameras had not documented either the crime or the stories about Burmeister told by witnesses, a particularly large amount of time was devoted to tabloid-style "reenactments" of what the witnesses were describing, each of which—as in the Lukaitis case—was presented in the most creepy style imaginable. Dark, shadowy, images of eerie, grim-faced young men lurking in barren landscapes, or rowdily, drunkenly planning their mur-derous missions as raucous, truly disgusting, racist, anti-Semitic, homo-phobic songs—recorded by members of this subculture—played on a stereo.

The wailing of the victims' loved ones, all decent working-class family people, was melodramatically repeated as a kind of refrain throughout the proceedings, making Burmeister's own family melodrama, as pre-sented by the defense, even less sympathetic as an "abuse excuse" case than the Lukaitis defense. Indeed, the only mitigating circumstance the defense could come up with seemed to be the death of his sister when he was in junior high school, and his mother's temporary turn to drink, in the aftermath of this tragedy, to soothe her grief. As for his reasons for becoming a Nazi, there was only the paltry suggestion that he "had al-ways wanted to belong" (as indeed do we all).

Throughout the trial this particularly unattractive, sullen young man sat stony faced. The jury, apparently in a state of extreme anger and ex-haustion because one woman refused to vote for the death penalty on the grounds that, in her view, "life in prison was a worse fate," finally rec-ommended life with no parole. And at the sentencing, Burmeister, who had not testified, uttered his first words to the jury: "The state has chosen to blame me; so be it for now," he said defiantly. But, "I'm not conced-ing; I'm not gonna quit; this is not over."

And then, as a last word, Moran commented again upon the troubling issue of "evil" in America. "One worries," he said thoughtfully, "about whether trying to understand the evil lessens it somehow; whether trying to get a handle on it takes away from the condemnation we feel." In other words, Moran, so evenhanded and reasonable about the Menendez brothers, was now, only a few years later, wondering whether this ratio-nal, social-constructionist view of "evil" did not in fact diminish our sense of moral outrage at its existence.

The most eerie of all the *Crime Stories* segments I viewed was surely that of sixteen-year-old Rob Ferrell, a self-proclaimed vampire, who admitted to bludgeoning to death the parents of one of the members of his vampire cult. There is no need, I think, to repeat the various visual, verbal, and dramatic techniques used to create a sense of horror, of alien beings too far beyond the pale of "normal" emotion or reason to be considered anything but inhuman monsters. Indeed, the opening words of Richard Belzer, the commentator in this segment, were, "Like characters in a horror movie," the defendant and his friends "acted out a set of rituals and actions which must surely boggle the minds of most Americans and fill them with terror and alarm." Later, one of police officers repeated this phrase, saying, "I thought I had walked into a horror movie," when describing the crime scene. Nor did Ferrell disagree. "I'm evil," he proudly stated in interviews. "I've been evil for some years. I enjoy being evil." And as footage—this time real footage—of the defendant crossed the screen, we saw him mugging, sticking his tongue out, and generally trying to appear as menacing as possible.

Witnesses, including the fourteen-year-old girl whose parents were killed, described her desire to "share blood" with Ferrell and so become a vampire because—like Burmeister—"I wanted to be a part of something instead of a nobody. I've been a nobody all my life." And even more startling was the absence of even the vaguest defense attempt to paint Ferrell in psychologically understandable, much less mitigating, terms. His own mother, in fact, was herself a vampire who had been convicted of soliciting sex from a fourteen-year-old member of the vampire cult. Needless to say, there was no sense of human remorse or any other emotion from Ferrell, except his apparent pride in being "evil." And with so little to go on, the jury, after four and a half hours, reached a guilty verdict. After hearing the victim impact statements at sentencing, they voted unanimously on a recommendation of death, with which the judge concurred.

These cases may seem particularly bizarre, and they certainly do fit that description. But they are not only true cases, they are the cases singled out—for obvious reasons—to be featured and debated, not only on Court TV but also on news and talk television generally. For it is always the most bizarre and sensational of cases that the media know will attract attention and garner ratings. Hate crimes committed by fringe groups of violent bigots, bizarre cults devoted to satanic, often violent rituals, and individual cases of teenagers like Lukaitis whose fantasies and actions are equally bizarre and terrifying are not unheard-of cases in America these days. Of course they exist and occur; and of course, on some level, they are socially troubling.

But what happens when the media, for their own reasons, exaggerate and overplay the numbers of such groups and individuals? What happens, in particular, when they choose—again for reasons of sensation and ratings—to portray these bizarre and unusual (and the operative word here is *unusual)* cases in the conventions of the most melodramatic, over-the-top, B-movie horror films? Consciously or unconsciously, audiences receive a terrifying and politically loaded message about American youth, American society generally, and especially the "rise" in youth crime in general across all sectors of the population. Cults and murderous madmen in America are a relatively small segment of the population. Moreover, they have—at least since the advent of cheap print media—always existed and always been hyped by media moguls.

What is different about these cases and these media representations is, first, the dramatic power of visual media, especially television, which is consumed, like the air around us, on a continuous, almost unconscious basis. But far more importantly, as we have seen, are the shifting visual and generic conventions through which these cases and characters and cults are presented. The ultimate significance of the Menendez case—among the first cases to become a major media event—was the valiant, but ultimate failure of the defendant-centered, psychologically and socially grounded defense of the brothers. For not only the courts and public opinion, but equally—if not more significantly—Court TV and the other media understood this failure as a signal that it was time to change representational strategies. They needed to fit the growing tide of sentiment that preferred, indeed seemed to get some sense of security and satisfaction from, a view of youth crime in which defendants were presented as evil demons, lost to the human race, and fit only for incapacitation or death. And so, once again, the inadvertent but powerful alliance of political and legal policy and television's representational strategies have created a simpleminded, distorted, and incredibly one-sided vision of crime. Now the "victims" are no longer—in any dominant ideological construction—society's neglected, abused, despised, envied, and thrown-away youth, but only those against whom they sometimes blindly and tragically strike out.

In an old folk song, "The Ballad of Donald White," the narrator, about to go to the gallows for murder, admits his guilt, tells his sad life story and ends with the following lines addressed to those "who think the worst of me" and whose minds he assumes "will be at ease when I'm on that hanging tree":

> There's just one more question before they kill me dead
> I'm wondering just how much to you I've really said
> Concerning all the boys who walk the road just like me
> Are they enemies or victims of your society?

The answer, one hundred and fifty years after the incident the song records, is clear. Not only are boys like White deemed "enemies" of society; they are no longer considered members of society at all, but demon creatures who must be expunged from society entirely in order to ensure our common "safety."

8

Television, Melodrama, and the Rise of the Victims' Rights Movement

In 1974 I saw a movie that sent chills down my spine. It was called *Death Wish*, and it told the story of a mild-mannered liberal businessman whose wife and daughter were brutally raped and murdered by a group of dark-skinned, near subhuman thugs. His response to his grief was to become a self-styled vigilante, stalking the New York City streets in search of other muggers and rapists, all young, apparently deranged, and dark skinned, and shooting them down in cold blood. The audience cheered more loudly at each burst of vengeful gunfire, for, as critic Leonard Maltin has rightly noted, the film was a masterpiece of "manipulation at its zenith."[1] It was also, I now see, the beginning of a slow but insidious trend in national consciousness and criminal justice policy away from the liberal policies of the Warren Court and its concerns that the rights of defendants be protected from possible abuses by the engines of the state. We have now reached a far more reactionary (in the truest sense of that word), often even bloodthirsty, concern for the "rights" of "victims" to have revenge, and we mete out punishment of the most extreme kind. The trend has been evident in a variety of ways and places, but it can be seen most dramatically in the rise of the increasingly influential Victims' Rights movement.

In this chapter, I want to explore the genealogy of this movement's rise to prominence. In its ideological thrust and in the popularity it has amassed among the general public and many legal practitioners and scholars, it speaks to the heart of what I have been discussing in the preceding chapters: the shift from a legal system, and a broad, media-supported, trend in national thinking, in which victims and victimization have become more and more central while the root causes of crime generally, much less the particular crime of any particular defendant, are increasingly receding in importance. And, as a corollary to this shift, of course, there is a parallel shift in legal and public sentiment away from issues of rehabilitation and redemption, or—more importantly—from attempts to get at root causes of crime in general. Vengeance and punishment are becoming good enough social responses to criminal acts and crime generally. Thus, the coming of this now powerful social movement has much to tell us about how we as a nation have come to see and treat all manner of disturbing, problematic behaviors and situations in terms of crime and punishment, judgment and revenge. And we must consider the role that television has played in helping to promote its success.

Indeed, while there were several contributing elements to the rise of the Victims' Rights movement—the shift to the right in national political sensibilities and its impact on criminal legal procedures being among the most obvious—it has been television, especially the coming of cameras in the courtroom and the rise of the televised trial as major media event, which has been most influential. For in transforming legal proceedings into dramatic spectacles, informed by the most melodramatic of pop culture genres and conventions, television has, not necessarily intentionally, given emotional aid to a movement which, like the so-called Right-to-Life movement, depends on sentimental, emotionally loaded images and narratives to influence our common understandings and attitudes about criminal justice in ways that are more politically dangerous than they may seem.

As a genre film, of course, *Death Wish* was not new. The revenge film genre has been around as long as Hollywood itself, and it has always incorporated themes and conventions informed by a recognizable set of assumptions about law and criminal justice. Thomas Schatz, in his influential study of *Hollywood Genres*, has described genre films as "sociological events," "objectified mass dreams" that work "to solve, if only temporarily, the conflicts which have disturbed the community welfare."[2] Crime and the fear of crime, especially violent crime, are certainly among the most emotionally loaded of those "disturbances of community welfare." And revenge, as acted out in such genre films as *Death Wish* and *Dirty Harry*, have an obvious emotional appeal. They satisfy our desire for the kind of instant gratification that the slowly grinding wheels of actual justice rarely provide.

William Ian Miller, in an interesting study of Clint Eastwood's revenge films, describes revenge as "a style of doing justice" made necessary when the state cannot or will not take effective action against crime.[3] "It is not just that popular culture invents the avenger, that it invents a more efficient style of justice for us, frustrated as we are by our fears, our anxieties, our perceptions of crime and violence," he writes. "Popular culture is also largely responsible for creating our image of the avenger's straw men: the legal system. . . . It constructs images of a largely inept law and in turn constructs a view of society desperately in need of efficient and effective mechanisms of social control."[4]

Miller sees these films as not in step with current attitudes in the real world of criminal justice. In our legal system, he argues, revenge is associated largely with "the ineffable vulgarity of young lower-class youth" and given little respect. "Revenge is not a publicly admissible motive" today, he argues. "Church, state and reason all line up against it." "Retribution," a related but far weaker concept, "can still be mentioned in polite society," he believes, " because it implies "a controlled, proportional" response to wrongdoing, and, since it is impersonal and administered by the state, involves no emotional tone.[5] But the demand for revenge as a legal remedy is considered far too extreme for rational, civilized societies.

A recent textbook on *Media, Crime, and Criminal Justice*—one of the few available, to my knowledge—seems to support Miller's argument about the marginalization of revenge in current criminal justice discourse. The author begins his chapter on "Media and the Construction of Crime and Justice" by defining the concerns of criminal justice as "the opposing ideas of due process and crime control,"[6] while making no mention at all of the concepts of punishment or retribution, much less revenge. Nonetheless, Miller argues, there is an emotional need in most of us for a more emotionally resonant way of doing justice, and the revenge genre fills that need. These films please us, he says, because they work as fantasies, satisfying that "repressed segment of us" that craves such gratifying emotional closure, no matter what the legal system says.

Miller's argument rests on the dubious assumption that revenge fantasies have traditionally reflected the subconscious need to gratify urges that civilized society represses. But even if he is right, I would argue that the repressed desires expressed in revenge genre films are in fact less and less repressed; that, on the contrary, there is a quite dramatic return to the fashionability of the revenge model of justice in this country, engineered in great part by the growing influence of the Victims Rights' movement, although it differs in important ways from Miller's generic model. For in the Victims' Rights movement's model, revenge is no longer associated with the disreputable "vulgarity of lower class youth," but with the most respectable, middle- and upper-class segments of our population. They see themselves as "victims," more often than not, of today's version of "vulgar, lower class youth"—usually poor inner-city blacks, the most demonized figures in media treatments of crime today. Indeed, it is this very model of revenge—the respectable, middle-class white citizen avenging himself on the vulgar, lower-class, dark-skinned youthful predator—that movies like *Death Wish* and *Dirty Harry* so ominously herald. And it is this model which televised trials more and more often present to the American public, whose growing hunger for vengeance it feeds and nurtures.

Interestingly enough, in an "Unconcluding Postscript," to his essay, Miller himself acknowledges the possible return of the revenge model and attributes it, quite rightly, to the increased merging of popular culture convention and legal reality. Indeed, he describes Court TV as the most seamless example of this merging of "the law of popular culture and the 'real' thing." For it is on Court TV that law most dramatically and explicitly becomes entertainment. Nor is he particularly alarmed about this turn. "Popular culture sees revenge as a necessary supplement to the law," he writes, "and it might well be that popular culture is not wrong."[7] I will argue that popular culture is indeed quite wrong. But I will be arguing against the grain of current legal sentiment and policy.

A Genealogy of Victims' Rights

Before turning to the ways in which TV has helped to create support for a model of criminal justice based more on revenge than rehabilitation or retribution, more on passion than reason, and more on concern for victims than for those whose life and liberty are threatened by the state, it will be useful to turn briefly to some of the legal and social factors that have given rise to these attitudes. For, as we have seen, mass media never single-handedly creates trends in popular sentiment. Rather, it works in tandem with other forces in the social and political environment to reflect and reinforce dominant sentiments and attitudes. In the case of victims' rights, however, television has played an especially important role, because, as a visual, dramatic medium, it has the power to forge larger-than-life images of human suffering and to elicit strong emotional responses which are in keeping with the rhetoric of victims' rights.

In an article entitled "Victims and Vengeance: Why the Victims Rights Amendment is a Bad Idea," Bruce Shapiro documents his contention that "in . . . American politics today, victims of violent crime are accorded uniquely sanctified status." He quotes Democratic attorney general Janet Reno's address to a victims' rights convention in which she attests to drawing "the most strength from victims, for they represent America to me: people who will not be put down, people who will not be defeated, people who will rise again and again and stand for what is right. . . . You are my heroes and heroines," she gushes. "You are but little lower than the angels." Shapiro insists that "this is not just rhetoric" and he is right.[8] In the 1996 elections, eight states added victims' rights language to their constitution, joining twenty-eight others; Carolyn McCarthy, the wife and mother of two of Colin Ferguson's victims won a seat in Congress; the Justice Department doubled its victims' assistance budget to $400 million; and President Clinton, speaking in the Rose Garden, added his support to the movement by insisting that "the only way to give victims equal and due consideration" would be to amend the Constitution of the United States. Thus the powerful influence of a movement that began as a small group of grassroots support and advocacy groups, but in the past fifteen years has ballooned into a major force of some eight thousand organizations, most of them funded by right-wing groups and politicians. Shapiro refers to the movement as a "vengeance-rights lobby," and indeed, many of its demands—for swifter executions and longer prison terms, for example—smack of the "style of justice" depicted and valorized in the revenge genre movies Miller analyzes.

Of course, there has been a trend toward harsher punishments and greater numbers of executions in this country for quite a while, and the trend is in keeping with the rightward drift of the nation around many issues, fueled in part by an increasing fear that society has become too permissive. But victims' rights advocates are among the major players in this trend, and their success in recent years has been notable. Among the more important markers of this success was the Supreme Court ruling in 1991, in *Payne v. Tennessee*, 501 U.S. 808, that victim impact statements would be permitted in sentencing hearings in death penalty cases. Only a few years earlier, in 1987, in *Booth v. Maryland*, 482 U.S. 496, the Court had narrowly defeated such a ruling. Nor was the 1991 decision unanimous. Justices Marshall, Stevens, and Blackmun all dissented, and Stevens, in his strongly worded dissent, expressed particular alarm. Among his concerns was that such statements would tell juries that "some of the murdered dead were more equal than others—and that defendants who killed 'important' people were more deserving of execution." But more importantly, he noted with concern, "the current popularity of capital punishment . . . the political appeal of arguments that assume that increasing the severity of sentences is the best cure for . . . crime, and the political strength of the 'victims' rights' movement." Given this turn in popular opinion, he wrote, "I recognize that today's decision will be greeted with enthusiasm by a large number of . . . citizens." But to him it seemed a "great tragedy" and "a sad day for a great institution" because, he said, "what Justice Holmes had called 'the hydraulic pressure' of public opinion . . . ha[d] played a role not only in the Court's decision to hear the case . . . but even in its resolution of the constitutional issue involved." Stevens was in the minority, however, and these statements are now a staple of death penalty sentencing hearings. Their impact, with the advent of televised trials, reaches far beyond the twelve jurors to whom they are immediately addressed.

As we have seen, the Supreme Court's ultimate reasoning, in finally allowing cameras into courtrooms at all, was to allay the fears, rising ominously by the late seventies, that the criminal justice system wasn't "working," that it was too "soft on crime" and that criminals were increasingly being allowed to go free, roaming the streets in search of ever more innocent victims. And it is just such a specter of justice as ineffective, as "soft on crime," as incapable of controlling street crime or punishing wrongdoers which Miller notes as a staple of the revenge drama.[9] But while the justices assumed that the airing of actual trials would somehow allay those fears by showing justice "at work," so to speak, busily and effectively punishing and even banishing the wrongdoers, this assumption has not always proven true. In fact, as we have seen, in the early days of Court TV the most high-profile trials, the ones that most caught public attention and engendered TV talk show debate, were not particularly good examples of justice at work—at least in the eyes of the public. The first Menendez brothers trial and the O. J. Simpson trial both tended to further inflame public outrage at a system in which people seemed literally to get away with murder. And because of this, judges and prosecutors had to learn to conduct their trials in ways that would produce the salutary results the justices hoped for when they allowed the cameras in. But as we have seen, the Menendez and Simpson trials did not in fact produce such closure, and, as a result, there was more and more apprehension on the part of judges and prosecutors about cameras in courtrooms.

And there was more and more effort, as the McVeigh trial showed, to make sure no high-profile case that garnered media attention, whether actually televised or merely reported on extensively, would give such an impression. The Menendez brothers' judge (who did indeed shift gears dramatically in the second trial), and their successors have indeed succeeded in shifting public perceptions of the justice system rather dramatically. So successful have they been that in March 1999 the American Bar Association conducted a survey of public opinion about the workings of the justice system. It found that, indeed, in the last decade, Americans' opinions of the court system has risen significantly, while other institutions—especially the media and Congress—were deemed even more corrupt and ineffective than in previous years. Their recommendation was that in order to further educate the public about the judicial system and thereby further improve its public image, the Supreme Court, so long adamantly opposed to being televised, should now allow cameras into its own proceedings.[10]

The Power of Televised Victimology

The power of televised trials to influence many voters' views of the justice system has thus been as successful as the justices had hoped. But this came only after a period of trial and error in which judges and prosecutors learned to use television in ways that were most likely to produce "hegemonic narratives" in which the system was shown to work. The role of victims in these made-for-TV spectacles has been particularly effective in creating this image, since audiences tend to empathize with feelings of victims and share their satisfaction in verdicts in which those convicted of victimizing innocent citizens are harshly punished. But even before the advent of televised trials, when the Victims' Rights movement was just beginning, it recognized that television could be a powerful tool in pleading its cause and found ways to make use of it. In fact, the ties between victims' rights and television date back to 1983, when a man named John Walsh—the father of a kidnaped child who quickly became a prominent spokesperson for the movement—became the first of what is now a long line of Celebrity Victims, as I think of them. The most well known are the fathers of Ron Goldman and Polly Klaas, both of whom have logged more airtime in recent years than even the most popular television actors and actresses. In that year, Walsh's story was made into a docudrama, called *Adam,* which was so successful that in 1986 it was followed up by a sequel called *Adam: His Song Continues.* Two years later, Walsh parlayed the success of these movies, in which the conventions of melodrama were used to instill pity for the victims and fear of the monstrous predators into media stardom by becoming the host of his own tabloid TV series, *America's Most Wanted.* The series, which featured reenactments of actual crimes followed by pleas to viewers to help catch the still-at-large perpetrators, was a success with audiences as well as the FBI, which worked with Walsh on the series and welcomed his help in catching alleged criminals.

But as Anna Williams explains in an article about the series, the format was not only sensational and melodramatic in form and style, it was explicitly oriented toward a view of crime as a family matter, for it invariably pitted victims of traditional nuclear families against the harrowing images of criminals as antisocial loners and lunatics preying on women and especially children.[11] Michael Linder, one of the producers of the series, explained in an issue of *TV Guide* the criteria for choosing cases for the series. "A drug dealer who shoots another drug dealer is not as compelling," he explained, "as a child molester or murderer." "If a man brutalizes innocent children, that definitely adds points," he said.[12] Such a hierarchy of victimization is a mainstay of the Victims' Rights movement, which plays upon notions of decent families besieged by violent amoral criminals.

When the series was renewed in 1995, after a brief absence, it had an even more programmatic focus on victims as a cohesive social grouping of good solid citizens and families, fighting the dark armies of antisocial predators. The former grouping of course included the assumed viewers, "we" out there in television land who—as is typical of the television announcer's address to audiences—were assumed to be members of middle class families among whose defining characteristics (along with the desire for, and money to afford, advertised commodities), was fear of crime. To make this point dramatically clear, Walsh even added a subtitle to the new series: *America Fights Back.* And America, in this case, included only those of us in the target audience of middle-class family members fearful of crime. Thus the series constructed itself as a leading component of what was by then a growing national trend, in media, in the courts, and in the growing Victims' Rights movement, dividing American society into two groups defined by their relationship to the criminal justice system: those who prey on others and those who "fight back." Indeed, it is arguable that television today—thanks to series like these as well as televised trials and the commentary they engender—is informed by a fairly new and prominent, if not dominant, thematic: the division of society into criminals and crime fighters. We are all either cops or robbers today, and for those of us on the side of the angels, vengeance for crimes against "innocent victims" is our virtuous stock in trade.

Docudramas like the *Adam* movies and tabloid TV series both employ the conventions of melodrama to engage viewers and elicit emotion and sympathy and a desire for harsh, vengeful punishment. The kidnaping of little Adam Walsh, the rapes and murders of innocent women and children on Walsh's *America's Most Wanted*, these are the images and narratives that fuel the kind of testimony that so moved jurors in the McVeigh trial. And as more death penalty trials are televised, we are seeing more of the power of melodrama to sway the public to the views of victims' rights advocates. Among other ominous trends is the increasing demand by victims to be present and witness the executions of those convicted of killing loved ones. On a recent local newscast, for example, I heard the mother of a murder victim say, with an intensity that was frightening, "I want to be there; I want to be in the front row when they kill that guy; I want to be the one to pull the toggle switch!"

This example is not atypical of what one hears in televised "victim impact statements." Emotion and passion are more and more present in courtroom proceedings, and their impact on jurors and viewers cannot be denied. But is this kind of melodramatic, often hysterical utterance actually appropriate to the adjudication of legal matters? It is certainly the pattern in death penalty sentencing hearings, in which shocking behavior and its impact on survivors is used to titillate, frighten, and enrage viewers. The final sentencing, especially if it is as harsh as the victims demand, offers a utopian fantasy of moral closure, in which the highly personalized resolution of one person's experience of victimization, through the court's revenge on a single perpetrator, suggests, disingenuously, that the larger problem of social violence itself has somehow been "solved."

Another important element of these sentencing hearings is their indulgence of "victims" speaking for harsh sentences for convicted defendants. They allow the use of sentimentality, a term which I believe gets at the heart of what is most frightening and dangerous about the movement for victims' rights and the media's complicity in furthering its goals. Sentimentality is generally understood to be a kind of false, excessive, insincere, and hypocritical form of emotion. It is what is meant by the term "crocodile tears," the often inappropriately excessive and insincere display of grief and sorrow by those who presumably have some other motive or agenda that the display of grief serves to mask. Indeed, Jungian analyst Marie-Louise von Fraanz, in defining the distinction between the sentimentality of melodrama and true grief notes, importantly, that "where there is sentimentality . . . there is also a certain amount of brutality." She uses the example of the Nazi general Hermann Göring who, she notes, "could sign the death sentence for three hundred people but if one of his birds died then that fat old man would cry. . . . He is a classic example," she writes, for "cold brutality is very often covered up by sentimentality."[13] I would certainly agree, for it is clear to me, having spent many hours studying tapes of victim impact statements, that there is a great deal of cold brutality masked by sentimentality in the rhetoric and displays of grief of many of the spokespersons for victims and their "rights."

This is an insight that needs to be more fully considered by those whose honest concern for the suffering of victims leads them to support demands for such legal remedies as the Victims' Rights Amendment. For beneath the compelling emotion that informs the demands of victims, there is all too often an ugly and irrational cry for blood that smacks of mob violence and vigilante justice. And of course such emotions and their ability to fuel desperate, irrational actions are the very stuff of revenge genre films like *Death Wish*, in which audiences cheer the cold-blooded murder of individuals for whom due process has become an annoying distraction from the true needs of society for immediate, harsh punishment.

Lauren Berlant, as I've noted, has written brilliantly about the dangers of sentimentality in the legal and political spheres. She labels the period we live in "an age of sentimental politics" in which "rhetorics of utopian/traumatized feeling"—which, as we have seen, are characteristic of the melodramatic imagination and its underlying assumptions—are dominant. Berlant believes that "utopian/traumatized subjectivity . . . has replaced rational subjectivity as the essential index of value for personhood and thus for society." "Revelations of trauma, incitements to rescue, the reprivatization of victims as the ground of hope, and above all, the notion that feeling itself is the true self, the self that must be protected from pain" are the marks of the politics of sentimentality. And they have led, according to Berlant, to a situation in which we are increasingly governed by policies based on an assumption of "the *self-evidence* and *objectivity* of painful feeling and the nation's duty to eradicate it." The danger here, says Berlant, is that questions of social inequity and social value are now adjudicated in the register not of power, but of "sincere surplus feeling."[14]

Berlant, whose focus is actually on the Right-to-Life movement but whose arguments apply equally well to the politics of victimology and victims' rights, argues that the political struggles in which sentimentality is deployed most effectively are those that find "validity in those seemingly superpolitical moments when a 'clear' wrong—say, the spectacle of children violently exploited—produces a 'universal' response." These are struggles informed by "a politics of protection, reparation, rescue." They "claim a hardwired truth, a core of common sense" which is "beyond ideology, beyond mediation, beyond contestation" and "which seems to dissolve contradiction and dissent."[15] The fantasy of reparation, the valorization of "surplus" or excess feeling, the tendency to substitute passion for reason in determining political and legal policy—all these of course are elements of the melodramatic imagination of which television, in fiction, in docudrama, in tabloids, and now in trials, makes such effective use. And as Berlant warns, a political movement based on such precepts must be viewed with grave suspicion. For when reason becomes overwhelmed by emotion, the rule of law itself is in danger of being usurped.

During the McVeigh trial I watched the nightly press conferences in which victims and survivors cried out for blood. What most struck—and frightened—me was that the most passionate of these people, the most, in their own minds, severely injured or bereft, were also the most vociferously contemptuous and proudly ignorant of the Constitution and the law. Like the fictional heroes of revenge genre films, they wanted swift and immediate reparation for their losses, and they had no trust at all in the wimpish ways of a legal system they saw as run by devious, sleazy attorneys and inept or corrupt officials. And like those heroes, these passionately articulate and righteously indignant individuals were all too easy to sympathize with. Who could not empathize with the grandmother who took her two small boys to a daycare center and never saw them again, especially when, as is as common in the Victims' Rights movement as it is in the Right-to-Life movement, heart-wrenching or horrifying images are deployed as the most powerful elements of the political argument. In the wake of the bombing, and then the trial, endless pictures of smiling children, only recently alive, along with carefully chosen images of a tiny shoe lying in the rubble or a tiny limb found lying far from the body of which it had only recently been a part, were shown on TV screens virtually twenty-four hours a day for several weeks. Such images do indeed seem to be "superpolitical," "beyond ideology," to use Berlant's terms. But they are deployed in the service of an agenda that is intensely political and ideological.

Victims' Rights and Legal Theory

Of course there are many prominent theoretical and legal defenders of the Victims' Rights movement whose arguments are neither sentimental nor melodramatic, but based on a particular view of the criminal justice system and how it should operate in ways that are fair and balanced. Paul Gewirtz and others associated with the storytelling trend in legal studies are among the most persuasive in their support for the role of victims in trials. Gewirtz argues that the use of victim impact statements corrects an imbalance in criminal proceedings that allows the victims to be doubly "silenced," by her or his murderer and then by the courts. For, he argues, in our current system the defendant alone has a legal spokesperson, or advocate, while the victim—whose injury is considered an injury to the state rather than a personal injury—is actually represented by no one. He rightly notes that "criminal trials have become a central moral arena for society," but he sees this arena as one in which the defendant is central because "the main dynamic . . . is to support the norms of socially acceptable behavior by defining otherness . . . the twisted deviance of Susan Smith, the apparently brazen evil of the Menendez brothers." Gewirtz believes that the true center of the trial should not be the defendant but the victim, for, in his view, "The victim is the actual subject of the trial and so the victim's place as at least a character in the criminal trial's narrative is definitional."[16]

In fact, the portrayal of the criminal trial as one in which the deviance or otherness of the criminal defendant holds center stage, and where the moral issue revolves around determining the extent of this "deviancy" and punishing or repairing it, has, until recently, been quite accurate. Indeed, it has been the tradition of liberal democracies to focus on the criminal as a deviant. In fact, the situation Gewirtz describes and deplores is the very one we have already addressed: the fact that shifts in social paradigms tend to overlap, so that old belief systems and traditions tend to coexist, at least for a time, with new paradigms that arise to fit new eras and new ways of thinking, both intellectually and morally.

I would argue that such is the case today, for we are living in an era in which dominant paradigms of belief and tradition of all kinds are increasingly up for grabs, and new models and attitudes are arising to replace the old. The Victims' Rights movement and the complementary legal and political movements and trends that accompany it, in particular, are signs that in matters of crime and justice, the liberal model of rehabilitation is increasingly being displaced by a new paradigm of justice more suited to our present era, which is far less marked by the traditions of liberal democracy and far more repressive and punishment oriented in every arena, especially that of criminal justice.

What is most disturbing about this trend, and what marks it as a dramatic turning point in American legal and media history, is its broad implications about what we as a nation stand for; what, in fact, is the measure of a true "American." This nation, after all, began as an experiment in the liberal principles that are the bedrock of our constitutional democracy. Coming from a country in which civil liberties were severely curtailed by an autocratic monarchy, the founding fathers wanted to insure that freedoms previously unheard of in the Western world would not only be guaranteed, but would in fact be the cornerstone of a new political philosophy based on the notion that mere mortals were capable of organizing their own social—and legal—systems and enforcing them in ways that would maintain order and harmony *without* resorting to notions of human nature as inherently evil, incorrigible, incapable of redemption. Thus we have the liberal tradition of trials by juries of one's peers, viewed by an educated public. And it was in this philosophical tradition—reborn in the sixties with the Warren Court, in the midst of the rebirth of liberalism after the horrors of the demonic McCarthy period—that so many of our most important legal precedents were set. The rights of defendants were important then, as in the Revolutionary era, because the definition of American liberalism included a clearly democratic bias toward giving every one of us the benefit of the doubt—the *reasonable doubt* that forces the burden of proof on the state rather than the defendant in criminal trials. In other words, Americans have a tradition—now largely forgotten, it would seem—that is based on the idea that it is better to let many criminals go free than to make the tragic error of sending even one innocent person to prison.

In everything I've been discussing in the previous chapters, we have seen the slow and complex decline of this notion and its replacement—in an age of fear, paranoia, and a vengeful kind of rage that seems to sprout up in many arenas of American life—by its very opposite. In case after case, and television series after television series, we have seen a dramatic shift away from reasonable doubt, from giving anyone the benefit of any doubt, as a bloodthirsty taste for a vigilante kind of justice seems to have seriously undermined many of our most important democratic assumptions, on TV and in the courts. More and more, it is, as we have seen, the victim that takes center stage in our national consciousness, and the ones who prosecute those presumed to have caused the victimization are the heroes, while defendants, especially their advocates, are increasingly distrusted and defiled. Goliath has replaced David as our national heroic prototype, and David is left to fend for himself, in a world increasingly filled with people ready to convict him of whatever trouble may be in the air, as quickly and brutally as possible.

In the summer of 2002, the Steven Spielberg film *Minority Report*, based on a story by the Orwellian science fiction writer, Philip Dick, put forth the image of a near future in which crime has been wholly eradicated in the nation's capital through a new "Pre-crime" police agency which, through the use of beings capable of foreseeing the future, can predict when a crime will be committed and arrest the targeted future criminal before she or he can act out her or his future crime. The agency has great public support because the residents of the capital are free of fear, protected by the patriarchal state in which so many feminists today seem to be similarly putting their faith.

What is lost here, as the film and the story make clear, is the possibility of a glitch in the system, which has two prongs. One of course is the possibility that the "precogs" who see the future may be wrong, or even disagree, at times. The other, more interesting glitch involves the possibility of human redemption through free will: the idea that a person may, in fact, at the moment of most intense provocation, change his or her mind and choose *not* to commit the crime after all. Of course, underlying both these problems is the more legalistic, constitutional issue of civil liberties and human privacy. As Steven Spielberg himself admitted in interviews when the film opened, the issue he raises in his entertainment piece is a vexed one. For we are—were then—living in an era when fear, not only of crime but of terrorism, has made many Americans, like so many feminists, willing to barter their own freedom for the trade-off of what seems to be increased security.

But security from what? And against whom? We began with the tabloid series *Cops* and ended with another tabloid, *America's Most Wanted: America Fights Back*. In both series, as in much of the rest of fictional and nonfictional television we have examined, the answer is a "them, out there" who are out to get "us" and whom we must stop at all costs—even our own freedom. More seriously, perhaps, we are jeopardizing our traditional belief in giving the benefit of the doubt, in the possibility of human error in judgment, in the idea that an injustice to even one human being is a truly horrible and inherently un-American event. In *Minority Report* the traditional liberal good guy—played by the irresistibly charming Tom Cruise—is transformed from an avenging member of the "Pre-crime" force to its enemy and nemesis. He had joined the program in a state of rage at the abduction and apparent murder of his own young son. He causes its downfall when he himself becomes the wrongful target of the vindictive program of which he is a major architect and enforcer.

In *America's Most Wanted* and the Victims' Rights movement to which it helped give birth lives much the same mentality that Dick describes as giving birth to, and popularizing, "Pre-crime" thinking, technology, and laws. The abduction and murder of Walsh's own son (another fair-haired, middle-class youngster), as melodramatically exploited on his series and docudramas as in the early scenes of *Minority Report,* helped to fuel the flames of an American mentality much like that seen in the movie. At the heart of this mentality *is,* of course, the idea that we have a right—indeed, a national need—to stop crime by any means necessary. And more importantly—since this is such a tricky business—we have a way of recognizing not only actual criminals, but potential criminals, and hunting them down like dogs.

We do not, of course, have the technology Dick dreamed up and Spielberg dramatized. What we do have, however, is a different kind of technology—television—which is capable not of predicting who among all human beings will commit crimes, but instead, *what types* of people are likely to do so. For it is, as we have seen, the great power of melodramatic drama to create monsters meant to terrify us, and heroes, heroines, and especially victims meant to move us not only to tears but to action. When a child—especially a pretty blonde privileged child like Polly Klaas, Jon-Benet Ramsey, or Elizabeth Smart—is presumed to have been taken, hoards of "good citizens" jump on board the volunteer vigilante forces promoted by television shows like *AMW* as well as news reports featuring pleas from frantic, tearful "victims" and rush off to find the criminal. Almost always—for these are the kinds of stories that make headlines—the suspected perpetrator is, like the people on *Cops* and *AMW*, of a certain unsavory "type," made-for-TV, to scare honest citizens to death.

Minority Report, which is liberal in its approach to such techniques and movements, ends by debunking this way of thinking. Unfortunately, however, it is indeed a "minority report" amidst a wave of current movies—and especially TV programs—in which criminals and terrorists are easily recognized and stopped in their tracks by heroic crime fighters, and increasingly, military and intelligence agents. What all this adds up to—and this is where this study will conclude—is a new national mentality in which "we" and "they" are clearly distinguishable, and "they" are inherently "bad" while "we" are indisputably "good." For what the Victims' Rights movement, aided enormously by trends in media and law enforcement, thrives on is a new "them" versus "us" mentality. With this attitude, as in the cold war, the rule of law, much less any sense of democratic doubt or compassion, is given shorter and shorter shrift, as fear and prejudice lead us all into a strangely media-produced "war on crime" in which we are all warriors, either "part of the problem or the solution," as someone in the sixties, in a dramatically different context, once said.

Conclusion

The Criminalization of American Life

Sometimes I think this whole world is one big prison yard
Some of us are prisoners, the rest of us are guards.   —Bob Dylan

In a December 2000 issue of the Sunday *New York Times*, a brief side piece, apparently meant to be amusing, in the "Week in Review" section described an amazingly fast-selling new toy called "Death Row Marv." The electronic toy, based on the anti-hero of Frank Miller's graphic comic *Sin City*, and marketed, for a mere $20, for "ages 13 and up," is a replica of the menacing-looking Marv strapped to an electric chair. The operator merely inserts a battery, pushes a button, and, according to the words on the box, watches Marv's "eyes grow red" and then "convulse as the switch is thrown" and he expires. It's apparently a big hit with the fifteen- to forty-five-year-old male consumer.[1]

In a related "Ideas and Trends" article in the very same issue, the *Times* put aside a half page to describe what it saw as a new trend in consumer product styling: "fear-of-crime design." The typically lighthearted article described such products as "a holster for a cellular phone that looks just like a holster for a snub-nosed pistol"; computers that "are no longer white and cheery-looking but black, sleek and faintly menacing"; "tall sport utility vehicles designed to intimidate other motorists," and other products designed to express what one Minneapolis designer describes as a puzzling, even alarming "aesthetic of meanness" developing in the visual American landscape.[2]

"Where this aggression is coming from is a mystery" according to the author of the piece, Keith Bradshear.[3] But is it really? In the previous chapters we have charted a growing trend in television programming, the most widely consumed and influential of the mass media, toward an emphasis on crime and punishment—especially punishment—as the dominant way of thinking about social issues and strategizing their possible "cures." Everything from family dysfunction and inept parenting to race and gender inequities, as we have seen, have become fodder for the criminal justice system—a system increasingly, by popular demand, hell bent on putting more and more Americans in prisons for longer and longer time periods and for less and less socially "dangerous" crimes. The coming of televised trials, of twenty-four-hour-a-day talk shows devoted, at every possible opportunity, to switching from actual news to sensational, but statistically and socially trivial, crime stories; and of a general tendency to view virtually every "big" news story in terms of courtroom drama and the juicy possibility of ferreting out criminal activity somewhere, by someone, are so commonplace now that we have come to accept them as legitimate approaches to every possible troubling event in American life.

In fact, as I have been arguing, the proliferation of discourse on crime and criminality, law and order, have overwhelmingly come to dominate media fiction and nonfiction. We have been lulled into a worldview—difficult to resist because it is, let's face it, sexy and enticing—in which virtually every issue on the public table has been transformed from being solvable through economics, social institutions, cultural and educational reform, treatment and rehabilitation, to being treated by the criminal justice system. We have reached a stage in American history, made possible only, I believe, by the complicity and support of mass media genres, images, settings, and dialogue in which there is very little room in the public sphere—and by extension the public mind—for any other way of thinking except the one set forth by the processes and discourses of crime and punishment.

As I have tried to demonstrate, this was easier to accomplish than it might have seemed to more liberal thinkers. After all, crime and punishment have been mainstays of dramatic art since the days of Greek tragedy. And understandably so. For the problems of violence, of social cohesion and harmony, of deviance from the humanitarian norms of human relationships are and have always been critical issues in every era of history. And rightly so. But as we have seen, in our survey of various genres of the past and present dealing with these lofty issues, the approach any given society takes to such issues varies greatly. And the variations, from era to era and from decade to decade, reflect radically different views of what a good society might actually look and feel like. We needn't go back to the

Greeks to see how perspectives on laws and outlaws, the imprisoned and the free, the "good citizens" and the "bad," have shifted radically in recent decades in our own era. It is after all, as we have seen, a very far cry indeed from the world of *Cool Hand Luke* to that of HBO's *Oz*. And an equally long leap in social perspective from the world of *The Defenders* to that of *Law and Order* and *The Practice*. *Cool Hand Luke, Bonnie and Clyde, Butch Cassidy and the Sundance Kid*—all heroes of popular movies of the late 1960s and early 1970s—were immensely, seductively, attractive figures *because* they defied the laws of an unjust society. But with the coming of the more recent TV series, especially the meant-to-scare-the-pants-off-you tabloid crime shows, "criminals" often guilty of no discernible infraction of law except for their failure or inability—almost invariably for social reasons—to conform to an increasingly harsh and inequitable social environment, are presented as evil alien beings, for whom no recourse seems possible except total expungement from the social order. Lock 'em up quick, the tabloids and news shows and cable talk channels keep telling us, before they come and get your Momma.

In fact, during the two or three years in which I have worked on this book, there has been—surprisingly even to me—an amazing proliferation of crime drama, crime talk, and crime "information." Almost all of it reinforces the trend toward viewing those caught on the wrong side of the law—no matter what the reasons or circumstances—as "evil" rather than unfortunate, disturbed, or ill. Nor has fictional programming been slow to keep pace with these other genres in inventing more and more varieties of legal series and more "respectable" crime series that draw heavily on the more creepy aspects of tabloid series like *Cops*. The most popular of these, *CSI: Crime Scene Investigation*, cleverly combines the scientific forensics so prominent in the *Law and Order* series with a far more ghoulish fascination with gorily enlarged, graphic images of decaying body parts, usually infested with a variety of flesh-eating insects and other unsavory creatures. The series, which spawned its own Miami-based spin-off within a year, is set in Las Vegas, the very kind of seedy setting favored by tabloid series. And its criminals, unlike the more typically troubled perpetrators of *Law and Order*, very often veer to the bizarre and alien types of the tabloids whom we can easily despise and distance ourselves from. Obsessed loners and psychopaths, with no apparent personal or social connections, are common, as are the kinds of weird, lost souls seen so often on the low-rent series. This new franchise is a kind of hybrid of the traditional realistic crime series and the far more lurid tabloid series in which criminals live in border territories—both physical and mental—and seem more grotesque and alien than the usual *noir* bad guys.

The FX network has its own hit series, *The Shield*, featuring a tough, brutal avenger-style cop who clearly puts himself above the law when it comes to catching and dealing with suspected criminals. He is a truly scary character, bulked up, with a shaved head and dressed more like a biker gang member than a law enforcement officer. And HBO, always given a wider berth than commercial networks, as we saw in the case of *Oz*, introduced a series in 2002 called *The Wire*, which features another rogue cop who doesn't let the policies or politics of the police department stop him from doing what he personally feels necessary to catch "bad guys." Showtime, not to be outdone by HBO, recently began its own criminal justice series, *Streetwise*, described by *TV Guide* as "a bleak dreary look inside the federal parole system" that shares with similar series "an unwillingness to provide easy answers to society's criminal ills."[4] In this series, parolees are shown to be clearly unrehabilitated and destined to return to old neighborhoods, old cohorts, and old habits.

Among the spate of other new series that debuted in 2002 are a laundry list of shows featuring hard-boiled, "take all prisoners" detectives, cops, and even vigilante-style private citizens who seek out and capture "bad guys" of the scariest sort. All borrow from the fear-inducing, "get them before they get you" spirit of reality series like *Cops*, if not their rough-edged, tabloid style. Among them are CBS's *Without a Trace*, about FBI agents who investigate missing persons cases; CBS's *CSI* spin-off, *CSI: Miami*, about forensic police investigators; CBS's *Robbery Homicide Division*, about law-abiding L.A. cops; Fox's *Fast Lane*, with two hip cops in L.A. and tons of gunplay; and CBS's *Hack*, about a disgraced Philadelphia cop who becomes a vigilante cab driver.

In case there is any doubt about the ideological direction of Dick Wolf's now legendary success in producing spin-offs as well as new series to build upon *Law and Order*'s phenomenal popularity, he is now taking us full circle. He has an updated version of the old sixties chestnut *Dragnet*, featuring the same old straight-arrow LAPD cops who wanted "Just the facts, Ma'am," and had never even heard of terms like "abuse excuse" or even "psychobabble." This update is a far cry indeed from the first season of his first series, in which feminism and race consciousness were at least serious concerns to be debated and over which the principals would agonize.

Law series too are proliferating more steadily, although their shelf lives are generally unpredictable. So far, *Philly*—whose ratings indicate it may not long survive after its two-season run—about a defense team not opposed to cutting legal corners in a system where the other side is as morally compromised, is still running as I write. *100 Centre Street*—another series among the many law programs that come and go, but mostly keep coming—is an original A&E series produced by Sidney Lumet. He produced such classics of left liberalism as *The Verdict*, about a truly heroic defense attorney up against a corrupt medical, legal, and religious establishment; and *Prince of the City* and *Serpico*, about heroic police officers turned whistleblowers on their own corrupt colleagues. But this series, now gone, was far less idealistic in its portrayal of defense attorneys than *The Verdict*. In fact, in the only legal series actually to feature a public defender as a major character, *100 Centre Street*'s guy was as irresponsible and unsavory as any on *Law and Order*. He was often shown cheating on his wife, once even with a prosecutor with whom he flirted outrageously during a trial in which she was prosecuting his own client. Sexual philandering caused him, on more than one occasion, to fail to meet with his client before trial and familiarize himself with the case. This series certainly did little to rehabilitate the already sleazy, incompetent image of defense attorneys, especially public defenders.

For the People, perhaps the most politically intriguing series since *Law and Order*, features prosecutor-heroes, this time two women. The more liberal of the two, in the style of *L&O*'s Claire Kincaid, has a liberal heart. She was married to a public defender, still on the scene as a major character, and they still carry a mutual torch, although their marriage ran aground, believably enough, because of the conflicts inherent in their oppositional roles within the justice system. This admirable woman tries her best to squeeze liberal justice from the system whenever possible, by working from within the belly of the beast and making whatever deals she has to, to achieve the best of two generally bad options. When a new D.A. is brought in, a black, upscale Republican with a truly nasty and reactionary protégé in tow, conflict seems inevitable and the more liberal woman expects to lose her job. By the end of the first segment, however, they bond. The D.A. respects the professionalism and efficiency of her ideological opposite, and they agree to work together to "do the job" they both went to law school to get done. Thus, do "liberalism" and extreme reaction make for very comfy, even sisterly (this is Lifetime, the women's network) bedfellows.

Finally, there was a series called *Girls Club*, in which three young women begin careers as trial attorneys in a large firm dominated by older white males. The good news here is that the young women are quite outspoken—as is the series—about the sexism of the traditional law firm. The bad news is that, like *Ally McBeal*, also created by David Kelley, the young women tend to be incredibly insecure, obsessed with men and prone to absurdly immature and unprofessional behavior. This is the latest fictional law series to surface, as I write, but more cannot be long in coming: so many have already proven to be successful for so many networks.

Even more pronounced, in part because they are so cheap to produce, are the nonfiction series and specials focusing on law and criminal justice. Court TV, to take the most glaring example, has virtually transformed itself into a prime-time tabloid schlock fest. Every night on that network— once usefully informative and even, at times, seriously controversial—we can now view a full hour of *Cops* reruns; endless B-level made-for-TV movies in which dangerously ominous criminals are pursued and imprisoned or, more often, killed by upright law enforcement heroes; original Court TV series with self-explanatory titles like *Mugshots*, *Inside Cell Block F*, and of course the increasingly punitive *Crime Stories*. MSNBC has eagerly jumped on the bandwagon with nightly series like *MSNBC Investigates* and *Lockup*, both of which "document" proceedings in the criminal courts and prisons in ways that are more sleazy and sensational than informative. The A&E network also runs such tabloid-inspired nightly series as *City Confidential* and *Investigative Reports*, which focus, like the others, on the seamier side of the "criminal element" and the valiant efforts of "crime fighters" to deal with them in ways that protect "honest citizens" like us. TNT, which has now picked up rerun rights for *Law and Order*, runs three episodes in a row every Tuesday night. And during the summer of 2002, Dick Wolf, who produces the franchise, began a new nonfiction series on the parent network, NBC, called *Crime and Punishment*. This series, labeled "fusion TV" in the *New York Times* because "it combines documentary film making with elements of reality TV and traditional dramatic fiction," is in fact a direct imitation of Court TV's *Crime Stories*, editing actual criminal trials down to a one-hour docudrama format. In the same week, ABC aired its own version of this new genre, called *State V.*, and Court TV began a new series called *Dominick Dunne's Power, Privilege and Justice*, hosted by the pulp novelist and *Vanity Fair* writer who became a television celebrity in his own right with his incredibly vitriolic, antidefense commentary on the first Menendez trial, followed by equally vengeful reports on the O. J. Simpson case and others.

The Discovery Channel—another network first introduced as a primarily "educational" and "cultural" addition to the world of television programming—by 1999 had, like A&E, come to devote virtually all of its prime-time hours to crime and criminal justice matters. Much of it—especially *World's Most Dangerous Car Chases*, which was sandwiched between *New Detectives* and *Justice Files*—was not only sensational, but downright sleazy, outdoing even *Cops* in its emphasis on the kind of cops 'n' robbers "reality programming" that was at once cheap to produce and heavy on action-filled images of heroic law enforcement officers in hot pursuit of "dangerous" criminals.

Even the E! Network, a twenty-four-hour-a-day entertainment industry channel, now devotes two hours a night to series involving crime and criminals. A series called *Mysteries and Scandals*—so popular that it runs twice nightly—chronicles the lives and mysteriously ominous, or obviously criminal, deaths of those connected with the entertainment industry, from major stars like Marilyn Monroe to has-beens and would-have-beens, unknown to any but the most obsessive crime or Hollywood buff. An equally popular series is *True Hollywood Story*, which similarly digs up and sensationally "reconstructs" the sordid details of every major or minor "celebrity" whose life ever involved any form of violence or run-in with the law, whether as perpetrator or victim. This is a really astonishing turn in news and entertainment programming, as is the emphatic turn from actual news stories or cultural programming on the part of twenty-four-hour news and "arts" channels.

But they are not the only networks—vying furiously for an audience now offered so many options as cable channels proliferate—which believe that the surest bet for luring viewers away from competitors is to switch their programming priorities away from their original schedules toward an almost exclusive focus on crime, sleaze, mysterious "unsolved" tragedies, and the like. Even Lifetime, the putative "women's channel," has a nightly prime-time series called *Unsolved Mysteries* in which, as in other tabloids, audiences are offered scary reenactments of murders, disappearances, and other gruesome, apparently criminal, incidents in which the still unknown solution to the "mystery" encourages the kind of paranoid, "they're out there" state of mind that has become *the* staple of nonfiction programming these days.

And the beat goes on, reaching even to the noncable networks, which are losing more and more of their ratings shares to cable and are forced to compete by offering their own imitations of the sleazy crime stories that are now the biggest audience draw across the board on TV screens. According to a survey reported in a June 2000 issue of *TV Guide*, "Crime does seem to pay, especially on TV." According to their own survey, "crime is by far the most popular story topic of the network news magazines," dominating the air time of such shows as *Dateline*, *60 Minutes*, *20/20*, and *48 Hours*. By necessity, they are pushing such issues as health, education, consumer safety, international news, and even entertainment off to the margins due to our national obsession with lawbreakers of all kinds—from mass murderers to celebrity drug users, to second-graders accused of sexual harassment for kissing little-girl classmates.[5]

Throughout this book I have been describing a huge mosaic of television programming, spanning genres and networks, from the most dominant to the most fringy, from the most watched to the most cultlike. A huge percentage of them have been increasingly focused on holding us together as a nation by defining "real" Americans—those who conform, succeed, consume, and, in the case of tabloids like *America's Most Wanted*, even aid in maintaining peace and harmony: they fight crime quite directly by looking for, finding, and reporting actual "wanted" criminals. This mosaic, which media theorist Nick Browne has called a "supertext,"[6] extends from entertainment networks like E!, which now feature celebrity and crime series, to religious programming hosted by the likes of Pat Robertson, which increasingly describe the "sinners" they have always tried to "redeem" in terms of criminal justice. Indeed, as we have seen on talk shows such as *Oprah*, religious programming too has moved from a traditional focus on helping viewers and guests "find Jesus," thereby saving themselves from damnation, to a more dramatic focus on the importance of not only "getting right with God" but also with your local police force. Sunday morning's *Hour of Power* with Robert Schuller, for example, increasingly offers testimony from "saved sinners" who found Jesus in prison and asks those viewers now incarcerated to redeem themselves, join the armies of God rather than Satan, and perhaps get a spot on a TV show. For those insomniacs or lonely Sunday morning viewers who watch them, even infomercials are increasingly selling products like "The Club," which insures against those who would try to break into our cars or homes, offering dramatic reenactments of such crimes.

One of the more interesting aspects of this phenomenon is addressed in an excellent book by Esther Madriz called *Nothing Bad Happens to Good Girls: Fear of Crime in Women's Lives*. In it, the author, a sociologist, analyzes the many ways in which our society instills an often highly unrealistic fear of crime in women, through a variety of institutions, from the family to the media themselves. An ideology based on terror managed to convince the great number of women she interviewed that they are in grave danger both in and out of their homes and that, therefore, crime itself is the greatest enemy they must fight, regardless of race and class difference. The race and class implications of this study are both frightening and saddening because, again, we, and in this case I mean women specifically, find ourselves being asked to put aside our concerns for equality and justice for all people—no matter their race, class, sexual orientation, or ethnicity—in favor of a widespread umbrella movement to commit ourselves to the fight against "crime."[7]

"But not so fast," say the producers of these shows. "To simply call something a crime story is to dismiss all the nuances and subtleties involved. They may be stories that involve the individual and the legal system, or that contain all sorts of other elements that make them so much more complex," for, after all, they argue, "crime is an important gateway to societal issues and the human condition."[8] But that is just the point. With all this focus on crime and punishment, cops and robbers, prosecutors and defense attorneys, we are narrowing the gateway to all issues of society and the human condition to a single—and, again, disturbingly attractive and simplistic—way of thinking of the myriad issues and problems involved in those two little concepts: societal issues and the human condition.

In fact, the real significance of this exaggerated, increasingly pervasive emphasis on crime and criminality as endemic, as the defining feature of all that ails our troubled and troubling society, is its polarizing effect on public debate about social issues and, by extension, public opinion in the population at large. This situation is verified by the endless polls showing that, as we have seen already, most Americans now believe, against the grain of actual facts, that crime is the most important issue facing our nation. And, as I have been arguing, this turn in public opinion has everything to do with the power of television—visual, melodramatic, filled with emotionally compelling and memorable images of violence and grief. It overrides the power of actual facts, whether they are reported in print or briefly noted elsewhere, usually with an accompanying graph or talking-head "expert." Neither of these can compete in emotional impact with the opposing if misleading messages of the tabloids, dramas, and news magazines and their sensational images and heart-piercing tales of danger and victimization.

How to explain the power of the images, the narratives, the terrifying or heart-wrenching dramas of these intellectually vapid but emotionally compelling programs to override the "facts" we can verify as true? To answer that question we need to understand the way in which television draws us into its way of seeing and feeling and thinking about reality. We live, after all, in an age of voyeurism in which more and more of our leisure time is spent *watching*—watching computer screens, watching movies at theaters and at home, and especially watching television. Things become real to us because they have been "seen on TV." This makes for an interestingly contradictory situation. On the one hand, there is something positive, even perhaps miraculous, about the powers of television to allow us literally to bear witness to any number of public events—from presidential inaugurations and royal weddings to natural and technological disasters—and so vicariously participate in these occurrences, as citizens, as mourners, even as learners. The concept of the public sphere, the arena within which great and/or meaningful human events and decisions are carried out, has historically been limited to the very few, until quite recently the propertied, wealthy white males. The rest of us were forced passively to suffer the consequences of these deeds and decisions with little or no access even to information about what has occurred and how it will affect us.[9]

With the coming of television, all that has changed. Now all of us, from the youngest to the most feeble, from the most erudite to the truly illiterate, from the most to the least powerful and wealthy among us, are invited to witness such events and feel more a part of them than ever in history. The Clarence Thomas confirmation hearings, the O. J. Simpson trial, the wedding and funeral of Princess Diana: all these events were witnessed by a global audience swept up in a long-running, round-the-clock spectacle around which swirled endless dialogue and debate about what the television news magazine producers refer to as "societal issues" and "the human condition."

Television producers always look for a "major" story, with "legs," to break the monotony of daily events and keep audiences entranced and captive for as long as possible. They endowed these events with enormous import, sometimes deserved, often perhaps not, each of which engendered—deservedly or not—impassioned emotions and debates about life and death, race and class, romantic love and sexual violence, and so much more. The Hill-Thomas hearings undoubtedly influenced public opinion and policy, especially legal policy, waking a sleeping nation to something feminists had tried to publicize for at least two decades: the problem of sexual harassment in the workplace and its impact on the status of women in the country generally. The Simpson trial allowed us to bear witness—if we were willing to look honestly—to the terrifying rift that exists in this country between those who are white and those who are not. Like that other amazingly watchable media event, the videotape of the Rodney King beating, the trial aimed a glaring spotlight on the issue of racism within the criminal justice system, from the rank and file police officer to the highest-ranking law enforcement officials.

These events were arguably healthy in the sense that they forced Americans to deal with serious social injustices, at least for the brief time they held our undivided attention. But not all major media events to which we are now privileged to bear personal witness through the technology of television have this kind of socially positive and enlightening impact. At least these events focused attention on the most serious social and human issues of their day.

But what, after all, is the ultimate impact of the global voyeurism that accompanies tragic events—storms and earthquakes, babies trapped in wells and mourning relatives of victims of hideous deaths, weddings and funerals of the rich and famous? The producers of these spectacles would have us believe that they too force us to confront profound issues of social and human import, of course. And they would not be wrong. The privilege of bearing witness to the weeping victims of hurricanes and tornadoes, ice storms and plane crashes, does indeed allow us to share vicariously in the suffering of those affected and even, quite often, to send our condolences and offerings of actual aid. The awesome power of nature is surely a monumental issue that profoundly impacts upon human experience and the human condition. We witness the sufferings of wartime refugees and famine victims with the same vicarious sense of sorrow and pity. Such televised events, as Dick Hebdige persuasively argues, may even be the catalysts for the kind of social activism that actually does involve a transferring of resources from those who have much to those who have virtually nothing.[10]

But there is a slippery slope that we must navigate while participating in these irresistible and in many ways socially useful media events. In certain cases—the Simpson trial, the King case, the Hill-Thomas hearings—we really are affected by the events and by the debate and dialogue that surround them. As American citizens, after all, we all have a stake in issues of race, class and gender, of justice and public policy. I remember clearly the exhilaration I felt, as someone who had been active in feminist battles since the 1960s, watching the Hill-Thomas hearings and bearing witness to a public conversation that had previously been limited to victims and activists but was now suddenly placed front and center on the public agenda, to be recognized and fought over by the entire nation, at last! While many feminists found the Thomas confirmation depressing, I found it merely anticlimactic, for to me—and I was ultimately proven right (more "right," as I've discussed earlier, in many cases, than I had wished to be)—it was only the beginning of a years-long process that would certainly change the way we felt, thought, and dealt with such issues in the future.

For one thing, while television persuasively convinces one of the opposite view, the truth is that crimes of all kinds, including violent crimes, juvenile and drug-related crimes, have steadily declined in quite impressive leaps and bounds in the last two decades of the twentieth century. One of the largest declines in history in all of these categories and others—a full 10 percent—came in 1999.[11] "Juvenile Violent Crime Falls to All Time Low,"[12] "Number in Prison Grows Despite Crime Reduction,"[13] are typical headlines that have been peppering the pages of major newspapers for years now, after all.

Nor is the failure and idiocy of the famous "war on drugs," which is responsible for keeping so many incarcerated for longer and longer periods of time, unknown to those who read the papers—or even go to the movies.[14]

And yet, the fear of crime and the popularity of harsh criminal law policy continues to hold sway among American voters and poll participants. There is something almost schizophrenic, in fact, about the disparity between what one "knows" to be fact and what one sees portrayed on television programs—from the most "serious" to the most schlocky. This logical disconnect in the public mind between what is documented fact and what people seem to fear and vote for, when it comes to criminal justice law, is in my view odd enough to bear some serious analysis—about social issues, about media representation, and about the consciousness and concern of thinking, progressive people about social issues in general.

In fact, as one watches the seemingly endless amount of television programming dealing with social issues—from televised trials, to talk shows, to news programs, to courtroom dramas, to tabloid schlock—one cannot help but feel the lull of the media, made explicit in shows like *America's Most Wanted*, toward a view of virtually everything in public and private life as a matter of crime and punishment. "We" are increasingly identified as "crime fighters," while "they" are the enemy against whom we are enlisted to fight, with our votes and our hotline phone calls, and by dedicating our hearts and minds to a worldview in which the police and courts are the only important public arena, and "we" are always on the side of those who represent law and order and against the "they" who defy it. Nor is television the only medium to explicitly appeal to this worldview and ask citizens to participate actively in crime fighting. The police in Utah have recently set up a Website in which information about ongoing criminal investigations is posted, and members of the public are asked to help solve the crimes.[15] By now it has become common when reporting on crimes in which children go missing for families to use television to enlist the help of their own communities in joining search parties to help the police find evidence and hunt down the criminal. This in spite of the little-known fact that only a mere 2 percent of kidnapings are actually committed by strangers; most often, it is angry noncustodial parents.[16]

If there is a unifying thesis here it is that television, coincidentally in concert with law enforcement and other government agencies, has "chosen" crime as the issue and "criminals" as the enemy against whom we as Americans can most readily and passionately unite—at a time when social fragmentation, disaffection, and alienation are increasingly serious threats to the national spirit. The role of television as a unifying power against the many forces of atomization, alienation, and fragmentation that industrialization (and later, postindustrialization) brought with it is hardly new. In fact, as Raymond Williams explained in a very early but still seminal work on television as a cultural and social force,[17] it was actually the need for such a unifying force that led federal agencies as well as corporate sponsors and manufacturers to strongly endorse and promote the new medium, which had already been invented but was largely ignored and even ridiculed in the *New York Times* in the 1930s, during the years immediately following World War II.[18] For it was at that point that what Williams terms "mobile privatization" took place: the accelerating movement of populations from city to city and job and job; the decline of both the extended and nuclear families; the rise of the divorce rate and its attendant problems of youthful disaffection and alienation. This sea change led the government to see the usefulness of allocating airwaves to an industry offering to broadcast national programming via a home-based technology with the ability to reach all Americans, no matter where they may be moving or traveling, with unifying messages and images of national import. And so, from the start, television appeared as a godsend to those trying valiantly to keep order in the lives of a population whose traditional ways of doing things had, by then, been sorely disrupted by the radical economic and social changes wrought by industrialization and the new corporate world order.

But it was not only the government but also the newly ascendant corporations now dominating the economy that by then had come to see television as a godsend. Corporate sponsors also saw the great appeal of such an industry for reasons equally connected to the rise of industrialization and its effects, although their motives were more economic than social. For in an era when the national economy had been largely transformed from one dependent on heavy industry to one based almost entirely on consumerism, a home-based visual medium that could sell consumer goods directly—and with visual and emotional power—to consumers right in their own living rooms was too good to resist.

Television, as has been mentioned, was always more than an entertainment form in America. For from the start, the entertainment programming itself had an ideological bent, meant to send a message to a confused, disoriented population, adrift in a new world order in which the old ways of keeping public and private order no longer seemed to apply. In the beginning, sitcoms such as *The Honeymooners*, *The Life of Riley*, and *The Goldbergs*, featuring working-class, often immigrant families and cultures learning to adjust to a new way of life, were common. And by the mid-fifties these early shows were largely replaced by others— *Father Knows Best*, *Leave It to Beaver*, *The Donna Reed Show*—which attempted to instruct all Americans in the values of corporate success and consumerism, a trend which survives to this day in most family-oriented comedy and drama series. Television, then, from the start, was set up as an institution through which Americans, living through social and cultural upheaval and change, might be informed about, and socialized into, the brave new world of postindustrial democracy.

But of course, then as now, entertainment genres may have been the most popular television programming, but hardly the only important ones.[19] News and documentaries were also important. In fact, those were the days when everyone really did watch the news because there were only three channels and, at 6:30, only one thing to watch on all of them: the news. Nor was there much more variety in theme or message on these news shows than on the sitcoms that followed. Each of them presented pretty much the same commercials as the entertainment genres, touting success and consumption, and pretty much the same stories with pretty much the same slant.

In fact, for all the changes in television's structure and content, there are certain things that have not really changed all that much. This is largely because the people who decide what we see and hear on our more and more sophisticated delivery systems are not all that different from their fifties' predecessors. Ratings, which drive the price of advertising on television, are still largely determined by the drama and sensationalism a program can deliver. The need for dramatic conflict, in both news and entertainment forms, remains dominant. And, not surprisingly, then as now, the dominant issue in nonfiction programming featured—in the interest of maintaining a sense of national unity and cohesion—a "them" against "us" central theme. In the Cold War fifties, of course, the "them" was Communism. The fear of Communist infiltration from within and attack from without was ubiquitous. And, throughout the last two decades of the twentieth century, as I have been arguing, with the Cold War over and no obvious global enemy to pit ourselves against, the "them" has been defined largely in terms of crime and criminality. But that has recently been changing.

Terrorism: The Media Finds a New Unifying "Enemy"

In 1996, one of the biggest summer blockbusters was a film called *Independence Day*, in which a giant alien "monster from outer space" attacked the world. Heroically, the president of the United States, who, as it turned out, was also a military hero, joined an interracial team of federal agents to destroy the monster. As is usual in such movies, this creature proved extremely difficult to annihilate. But when at last it had breathed its last breath and lay in a squishy mass of mush on the ground, the world rested easy. In fact, in a finale to end all such finales, the camera panned from continent to continent as, one after another, residents of every continent and culture, dressed in traditional garb, rose to salute the United States of America, savior of the world.

At the time I remember thinking that it was a clever ploy; that Hollywood—at a time when representatives of most minority groups, especially Arab Americans, had been protesting Hollywood's racial stereotyping of criminals and terrorists—found a politically correct "enemy" for such films. Within five years, of course, all that had changed. The terrorist attack on the World Trade Center in 2001 gave us back a terrific, authentic enemy to unite against, one which, it would seem, might serve to push plain old-fashioned American "crime" at least to the margins of TV screens, as the "War on Terror" replaced the "War on Crime" as our biggest, scariest, most immediate national problem.[20]

But of course, as I suggested in chapter 2, the rhetoric of terrorism and crime has always been remarkably similar, as have the representations of the "international terrorist" and the contemporary criminal. As things have turned out, I was quite right. For far from edging crime and criminal justice off the media map, the "War on Terror" has been waged in Washington and on TV as, in many respects, a mere extension of the ongoing "War on Crime." Of course, the battlefield for this war is broader than the courtroom this time around. Real live warfare, in a variety of global locations, mostly in Asia and the Middle East, is back full force on news channels, as well as on movie screens. In fact, the war movie—a genre largely gone from theaters since the debacle of Vietnam—is now back in all its red, white, and blue glory. From revivals of World War II heroics like *Saving Private Ryan* and *Pearl Harbor,* to revisionist versions of Vietnam itself, like *We Were Soldiers*, to any number of movies set in a variety of Arab and other Asian nations, such as *Terms of Engagement* and *Black Hawk Down,* it has become more than acceptable to portray the actual killing of large numbers of primarily darker skinned foreigners as heroic deeds. Many of these films have not only been aided by the government but honored by top administrators, including President George W. Bush himself. And while it may be true that "Hollywood jumped into bed with the Pentagon in the fall of 2002," according to critic J. Hoberman, "the ongoing courtship" actually "dates back to the Clinton administration,"[21] when the winds of war were, apparently, already blowing. It is this spate of war-glorifying movies, then, that—like the TV programs we have been analyzing—actually characterize the tenor of the times, while films like Steven Spielberg's liberal *Minority Report* are much rarer. The combination of Spielberg and Cruise, two of Hollywood's most bankable men, made the opening of *Minority Report* one of the biggest in a recent series of truly blockbuster summers for Hollywood. But again, its message was not a majoritarian one, in Hollywood or, certainly, in Washington, where no funding or government cooperation was either sought or received, for obvious reasons.

But two of the other big opening films that preceded *Minority Report* in the weeks before it opened were very different in focus and implication. *The Sum of All Fears*, a Tom Clancy novel adaptation starring Ben Affleck, featured an actual nuclear attack on Baltimore staged by terrorists in a way that attempted to begin a full-fledged nuclear war between Russia and the United States. The hero, Clancy's Jack Ryan was an ex-Marine, turned historian, turned CIA operative, who managed to thwart the plot and avert further, perhaps total, nuclear destruction. In pre-opening interviews, the standard question for Affleck concerned the ethical dimensions of staging so terrifying a terrorist attack so soon after the one on the World Trade Center. The standard answer was that the film was done "with integrity," and that those to whom it might cause anxiety were advised not to see it. Those who did see it were given a drama in which the "them" were very scary indeed, while the "us" were about as attractive and reassuring as Hollywood, short of getting Cruise himself, could have made him.

The other blockbuster of that June was another spy thriller, this time featuring another unusually young and attractive hero. *The Bourne Identity*, based on a Robert Ludlum novel, starred Matt Damon as another charming all-American guy, dressed, like Affleck, in casual Gap-style pants and sweaters, who manages to overcome great odds without breaking a sweat in a winning effort to separate the good guys from the bad, outsmart and destroy the latter, and—as in *The Sum of All Fears*—walk into the sunset with the girl of his dreams, having saved the world from evil. This time, the evil actually is within, since the villains are themselves part of a rogue CIA branch whose targets and tactics are vile. But this is no *Minority Report*. For there is no hint at all—as there is also not in *The Sum of All Fears*—that any political or legal issues are at stake. Instead, these films, typical of what Hollywood summer films have lately been giving us, present the simplistic view that good and evil, whether within or without our own borders or institutions, are easily identified and defeated—permanently, violently, and without recourse to any legal proceedings or precedents. All this can be done by decent, now extremely boyish and wholesome middle-class white males, heroes, representing what "real Americans" like "us" stand for and look and act like.

And so the blurring of the line between crime fighting, warfare and antiterrorist actions grows murkier. In fact, this is not surprising, nor does it confuse the thesis that was the impetus for this book. On the contrary, this return to full-blown, full-time war and spy coverage and dramatic fiction is almost by definition an extension of the themes we have already been discussing in relation to legal programming. For the turn to physical punishment, including the death penalty, and revenge and retribution rather than other forms of "solving" social problems—now on a global rather than local scale—is in a real sense what war has always been about. All the posters and bumper stickers with slogans like "These Colors Don't Run" and "Avenge September 11" are not rhetorically different from the calls of legal commentators, government officials, and survivors of crime victims for the harshest punishment, in the name of sheer revenge.

Even more to the point, as far as the link between "wars on crime," wars on enemy nations or groups, and "wars on terrorism" goes, there is a very specific aspect to this "war on terror," especially as it is presented on television news and current fiction, which is quite overtly being framed—and executed—in the juridical context of criminal justice discourse and process. Spy films, like the television series and newscasts we've been studying, may strongly imply that those who seriously threaten our security deserve no rights or liberties and need only be stopped in their tracks, violently, by all-American heroes. But they do not politically engage us in serious debate about legalities or procedures, for which television is a far more effective medium. It is television, not summer movie blockbusters starring young hunks in Gap attire, that has taken on the task of making real arguments for the extension of government and law enforcement powers in the interest of national security. It is television that presents the news and debates that push these ideas through when they seem necessary. And it is television that, in its blurring of fiction and reality, also presents these arguments—one way or another—in its parallel fictional and entertainment forms. It is, after all, a fact that since 9/11 the government and the courts have indeed been pushing the legal envelopes they control in the direction of fewer liberties and greater "security" measures. For the idea that terrorists have infiltrated our own borders is not mere rhetoric anymore. We have been attacked and we have every reason to believe—unlike during the anti-Communist

McCarthy years—that our borders will again be compromised by foreign agents plotting more violent attacks.

Nonetheless, the scariness of this scenario does not necessarily fit with the solutions being proposed, and actually enforced, by the Bush administration, and then implicitly endorsed by newscasters and in fictional series. In the real world, serious discussions about such things as holding suspected terrorists without access to counsel or the right to meet accusers indicate that civil liberties that affect all of us are in danger.[22] Immigrants are being detained for indefinite periods of time for a variety of reasons that make the newcomers seem "suspicious." Their names are being withheld in many cases and their numbers are unknown. In the case of American citizens suspected of conspiring to commit terrorist acts, President Bush has reserved the right to hold such persons for as long as he deems them "dangerous." In fact, one of the nightly MSNBC "crawls" discussing the American, Jose Padilla, accused of conspiring with the terrorist Al-Qaeda, seemed almost funny. "Suspected terrorist Jose Padilla will be held in detention until President decides that the war on terror is over," it read. For how will it be possible for a president to somehow decide that an undeclared, undefined "war" is "over"? And how, when, and under what circumstances can we expect him to make such a decision?

No matter. This is in fact being announced on "serious" news programs. And in keeping with television's blurring of reality and fiction, it is similarly, as of late, being bolstered by a newly popular television genre: the spy series. So far, we have *The Agency* and *Alias*. But increasingly, even in episodes of the White House–centered *The West Wing*, there is a major new element for the White House staff to contend with: the threat of terrorism. And with this new White House problem of course comes a new element of the White House: the relations between the president's offices and intelligence agencies like the CIA, which must join forces in the fight against terrorism in ways that glamorize and idealize that agency.

Unlike their more simplistic theatrical counterparts, these television series actually do employ a good deal of sophisticated legal discussion and debate in portraying the ways these agencies operate in fighting this fight. For if crime and criminals have been serving so well as media-generated "enemies" against which we all must rally together in fighting the good fight, then terrorism and terrorists serve all the better. It is television, rather than film, that has become the medium through which legal discourse and debate have become the dominant modes of presenting all social and political issues and conflicts. It is, therefore, not surprising that it is television that has taken on the more serious task of convincing us, through the blurry combination of melodrama and debate, that the extensions of government and juridical powers, at the expense of civil liberties, is necessary if we are to save ourselves from the terrifying creatures pushing at our gates, or already hiding inside our porous borders. For unlike the spy movies just discussed, even series like *Cops* and *AMW* work to convince us, albeit primarily with the use of melodramatic scenarios and expressionistic techniques, that law enforcement still matters. But now its powers must be extended to do the job needed, and of course its forces must be expanded to include ordinary citizens like you and me. Matt Damon and Ben Affleck may not need us, but John Walsh and his colleagues at the FBI certainly do, as is evident by the weekly scoreboard of "solved cases" made possible by the army of deputized viewers who watch out, seek, and report to the authorities through the *AMW* hot line.

And so, while the messages of recent film and television productions have much in common politically, there is a significant difference in focus. Movies still are primarily escapist, hero-centered, spectator sports. But television creates a viewing community of active Americans, held together by a common sense of identity as "real Americans," forming a community ready to help in the struggle against evil "outsiders." And what could make for better television? It's all there: the melodrama, the hyperbolic rhetoric, the permission to express the kind of vengeful rage that, it seems, a lot of Americans are feeling and acting out these days in all sorts of ways, anyway; and most importantly, there is a common enemy, to give us a sense of belonging to a real community of real American brothers and sisters. That is after all what television has always been about: telling us what it means to be a real American and drawing clear lines between "us" and "them," at a time when community, shared values, and mutual feeling are in increasingly short supply in our daily lives.

Notes

NOTES TO THE INTRODUCTION

1. Steven Donziger, ed., *The Real War on Crime: The Report of the National Criminal Justice Commission* (Washington, DC, 1996); Mike Males, *Framing Youth: 10 Myths about the Next Generation* (Monroe, ME, 1999). While I don't have space to go into greater depth on this point, these two books should be read carefully for an eye-opening look at how radically public opinion—circulated through media and government outlets—reflects incredibly distorted and terrifying myths about the rising extent and danger of criminal behavior.

2. L. Friedman, *Crime and Punishment in American History* (New York, 1993), Section Three, "Crime and Punishment in the Twentieth Century," 262–323.

3. Ibid.

4. Erika Doss, *Elvis Culture: Fans, Faith and Image* (Kansas City, 1999); see also Karal Ann Marling, *As Seen on TV: The Visual Culture of Every Day Life in the 1950s* (Cambridge, MA, 1994).

5. "Constitutional Argument in a National Theater," in R. Hariman, ed., *Popular Trials: Rhetoric, Media and the Law* (Tuscaloosa, AL, 1990), 31–54.

6. Racism, too, entered the courtrooms as an issue in those years, as accusations of racism, brutality, and general corruption within police departments became more and more common. As shall be discussed in greater detail later, this of course became a major issue in the O. J. Simpson case.

7. My thanks to Lee Quinby for this priceless anecdote.

8. Paul Thayer, *The Watchful Eye: American Justice in the Age of the Televised Trial* (Westport, CT: 1994), 67.

NOTES TO CHAPTER 1

1. Summaries of all series mentioned here and throughout the book can be found in Earle Marsh and Jason Brooks, *The Complete Directory to Prime Time Network and Cable TV Shows* (New York, 2000).

2. V. Sobchak, "Lounge Time," in N. Browne, ed., *Refiguring American Film Genres* (Berkeley, CA, 1999), 130–131.

3. Ibid., 135.

4. Given the enormous turnover in cast and characters over the long run of the series, this listing of characters is necessarily somewhat incomplete and probably already needs updating. For a thorough archival history of the cast and characters, see the series Website, www.lawandorder.com.

5. D. Keetley, "Law and Order," in Robert Jarvis and Paul Joseph, eds., *Prime-Time Law* (Durham, NC, 1998), 33.

6. Ibid., 38.

7. Alison Young, *Imagining Crime* (London, 1996), 9.

8. Ibid., 143.

9. T. Elthaesser, "Tales of Sound and Fury: Observations on the Family Melodrama," in Marcia Landy, *Imitation of Life: Melodrama in Film and Television* (Minneapolis, 1999), 73.

10. Ibid., 89.

11. E. Rapping, "Daytime Utopias: If You Lived in Pine Valley, You'd Be Home," in H. Jenkins and J. Shattuc, eds., *Hop on Pop: The Pleasures and Politics of Popular Culture* (Durham, NC, 2003), 33–59.

12. E. Taylor, *Prime Time Families* (Berkeley, 1989).

NOTES TO CHAPTER 2

1. "Crime and the Media: From Media Studies to Post-Modernism," in David Kidd-Hewitt and Richard Osborne, eds., *Crime and the Media: The Post-Modern Spectacle* (London, 1995), 42.

2. For a thorough survey of the state of crime and crime control in the late 1990s, see Steven Donziger, ed., *The Real War on Crime: The Report of the National Criminal Justice Commission* (New York, HarperPerennial, 1996). Donziger documents the actual incarceration rates of various age, race, and gender groups as well as the actual figures on crime rates that are not easily found in a credible form. He also documents the various penalties and even many of the atrocities committed against defendants and prisoners, and the various legal initiatives pending or passed which will alter criminal trial as well as arrest and prison procedures in ways that give prosecutors and police officers more advantage and defendants and suspects less. While I was writing this essay, a number of new bills, exacerbating this ominous trend, were being discussed as well. A federal bill to try thirteen-year-olds as adults, for example, and induce states, through the offer of large block grants, to follow suit, in cases of violent crime and "serious" drug offense, is only one of many such trend-setting ideas looked upon more and more favorably by Democrats and Republicans alike.

3. Donziger, *The Real War on Crime*, 102, 288.

4. Ibid., 146.

5. See Jean-Marie Guehenno, *The End of the Nation-State* (Minneapolis, 1995), for an interesting overview of decline of the nation-state, its causes, and implications.

6. Stanley Aronowitz, *The Death and Rebirth of American Radicalism* (New York, Routledge, 1997), 138.

7. I am not suggesting that the traditional paradigm of crime and punishment is on the way out. New paradigms have a way of overlapping and coexisting with the new, as social change occurs, in all areas of social life, although there is no doubt that traditional crime dramas have themselves been increasingly inflected by the move to the right. I am only suggesting that the tabloids do indeed represent a dramatic example of a rather pure version of a new paradigm of crime and punishment that is at the cutting edge of an ideological and cultural shift seen more mildly and subtly elsewhere.

8. Stuart Hall et al., *Policing the Crisis: Mugging, the State and Law and Order* (London, 1978), 145.

9. No crime series charts the dangerous after-story in which the actual fate, and future, of the convicted offender is portrayed. Even the "punishment phase" of criminal trials is omitted on series like *L&O*, for it is enough for audiences to know that "the problem" has been "taken care of." Such is the trust TV genres would have us place in the correctional system, which—it should be noted—is virtually absent, even on newscasts, from mainstream TV representation.

10. See Anna Williams, "Domesticity and the Aetiology of Crime," *Camera Obscura* 31 (January–May 1993): 97–121, for an interesting discussion of another form of tabloid, *America's Most Wanted*, which documents and reenacts unsolved crimes and asks viewers to help catch the criminals.

11. As I write, a new series has just aired on Fox that is far more disturbing than *Cops*, called *Video Justice: Crimes Caught on Tape*. For a full hour, the series plays for the audience actual videotapes of actual crimes, some acquired from vandalized stores, some from private citizens' videotapes, and some from police surveillance tapes. As the tapes—generally lurid and often horrifying in their vivid detailed footage of shoot-outs, acts of physical destruction, and brutal beatings—roll, the narrator provides rhetorically excessive commentary: "These creatures, cold-hearted and steely, have not an ounce of human fellow feeling, as you can see as they wildly attack their prey," is typical. Since this series has only aired a few times, I am not including it in this essay. If it survives, however, it will push the thesis of this essay to an outer extreme even more alarming.

12. George Lipsitz, "The Greatest Story Ever Sold: Marketing and the O. J. Simpson Trial," in Toni Morrison, ed., *Birth of a Nation'hood: Gaze, Script and Spectacle in the O. J. Simpson Case* (New York, 1997), 15.

13. I am using the masculine pronoun to refer to the cops in this series because, for the most part, the cops who serve as "hosts" on this series are white and male. Minority and female cops do figure at times, of course, sometimes as central figures, more often as backup. But it is significant that the standard figure of the police officer on this series—as of course is still the case in the actual police forces who participate in the series—is a white male.

14. Since the series moves from place to place and presents an endless series of police encounters, there are of course exceptions to these generalizations. Sometimes cities are visited—Boston, or Chicago, or Pittsburgh—in which urban settings figure at least to some extent. And sometimes a violent crime—a robbery or murder—may actually occur. The producers certainly welcome such sensationalism when they can get it. But for the most part what occurs on these routine shifts is much more mundane. And so footage is selected for the most drama possible, and this, usually, involves drunks, druggies, prostitutes, bar fights, and domestic upsets of one kind or another.

15. For an interesting book-length study of the structure and signifying practices of traditional crime drama in the United States and Britain, see Richard Sparks, *Television and the Drama of Crime: Moral Tales and the Place of Crime in Public Life* (Buckingham and Philadelphia, 1992).

16. Ray Surette, "Predator Criminals as Media Icons," in Gregg Barak, ed., *Media, Process, and the Social Construction of Crime* (New York, 1994), 131–132.

17. Ibid.

18. The relationship between documentary and "reality," and the ways in which the documentary form—in its "highest" and "lowest" generic manifestations—is both a *fictional* text and yet different from other fictional texts in that "it addresses the world in which we live rather than worlds in which we imagine living," is explored fully in Bill Nichols, *Representing Reality* (Bloomington and Indianapolis, 1991).

19. Herman Gray has thoroughly analyzed the way in which race and criminality have been constructed and deployed in mass media. The fullest treatment is in *Watching Race: Television and the Struggle for Blackness* (Minneapolis, 1995).

20. John Dilulio, *Courts, Corrections and the Constitution* (Princeton, NJ, 1999).

21. See Gray, *Watching Race*, for a more thorough discussion of the changing nature of racial representation during the Reagan years and the ways in which demographic imperatives affected the representation of race in terms of difference and assimilation.

22. Actually, several other tabloids—*America's Most Wanted; Hard Copy*, for example—employ just this stereotype quite often. In fact, I would argue— and would have, had space allowed, in this chapter—that this form of tabloid,

in which vicious predators suddenly and incomprehensibly turn on neighbors or even family members in the most repellent and horrifying of criminal acts, represents a kind of middle ground between traditional crime drama and the more radical version represented by *Cops*. For in these cases the "family in danger" theme is maintained, as is the focus on specific, usually even planned and motivated acts and the police's search for the offender. The difference—and the reason they figure as tabloids—is primarily stylistic. Documentary footage and reenactments are employed to give the same expressionistically aberrant image of crime and criminality. The saintly behavior of the cops contrasts sharply with the representation of criminals and even victims, whose environments—due to the "low rent" production values—have the same seedy, unsavory quality as on *Cops*. These tabloids seem to be set somewhere between the landscape of traditional urban crime drama and the border territory visualized on *Cops*.

23. It is worth noting here that as cases that are often videotaped by private citizens, in which cops in cars or on bikes are charged with beating and killing usually black suspects on roads or streets like these, the public is increasingly given evidence, often documented evidence, of police behavior that is itself wild, uncivilized, out of control, and vicious. It is not surprising, then, that these ideologically "corrective" tabloids should be appearing at just this moment, in which the tables are visually turned and the cops are seen, week after week, as icons of kindness and peacefulness while those they must arrest or subdue are the ones who seem vicious, out of control, and hostile.

24. Jeff Ferrell, "Culture, Crime and Criminology," in Jeff Ferrell and Alan Sanders, eds., *Cultural Criminology* (Boston, 1995), 7–8.

25. In *Policing the Risk Society* (Toronto, 1997), a detailed study of the work of police officers in contemporary society, Richard Ericson and Kevin Haggerty demonstrate this very point—a point that *Cops* illustrates eloquently. "It is extremely rare for a police officer to encounter a serious crime in progress," they say. It is "traffic and liquor violations" which make up most routine patrol work, while on house calls "what officers typically find . . . is not serious crime but a kaleidoscope of trouble that requires them to provide some combination of counsel, assistance, expertise, coercion, referral, and persuasion." Indeed, "direct involvement in crime work takes up as little as 3% of their working time" (pp. 19–20). "This emphasis entails a lessening of crime control in favor of surveillance," they argue, and creates a system in which "due process protection for suspects is eroded in favor of 'system rights' to the kind of knowledge useful to surveillance" (p. 18). While the authors argue that this kind of system is less "repressive" than simply managerial, the distinction—especially as acted out on shows like *Cops*—seems merely semantic. Repression of serious crime merely gives way to a far greater, more all-encompassing form of "repression" of a far greater range of personas and behaviors.

The authors mention the mass media's "dramatization of crime"—"*the* staple cultural product of their industry"—as important in creating the idea in the public mind, and even in the mind of the police themselves, that crime work is what cops *really* do. Thus, the implication goes, the media obscure the true surveillance nature of most police work today. Certainly in most crime drama this is true. But what is so intriguing about *Cops* is how it works to subtly *redefine* the very idea of crime to now include these essentially managerial functions—and, by extension, to redefine the definition of "criminal" to include those who need to be controlled.

26. Ileana Porras, "On Terrorism: Reflections on Violence and the Outlaw," in Dan Danielson and Karen Engle, eds., *After Identity: A Reader in Culture and Law* (New York, 1995), 295.

27. Ibid., 305–309.

NOTES TO CHAPTER 3

1. *New York Times,* August 10, 1999, A7.

2. Ibid.

3. See Steven Donziger, ed., *The Real War on Crime: The Report of the National Criminal Justice Commission* (Washington, DC, 1996), 103.

4. Philip Jenkins, "Myth and Murder: The Serial Killer Panic," in V. Kappeler, M. Blumberg, and G. Potter, eds., *The Mythology of Crime and Criminal Justice* (Prospect Park, IL, 1996), 75–76.

5. As I will discuss in greater depth in the concluding section of the book, there are great and disturbing parallels between the "war on crime" embarked upon by President George Bush and expanded with undue relish by his successor; and the more recent "war on terrorism" of George W. Bush begun after the attack on the World Trade Center in September 2001. Indeed, as I will argue—and as was suggested in the second chapter of the book—the rhetoric of crime and that of terrorism have always been disturbingly similar. So it is in no way surprising that terrorism and terrorists have so easily been incorporated as logical—indeed, predictable—extensions of an already existing set of media images and rhetoric. What sells time on television is equally profitable for those who benefit, economically or politically, from the criminal justice industry.

6. See Michel Foucault, *Discipline and Punish: The Birth of the Prison* (New York, 1995).

7. Ibid.

8. Emile Durkheim, *The Division of Labor* (New York, 1974).

9. Alison Young, *Imagining Crime* (London, 1996), 10.

10. Dinitia Smith, "'Oz': Prison Series Seeks to Shatter Expectations," *New York Times,* July 12, 1999, E1, 7.

11. F. Zimring and G. Hawkins, *Incapacitation: Penal Confinement and the Constraint of Crime* (New York, 1996); K. Haas and G. Alpert, *The Dilemma of Corrections* (Prospect Heights, IL, 1999).

12. A. Lewis, "The Clinton Administration and Civil Liberties," *New York Times,* January 7, 1997, A18.

13. Zimring and Hawkins, *Incapacitation,* 3–17.

14. L. Friedman, *Crime and Punishment in American History* (New York, 1993), 329.

15. Ibid., 334.

16. Ibid.

17. S. Rosenblatt, *Criminal Injustice: Confronting the Prison Crisis* (Boston, 1996), 100–108.

18. Ibid.

19. K. Haas and G. Alpert, *The Dilemma of Corrections* (Prospect Heights, IL, 1999), 11.

20. Rosenblatt, 301.

21. That the audience for this series is in fact liberal is important to explain, for there is a great irony here. Conservative groups have roundly condemned the series as one of the most violently brutal of all TV programs, which in fact it is. But the more sophisticated liberal viewer is willing to accept this kind of realism in a program deemed "serious art." What is ironic is that neither the producers nor the critics and viewers who have made it a hit have commented upon, nor apparently noticed, the incredibly reactionary subtext of the series and its uncomfortable fit with the most right-wing of political agendas. In fact, one of the great ironies of this series is that—if one follows the Internet chat groups about the series as I have done—the series is a major hit among a particularly interesting social subgroup: those male viewers interested in particularly brutal portrayals of good-looking, muscled men engaging in the most brutal sexual and other acts, especially rape, a common occurrence on *Oz.* A great number of these viewers actually seem to log on in order to gain access to "nude photos" of the actors themselves, culled from heaven knows where, but on offer virtually daily in online chat groups for *Oz,* which is now seen in reruns on the HBO spin-off network, HBO2.

22. Rosenblatt, *Criminal Injustice,* 307.

23. Connie McNeeley, *Public Rights, Public Rules* (New York, 1996), 61–63.

24. Stuart Hall et al., *Policing the Crisis: Mugging, the State and Law and Order* (London, 1978), 145.

25. C. James, "Hot New Series," *New York Times,* July 7, 1999, E1, 7.

26. Haas and Alpert, *Dilemma of Corrections,* 105.

27. Quoted in ibid., 17.

28. Donziger, 146–158.

29. Ibid., 35.
30. Ibid., 36.
31. Ibid., 304–307.
32. Ibid., 31.
33. C. Segal, *Tragedy and Civilization* (Norman, OK, 1999), 4–6.
34. Ibid., 316.
35. Quoted in ibid., 233.
36. Ibid., 234.
37. Ibid., 33.

NOTES TO CHAPTER 4

1. See E. Rapping, "Daytime Utopias: If You Lived in Pine Valley, You'd Be Home," in H. Jenkins and J. Shattuc, eds., *Hop on Pop: The Politics and Pleasures of Popular Culture* (Durham, NC, 2003), 31–60, and E. Rapping, "The Politics of Soap Operas," *Media-tions: Forays into the Culture and Gender Wars* (Boston, 1994), 176–192.

2. See Cynthia Lucia, "Female Lawyers on Film," in Martha Fineman, ed., *Feminism, Media and the Law* (New York, 1995), 221–255.

3. It is important to note that every trial, and indeed the entire criminal justice system, is inherently political, although it is only when a particular case makes that glaringly and dramatically obvious that most people realize it. But that is of course the very nature of American political institutions generally. We are educated to see them as "objective" and "neutral" when they are fraught with all the race, gender, sexual, ethnic, and class inequities that inflect every other aspect of American life.

4. That the 1980s and 1990s marked a period of relative—and deceptive— political calm in America is important here. For the Reagan-Bush and then the Clinton years were unusual. So unusual that when, in 2001, we found ourselves under attack in our own homeland and involved in the most intense global military adventures since Vietnam, the age group most emotionally distressed by all this was what used to be called Generation X. Having never experienced any national or international upheaval serious enough to affect their sense of physical and emotional security, these young people, according to a study reported in the *New York Times*, October 25, 2001, A18, tended to suffer the most severe symptoms of anxiety and depression.

5. Lawrence Friedman, *Crime and Punishment in America* (New York, 1993), 305–307.

6. Ibid.

7. These statistics are well known to those who practice law. Rikki Klieman, a former defense attorney now working as a Court TV anchor, for one, has

stated them several times. They are borne out, however, by simply studying the outcomes of the hundreds of trials aired and available on video from Court TV itself. In fact, my own analysis of Court TV catalogs describing the trials they have aired since 1991 brings the figure to 96 percent, a very high number, which includes many sentenced to life with no chance of parole.

8. Charles R. Nesson and Andrew Koblenz, "The Image of Justice: *Chandler v. Florida*," *Harvard Civil Rights–Civil Liberties Law Review* (Fall 1981).

9. Ibid., 405.

10. Ibid., 408.

11. Lisa Cuklanz, *Rape on Trial* (Philadelphia, 1996), 85–114.

12. Ibid., 74.

13. Hazel Thornton, *Hung Jury: Diary of a Menendez Juror* (Philadelphia, 1993), 3.

14. On many campuses, according to the *Washington Post*, students wore T-shirts that read "Free the Menendez Brothers." See J. Young, "Campus Groupies Identify with Young Killers," *Washington Post*, October 23, 1994, A14.

15. The trials of the Menendez brothers were complicated. There were two juries and two defense teams, one for each brother, but one trial. When testimony relevant to only one or the other was given, the other jury left the courtroom.

16. Thornton, *Hung Jury*, 8.

17. As we shall see in later chapters, battered woman/abused child defenses are hardly as successful in most cases—especially when the defendants are poor and/or black and must rely upon court-appointed counsel, as was this one. Which is not to say that money was the reason for the Menendez's mistrials, but rather quite the opposite: the fact that most defendants do not receive the kind of legal counsel that the brothers could afford makes for a legal system which is less than fair to defendants, all of whom, in a truly democratic system, would have access to "the best possible counsel," as those who drew up our Constitution clearly intended.

18. Thornton, *Hung Jury*, 12.

19. Ibid., 31.

20. Ibid., 35.

21. Ibid., 83.

22. Ibid., 80–85.

23. As I learned when one peer review reader for an article I wrote for a feminist journal advised that the entire article be rejected because of a single footnote in which the Menendez case was mentioned as an example of a defense that employed the "Battered Woman/Child Syndrome."

24. George Lipsitz, "The Greatest Story Ever Sold: Marketing and the O. J. Simpson Trial," in Toni Morrison, ed., *Birth of a Nation'hood: Gaze, Script and Spectacle in the O. J. Simpson Case* (New York, 1997), 54–57.

25. See A. Leon Higginbotham, "The Simpson Trial: Who Was Playing the Race Card?" in Morrison, *Birth of a Nation'hood*, 31–56.

26. See Drucilla Cornell, "Dismissed or Banished? A Testament to the Reasonableness of the Simpson Jury," in Morrison, *Birth of a Nation'hood*, 72.

27. See Herman Gray, *Watching Race* (Minneapolis, 1998).

28. Lipsitz, "The Greatest Story Ever Sold," 54–74.

29. Cornell, "Dismissed or Banished?" 132–156.

30. Steven Russell, "Undercurrents of Judicial Policy: Demystifying the Third Branch of Government and the O. J. Simpson Case," in Gregg Barak, ed., *Representing O.J.* (Guilderland, NY, 1998), 174.

31. Contributors to online Website newsgroups and chat rooms devoted to the trials and the brothers themselves, of which there were many at the time, most of which I kept up with, overwhelmingly voiced hatred and fear of them and support for the most harsh punishments possible within the law.

32. In the wake of the McVeigh trial and the rise in support for the death penalty, it is not surprising that even liberals are, in the wake of the terrorist attack on the World Trade Center, "now raising the issue of torture of criminal suspects in particularly heinous crimes as a reasonable policy." W. Glaberson, "Torture for Terrorists?" *New York Times*, November 5, 2001, E3.

33. Again, I am not suggesting that McVeigh was not guilty. Rather, I am merely suggesting that it was not "evidence" of the kind typically demanded by prosecutors that clinched the case for jurors or the public, but rather that other—more melodramatic, televisually compelling—features of the crime, namely the suffering of the victims themselves, became the primary focus of the trial. The suffering of victims, as we shall see, has in fact become increasingly replaced in trials as well as in public sentiment, policy, and certainly in television drama and reportage of crime as far more compelling and relevant than factual "evidence" or, more importantly, the social and psychological factors leading defendants to commit crimes in the first place.

34. At the time of his election to the presidency, George W. Bush, then governor of Texas, had approved the execution of almost as many death-row inmates as were killed in Oklahoma City. Since then, many federal executions, as well as deaths of American military personnel, have taken place in Bush's War on Terrorism.

35. Andrew Cohen, "Lessons from the Timothy McVeigh Trial," *Media Studies Journal*, Winter 1998, 11.

36. Linda Greenhouse, "ABA Studies Its Image," *New York Times*, February 2, 1999, A12.

NOTES TO CHAPTER 5

1. I analyze these early docudramas at length in *The Movie of the Week: Private Stories/Public Events* (Minneapolis, 1992).

2. Sarah Projansky, *Watching Rape: Film and Television in Postfeminist Culture* (New York, 2001), 90. Projansky, in her Introduction, also speaks of the ways in which "some . . . feminist concepts . . . had some success at infiltrating mainstream popular culture . . . [which] marked a partial acceptance of some arguments about rape." She lists, as do I in what follows, some of these progressive arguments (p. 11). In what she, and I, would consider a postfeminist turn in the 1990s, however, much of this explicit if limited incorporation of feminist thinking and practice has been reduced to "accepted" if not clichéd bits of common knowledge, about which not much is left to say—and much more is left unsaid, or perverted to fit far from progressive goals.

3. Robert Hariman, *Popular Trials: Rhetoric, Media and the Law* (Boston, 1994), 19.

4. Ibid., 22.

5. Lisa Cuklanz, *Rape on Trial* (Philadelphia, 1996), 36.

6. Nancy Fraser, "Rethinking the Public Sphere," *Social Text* 8, no. 3 (1991): 56–80.

7. Kathleen Jones, "On Authority, or, Why Women Are Not Entitled to Speak," in L. Quinby and I. Diamond, eds., *Feminism and Foucault* (Boston, 1990), 119, 130–131.

8. Cuklanz, *Rape on Trial*, 7.

9. Quoted in ibid., 9–10.

10. Wendy Brown, "States of Injury," in Joan Landes, ed., *Feminism: Public and Private* (Oxford, 1998), 461–463.

11. Projansky, 114.

12. Henry Louis Gates, "The Authority of the Jury," *New Yorker*, March 23, 1998, 11.

13. All the cases mentioned in this chapter and succeeding chapters are available on videotape from Court TV.

14. The power and charisma of the Kennedy men certainly contributed to the jurors' inclination to disbelieve the plaintiff and decide in favor of the Kennedy cousin.

15. "Female Serial Killer Dies," *New York Times*, October 9, 2002, A16.

16. Alison Young, *Watching Crime* (London, 1998), 255.

17. Brown, "States of Injury," 468.

18. Lauren Berlant, *The Queen of America Goes to Washington* (Raleigh, NC, 1997), 235.

19. Brown, "States of Injury," 469–473.

20. Ibid., 467.

21. Franklin Zimring, *Incapacitation* (Oxford, 1999).

NOTES TO CHAPTER 6

1. Raymond Williams, *Television: Technology and Cultural Form* (New York, 1993).

2. See E. Rapping, *The Culture of Recovery* (Boston, 1997).

3. See E. Rapping, *The Movie of the Week: Private Stories/Public Events* (Minneapolis, 1994).

4. Jacques Donzelot, *The Policing of Families* (New York, 1997), 88–89.

5. Ibid.

6. More recently, the case of Andrea Yates, who drowned her five children during a period of postpartum depression, complicated this theory. Despite a barrage of expert defense testimony supporting her plea of "not guilty by reason of insanity," Yates was convicted. Her husband, however, was indeed attacked by some commentators for his alleged failure to take his wife's condition seriously and his alleged pressuring of her to have more children, even though she had previously suffered this kind of depression. Yates was seen, then, as being both "absent" in some sense, and overly "present" in another. Nonetheless, his wife was the one punished, severely. Her sentence was life with no chance of parole.

7. Erika Doss, *Elvis Culture: Fans, Faith and Image* (Kansas City, 1999); see also Karal Ann Marling, *As Seen on TV: The Visual Culture of Every Day Life in the 1950s* (Cambridge, MA, 1994).

8. Alison Young, *Imagining Crime* (London, 1996), 103–104.

9. Linda Greenhouse, "Tennessee's New Criminal Laws," *New York Times*, February 23, 1996, A16.

10. Young, *Imagining Crime*, 105.

11. Ibid., 106.

12. G. Bozanovich, "Are Parents to Blame?" *Buffalo News*, January 17, 2000, 8.

13. W. Glaberson, "The Law and Parental Neglect," *New York Times*, December 21, 1999, A31; Bernard Schissel, *Social Justice*, Summer 1997, 165. This article makes the interesting point that while government agencies increasingly criminalize parental neglect or abuse, there is no such effort to hold state agencies in charge of child welfare for their own, often much worse abuse of the children for whom they are designated guardians.

14. Lisa Belkin, "The Crisis of the Family," *New York Times Magazine*, October 20, 1999, 24–56.

NOTES TO CHAPTER 7

1. A. Wolfe (Berkeley, CA, 1991).

2. Kevin Harner and Mark Drakeford (London, 1998).

3. See Steven Donziger, ed., *The Real War on Crime* (Washington, DC, 1996); M. Males, *Framing Youth* (Monroe, ME, 1998); F. Zimring, *American Youth Violence* (New York and Oxford, 1998).

4. H. Gray, *Watching Race* (Minneapolis, 1999).

5. Harner and Drakeford, 27–29.

6. A. Carnes, "Out of the Carceral Straitjacket: Under Twelve and in Jail," *Canadian Journal of Criminology*, July 1994, 305–327.

7. See E. Rapping, *The Culture of Recovery* (Boston, 1998), 65–94.

8. W. Claiborne, "Youth's Trial Puts Focus on Trend," *Washington Post*, November 5, 1999, A3; see also Zimring, *American Youth Violence*, 10–12.

9. Ibid.

10. Donziger, *Real War on Crime*, 188–190.

11. Zimring, *American Youth Violence*, 14.

12. Ibid.

13. J. Gonnerman, "Inside Riker's Island," *Village Voice*, August 8, 1999, 41–44.

14. L. Friedman, *Crime and Punishment in American History* (New York, 1993), 504.

15. Ibid., 169.

16. Ibid., 165.

17. Anthony Platt, quoted in Friedman, *Crime and Punishment*, 414.

18. Friedman, *Crime and Punishment*, 415.

19. Ibid., 416.

20. Ibid., 417.

21. S. Ewen, *Captains of Consciousness* (New York, 2000), 56.

22. Ibid., 13.

23. S. Frith, *Sound Effects* (New York and London, 1992).

24. Ewen, *Captains of Consciousness*, 114.

25. Ibid., 189.

26. Ibid., 143.

27. The targeting of youth markets on television, in movies, in clothing, cosmetic, and even automobile and other big ticket item ads has become so ubiquitous as to reach a point of absurdity. The ways in which advertising and marketing implicates parents, overly eager to please and/or placate children, as well as youth themselves, with spending power that is itself increasingly amazing, is evident in everything from the Baby Gap stores which feature high-fashion, high-priced togs for infants, to Saturn car ads, which encourage parents to buy the "right" car for their teenagers.

28. It is astonishing to note that this young man, who died at the age of twenty-six after having completed only two and a half movies (*Giant* had to be completed after his untimely death), has remained the very image of what youth culture, and the entire complex and contradictory idea of "the teenager," has come to mean in American society even today.

29. See E. Rapping, "Gender, 'Melrose Place' and the Spelling Legacy," in M. Meyers, ed., *Mediated Women* (Cresskill, NJ, 1996), 271–297.

30. Thomas Doherty, *Teenagers and Teenpics: The Juvenilization of American Movies in the 1950s* (Philadelphia, 1994), 42.

31. Thomas Doherty, 55, 115, 128–132.

32. H. Giroux, *Channel Surfing: Racism, the Media, and the Destruction of Today's Youth* (New York, 1997), 35.

33. See E. Rapping, "The Malling of Youth Culture," in *Media-tions: Forays into the Culture and Gender Wars* (Boston, 1997), 178–187.

34. These two attorneys were prominently featured on television debates during the Menendez brothers' trials.

35. Rapping, "The Return of the Bad Seed," in *Media-tions*, 201–222.

36. H. Gray, "Television, Black Americans and the American Dream," in H. Newcomb, ed., *Television: The Critical View*, 5th ed. (Oxford, 1994), 185–186.

37. See Donziger, *The Real War on Crime*; and Zimring, *American Youth Violence*.

NOTES TO CHAPTER 8

1. Leonard Maltin, *Leonard Maltin's 1999 Movie and TV Guide* (New York, 1999), 325.

2. Thomas Schatz, *Hollywood Genres* (Philadelphia, 1981), 22.

3. William Ian Miller, "Clint Eastwood and Equity: Popular Culture's Theory of Revenge," in Austin Sarat and Thomas R. Kearns, ed., *Law in the Domain of Culture* (Ann Arbor, MI, 1998), 198.

4. Ibid., 199–200. Thus the genre typically reflects great hostility toward the concept of the presumption of innocence and no sympathy whatever for the insanity defense, under any circumstances. These are also characteristics of the Victims' Rights movement, as the trial of Colin Ferguson, in which the most passionate and vengeful victim impact statements were hurled at a defendant clearly incapable of understanding what was being said.

5. Ibid., 168. See also Robert Nozick, *Philosophical Explanations* (Cambridge, MA, 1982), 169.

6. Ray Surette, *Media, Crime and Criminal Justice* (Belmont, CA, 1998), 1.

7. Miller, "Clint Eastwood," 201.

8. Bruce Shapiro, "Victims and Vengeance," *Nation*, February 10, 1997, 11–15.

9. Charles R. Nessom and Andrew Koblenz, "The Image of Justice: *Chandler v. Florida*," *Harvard Civil Rights–Civil Liberties Law Review* (Fall 1981).

10. Linda Greenhouse, "ABA Studies Its Image," *New York Times*, February 2, 1999, A12.

11. Anna Williams, "Domesticity and the Aetiology of Crime in *America's Most Wanted*," *Camera Obscura*, January–May 1993, 97–120.

12. Gordon van Sauter, "Rating the Reality Shows and Keeping Tabs on the Tabloids," *TV Guide*, May 2, 1992, 18.

13. Quoted in Margaret Bullitt-Jonas, *Holy Hunger* (Boston, 1999), 253.

14. Lauren Berlant, *The Queen of America Goes to Washington City* (Durham, NC, 1997), 35–37.

15. Ibid.

16. Paul Gewirtz, "Victims and Voyeurs: Two Narrative Problems of the Criminal Trial," in Peter Brooks and Paul Gewirtz, *Law's Stories: Narrative and Rhetoric in the Law* (New Haven, 1996), 148–149.

NOTES TO THE CONCLUSION

1. H. Jones "A Scary Merry Christmas," *New York Times*, December 10, 2001, A16.

2. "Ideas and Trends," *New York Times*, December 10, 2002, A24.

3. Ibid.

4. *TV Guide*, "The Roush Report," June 21, 2002, 7.

5. Ibid., June 13, 2000, 11.

6. Nick Browne, "Television's Supertext," in Horace Newcomb, ed., *Television: The Critical View*, 4th ed. (Oxford, 1994), 344–383.

7. Esther Madriz, *Nothing Bad Happens to Good Girls: Fear of Crime in Women's Lives* (Berkeley, 1997).

8. "The Roush Report," *TV Guide*, June 21, 2002, 7.

9. See E. Katz and D. Dayan, *Media Events: The Live Broadcasting of History* (New York, 1994).

10. Dick Hebdige, *Hiding in the Light* (London, 1989), 271–274.

11. B. Weiser, *New York Times*, August 10, 1999, A10.

12. H. Harrison, *New York Times*, November, 24, 1999, A19.

13. B. Weiser, *New York Times*, August 10, 2000, A14.

14. The 2000 film *Traffic* did a superb job of revealing, to a mass audience, the corruption and ineffectiveness of the so-called War on Drugs. Indeed, it showed the entire policy to be counterproductive, not only in increasing the flow

of drugs into our borders, but in corrupting officials, agents, and others in the process because of the huge sums of money involved.

15. Mindy Sink, "Utah's Crime Mysteries Go Online," *New York Times*, October 26, 2000, D8.

16. This fact was inserted briefly, amidst a host of far more rabble-rousing tidbits of crime news, in the "crawl"—the text that runs continuously across the bottom of the screens of twenty-four-hour news networks—of an MSNBC evening news program after the Elizabeth Smart kidnaping in the summer of 2002.

17. Raymond Williams, *Television: Technology and Cultural Form* (New York, 1993).

18. Ibid.

19. See Erik Barnouw, *Tube of Plenty: Evolution of American TV* (New York, 1982).

20. The proposals and discussions of possible and probable attacks on civil liberties in post-9/11 America are a constant in print and electronic news and opinion. The various controversial measures include unlimited detention of "suspected" terrorists entering the country, military tribunals in which defendants are not permitted to meet with counsel, infringements on the privacy of all citizens, and any number of other possible, problematic policies. See especially Adam Liptak, Neil A. Lewis, and Benjamin Weiser, "After Sept. 11, a Legal Battle on the Limits of Civil Liberty," *New York Times*, August 4, 2002, A1.

21. J. Hoberman, "The Art of War: How Hollywood Learned to Stop Worrying and Love the Bomb," *Village Voice*, June 25, 2002, 45.

22. All of these issues were and are still being widely reported and discussed in major newspapers and on virtually every television news and commentary program since shortly after the September 11 attack made the War on Terror a top news topic.

Index

About the Author

ELAYNE RAPPING is Professor of Women's Studies and Media Studies at SUNY Buffalo and a nationally known media critic and analyst. Her works have appeared in the *Village Voice*, *Newsday*, the *Nation*, *Cineaste*, and other publications, scholarly and mainstream. Her most recent books include *Media-tions: Forays into the Culture and Gender Wars* and *The Culture of Recovery: Making Sense of the Self-Help Movement in Women's Lives*. She lives in Buffalo and Manhattan.

CPSIA information can be obtained
at www.ICGtesting.com
Printed in the USA
LVHW031556020119
602485LV00006B/982/P